Evolving the Forest

editors:

Simon Lloyd, Richard Povall & Jeremy Ralph

To my brother, friend,
and great artist.
With love & thanks,
Marchant

TIMBER STRATEGIES

RFS
ROYAL FORESTRY SOCIETY

art.earth

First published 2020

art.earth, Kingsbridge, Devon, England.   www.artdotearth.org

Design: art.earth; set in Myriad Pro Light

Printed in Italy on 100% 120gsm recycled paper

A catalogue record is available from the British Library. ISBN: 978-0-9957196-3-7

Published by artdotearth CIC, Kingsbridge, Devon, England www.artdotearth.org | publications@artdotearth.org

photo: Richard Povall

Table of Contents

Table of Contents

art earth
artearth 07
Evolving the Forest
@royal_forestry

Foreword

Sir Harry Studholme

There is poetry in forests; a poetry hidden in plain sight. Trees bring shade and beauty to the streets and parks of our cities. They provide habitat and employment in our countryside even as they frame landscapes. Trees are complex living organisms; they absorb carbon dioxide and pollution and stabilise soils even as they grow the raw material for the paper in our books and the beams in our houses. Trees dwarf and outlive us, while their roots delve deep underground their branches reach for the sky and their leaves whisper to the wind. No surprise that there is much passion evoked when people come together to talk about trees as they did in June 2019 for the *Evolving the Forest* Conference at Dartington. Jeremy Ralph of Timber Strategies, Simon Lloyd of The Royal Forestry Society, Richard Povall of art.earth and others brought together a widely-drawn international cast of expert speakers, to debate with participants, learn and break down boundaries over three days of discussion. This book is both a record and a development of that discussion.

2019 was a year of celebrating forestry in Britain. 1919, one hundred years earlier, was the first year of peace after the Great War. In the turmoil of that war a plan to rebuild the then devastated forests of these islands was set in motion. When war began the consequences of millennia of converting land from forest to farm, had left less than one acre in twenty of Britain wooded. The once-thriving markets for forest products had fallen away decades earlier and most of this remaining woodland was uncared for. Some forestry enthusiasts remained, many of whom were members what became the Royal Forestry Society, but by the end of the second decade of the 20th century the country had become almost entirely dependent on imported timber — imports disrupted by Germany as an act of war. Demand for timber from pit props for mines to duck boards for trenches was greater than in peacetime. Raw material was taken from the already depleted forests as four years of war effort scoured British forests for timber. The Forestry Act of 1919 and the Forestry Commission it created were addressing an essential need to regrow the forests. It began a movement that, over the next 100 years, has more than doubled the area of forest in Britain, and rebuilt a forest economy.

What began in 1919 was not new, merely the reinvigoration of an ancient relationship. Our hunter-gatherer ancestors arriving 11,700 years ago, following the retreating ice, were already experienced users of wood — they had fifty thousand years of living with European trees. Axes, perhaps unsurprisingly, are among our earliest tools. By 5,800 years ago people were managing coppice in southern England and thousands of years before the Roman invasion humans were clearing land for agriculture.

The forests of Britain have been made and managed by man for millennia, embedded into our existence and woven into our cultural psyche. The forest landscape may evolve but the roots of connection run deep.

Today our woods are perhaps more precious, more important and yet more fragile than ever; as central to the future of man as their ancestors were to our own ancestors. How we plant and manage forests is essential not only to man's response to climate change but also to protecting biodiversity and growing renewable raw materials, yet how to do this is fraught with paradox. The threats to trees from pests, diseases and climate change are unprecedented. Out of our small pallet of 'native' forest trees, virtually all mature elm died over 30 years ago, ash is in serious decline and even oak is threatened in some parts of the country. There is public pressure to plant only native species, even though non-native conifers provide virtually all the wood we use. Practical foresters are deeply concerned that new plantations of native trees will, like the plantings of recent decades, be stunted by non-native grey squirrels. Nature solves problems through putting forward a diversity of solutions; tropical forests for example resist diseases through being diverse, with a single acre of rainforest holding more native species than our entire country. Seeds experiment by being different to each other. Taking nature as a model, *Evolving the Forest* was rich in ideas; from the artistic to the scientific, from the sensory to the cerebral, and from explorations of tree sentience to commercial forestry. These ideas drove a wealth of discussion.

Publicly this debate takes place at a time when the population are more engaged with trees than ever. Cities can be as wooded as the surrounding countryside; with urban trees an echo of the wild, their birds are woodland birds. In the countryside, although few jobs are land-based, woods are the most common and visible habitat of wild things. Despite this there is little public understanding of the dynamics of forestry. As in much of modern life, there is a shallow polarisation of views in the echo chamber of electronic media and a culture swift to close down debate — so in order to create a viable forest future, we must have debate and we must build bridges. We need writers, artists and ecologists, and also the earthy expertise of the tiny portion of the population who make a living from managing forests. They must talk together. We need to be humble and listen and learn and at the same time communicate what we know. *Evolving the Forest* provided a space to do this.

The future of managing our forests is not simple, but a Gordian knot. To cut through this knot and weave a realistic way forward the views of all parties will be needed; the scientific, the practical, the creative and the visionary. The magic of the mingling of art, ecology and forestry at the conference empowered conversations that will live long in the memories of those that were there. I hope that the ideas in this book, rooted in those discussions, will help build the connections to evolve our forests to thrive in 100 years' time.

Sir Harry Studholme

Chair of the Forestry Commission (2013 to 2020)

This stricken Hornbeam in Białowieża Forest's Strict Protection Area is the epitome of regenerating woodland life. October 2019 (photo: Simon Leadbeater)

Introduction

Richard Povall, art.earth

*E*volving the Forest* was an international conference developed by art.earth, the Royal Forestry Society and Timber Strategies spearheaded by our three editors, respectively Richard Povall, Simon Lloyd and Jeremy Ralph.

The event weaves its way through the book, with a final framing in Jeremy Ralph's epilogue. Like all such events produced by art.earth, this one was characterised by breadth as well as depth, bringing together many voices who are often ignorant of one another or, when they are not, are sometimes in discord — the event, and this publication, provided an opportunity to share and to observe the unknown familiar.

The event was held at Dartington Hall in southwest England from June 19-21, 2019.

art.earth Books (artdotearth.org/bookshop/) always represent a breadth of opinion about art, culture, ecology and life and we're delighted to be publishing this book on behalf of the *Evolving the Forest* collaborative partnership.

There was a significant gap between the event and the design of the book, so we opened up the call to those who were not delegates, meaning that some of the contributions here were not part of the conference event. This, then, is more than a Proceedings in any conventional sense: it is a commingling of opinion and thought about woods, trees and forest, often (but not always) referencing the frame of the 2019 centenary of the UK Forestry Commission. It's a book about the past and the future of our relationship with woods and trees.

Such breadth becomes challenging when attempting to curate a shape for the publication. After much debate we decided to bring chapters together under three major headings: Ecology and Forest Management, Philosophy and Polemic, and Creative Responses. However like any attempt to catalogue, and particularly given the fluid nature of many of the contributions, some pieces sit more comfortably under their section titles than others. Some could have been included under all three.

Beyond the conference event another major influence on the contents of this book was the 2020/21 coronavirus pandemic that, as we publish, still holds the planet in its grip. Most countries endured one or more periods of 'lockdown' when movements were restricted, sometimes totally, in order to control the spread of the Covid-19 virus. This had a significant impact on people's lives and both decreased their access to nature and (for the fortunate) simultaneously increased it. As traffic levels diminished the sounds of nature — particularly the birdsong so synonymous with our woods and cityscapes — became much more of a focus in our lives. We hope, as you read this book, that the world has moved on from this terrible time of pestilence, but its flavour and tenor can be felt and heard throughout these texts.

Richard Povall
November 2020

Workshop in the Gardener's Cottage *Evolving the Forest* (photo: Oliver Raymond-Barker)

Woodland at Coleridge, South Devon (photo: Richard Povall)

I: Ecology & Forest Management

Andreas Rutkauskas was born in Winnipeg, Canada. He currently resides in Kelowna, where he is a Lecturer in the Faculty of Creative and Critical Studies at The University of British Columbia's Okanagan campus. His projects involve photography and video, often focusing on landscapes that have undergone changes due to a range of technologies; examples include surveillance along the Canada/U.S. border, cycles of industrialization & deindustrialization in Canada's oil patch, and most recently, the aftermath and regeneration following wildfires in Western Canada.

Rutkauskas is the inaugural recipient of a residency with the Fondation Grantham pour l'art et l'environnement in 2020. In 2018, he was a Research Fellow with the Canadian Photography Institute, and he was a finalist for the Gabriele Basilico International Prize in Architecture and Landscape in 2016. His work has been exhibited in public art galleries and museums across Canada, as well as internationally.

photo: Oliver Raymond-Barker

Wildfire in an uncertain time

Andreas Rutkauskas

Elephant Hill Wildfire, ashcroft, British Columbia

As an artist and Lecturer at The University of British Columbia's Okanagan campus, I am writing from the unceded traditional territory of the Syilx. I acknowledge that the images reproduced here were made on the territories of the Syilx, Secwépemc, Nlaka'pamux, Ktunaxa, Blackfoot and Tsuu T'ina, each were sovereign and unique nations prior to the formation of the country now called Canada.

These words and images present my research on the topic of wildfire in Western Canada, particularly the role of fire as an agent of renewal within fire-adapted ecosystems, as well as the increased threat of wildfire due to environmental degradation and climate change. Through photography, I employ a documentary-aesthetic in an effort to facilitate dialogue regarding various landscapes. My primary tool is a 4x5' view camera. Shooting on sheet film and scanning my negatives allows for the creation of large-scale prints with a great amount of description. The subject of my work focuses on landscapes that have been affected by technology. This may refer to physical alteration of a landscape, or the psychological effects of such changes.

Aftermath of the Kenow Fire, Waterton Lakes National Park

My understanding of wildfire has been shaped through four years of living in a fire-prone environment. The summer of 2017 was my first in the Okanagan Valley and it was prototypically hot and dry. The Okanagan lies within the pronounced rain shadow of the Coast Mountains. Its vegetation zone consists of an arid basin, predominated by dry forest and grass-lands (Mann & Lee 2015:145). While it is natural for forests to burn within the Central Interior of British Columbia, increased drought, decreased winter snow-pack, earlier melt, and increased fuel load in forests are some of the factors that will compound human vulnerability to wildfire. My interest in wildfire began through unexpected first-hand experience. I began making photographs of the scorched earth and charred bark of Ponderosa Pine when a small fire occurred on Knox Mountain, directly within the City of Kelowna. A few days later I returned to the area and was astonished to find green tufts of wheatgrass and fescue pushing up out of the blackened earth. Renewal appeared to be immediate. Shortly thereafter, I photographed the aftermath of a larger fire in the District of Peachland. A thick line of fire guard had been bulldozed around the perimeter of the burn and the vegetation was coated with a waxy, resinous substance, which had dyed the landscape bright red. Chemical retardant is comprised primarily of ammonium phosphate and works by coating vegetation in the path of an active fire. The red colouring allows pilots of air tankers or helicopters to gauge whether the retardant was dropped in an appropriate swath, and the colour is fugitive, meaning that it fades over time with exposure to sunlight .[1]

---

1 'Wildland Products', Perimeter Solutions Canada Ltd, PHOS-CHEK Fire Retardant, accessed November 6, 2019, https://phoschek.com/industry/wildland/.

Chemical retardant coating vegetation

Since 2017, I have witnessed firsthand the two most devastating wildfire seasons on record for the province of British Columbia. Yet there is great unpredictability in recent climate patterns. Following these two extraordinary seasons of burning, the 2019 fire season was marginal, and the 2020 season is following this trend. As with many scholars, uncertainties brought about by the Covid-19 pandemic have affected my research, but this pandemic will also have extensive implications on the future management of wildfire risk. Across Canada, the pandemic resulted in a large portion of the public exploring new recreational opportunities, venturing deeper into forests as international travel remained an impossibility for most. The 2020 fire season was cooperative, insofar as wet and cool weather meant that the few fires that did ignite in British Columbia were caused by lightning rather than by anthropogenic sources.

The Syilx have inhabited the Okanagan for thousands of years, and they have a deep-rooted connection to fire wisdom. Historically, firekeepers would purposefully ignite the landscape at critical times of year, in order to rejuvenate the understory, renew berry crops, and create natural fire guards (Brend 2017). In other words, Indigenous populations of the Okanagan have been living cooperatively with fire for millennia. It is surprising then, that this traditional ecological knowledge has not been recognized by many settlers; even more unexpected is our lack of familiarity that the region's biome is fire-adapted. For instance, one of the most abundant species of conifer in the Okanagan is Lodgepole Pine, whose survival is dependent upon conflagration to open the tree's resinous cones. Another common species is the Ponderosa Pine; the bark of mature Ponderosa is thick enough to permit the tree to survive even moderately intense fires. These two species, along with Douglas Fir are also drought-tolerant and have evolved techniques such as self-pruning as a strategy for fire protection (Parish 1996). Today, prescribed burning is executed by The Ministry of Forests throughout the Okanagan Valley during the spring and autumn as a means of reducing fuel load along the forest floor, particularly in areas where the forest abuts suburban or industrial development. This spring however, a burn ban took effect in mid-April. This ban was directly in response to the Covid-19 pandemic and the effect pollutants have on viral respiratory infections (Health Link BC 2020). While these measures consider the best interests of vulnerable members of the public, actions that impact the Wildfire Fuel Risk Reduction Project may have broad-sweeping implications on future wildfire seasons.

Smoke from the Blazed Creek Wildfire, Kootenay Lake

Our fascination with fire, whether it be naturally caused or as a means of satisfying pyromania, is rooted in the sublime. No matter how controlled a wildfire is thought to be, it is ultimately a phenomenon that has a life of its own, which can inspire awe and terror. In North America, a lengthy history of fire suppression as a method of protecting natural resources as well as infrastructure has led to media representations of wildfire as inherently destructive. Walt Disney Productions' 1942 film Bambi has been impactful to generations of children, particularly the penultimate scenes depicting the wildfire that forces Bambi and his father to jump over a raging waterfall in an effort to avoid being incinerated. The cause of the fire was anthropogenic; a campfire started by hunters quickly spread out of control. Perhaps no campaign has caused greater detriment to forest ecology than that of Smokey Bear however. The U.S. Forest Service's advertising figure has been used to support a century-long preoccupation with fire suppression, which has resulted in fuel loads in North American forests being increased to dangerous levels and homogenous species population. While these examples date back to the 1940s, popular media continues to demonize wildfire and even equate it with acts of terrorism. Take for example the 2017 Hollywood film *Only the Brave*, which tells the story of the Granite Mountain Hotshots of Arizona, who 'defended thousands of acres of National wildlands, protected countless homes and saved lives all across the United States' (Nolan 2017). Nineteen members of the crew were killed due to a tactical error while fighting the Yarnell Hill Fire in Arizona during July of 2013. As the film's credits highlight 'The Yarnell Hill Fire is the greatest loss of firefighters in the U.S. since the September 11 attacks'(*ibid.*). In a similar manner, the PBS Nova documentary *Inside the Megafire* (Toubman 2019) relies on a cinematic discourse of coercion and fear. This forty-five-minute documentary examines the Camp fire, which destroyed the town of Paradise, California during the 2018 fire season, as a case study for the increased intensity and scale of wildfires in North America. While Inside the Megafire addresses practices of prescribed burning to benefit the land, the overarching tone supports destructive stereotypes, focusing on the central narrative of resident George Gold, who lost his retirement home in the fire, yet returns weeks later to find his beloved sports car unscathed.

Mount Eneas Wildfire

While the rhetoric of terror and heroism persists within popular media, a number of agencies in Canada have made efforts to counteract these perceptions through the increased provision of information to the public regarding the positive effects of fire on the land. Parks Canada undertook initial experiments with controlled burning in the early 1980s in Banff and Wood Buffalo National Parks. Initial burns yielded inconsistent results, yet reliability has improved significantly with time. Parks Canada now maintains a website dedicated to the tools and techniques involved in prescribed burning and publicly announced the locations of seventeen planned burns throughout national mountain parks in 2020 (Parks Canada 2020). Their website also includes photographs, information regarding fire status updates, health risks, and a glossary of fire terminology. Fire management strategies differ widely between national parks and interface areas however. Within parks, wildfires of natural origin are left to burn so long as they do not pose a threat to structures or resources, while suppression tactics remain dominant in the wildland urban interface.

Kettle River Recreation Area

My artistic approach to this subject seeks to reveal diverse perspectives, act as a critical foil to dominant media representations, and open up space for the consideration of practices of resiliency, including the reintegration of fire within fire-adapted ecosystems. In one of my images, the Kettle River can be seen winding its way through the unincorporated community of Rock Creek, nestled against the Canada/U.S. border. In 2015, campers at Kettle Valley Provincial Park were evacuated on short notice as wildfire consumed over two dozen homes in the area. Three summers later, it was a challenge to find an unoccupied campsite for the night, as crowds had returned to float down the Kettle River and cook over open campfires despite an active fire ban. In many regards, life resumes where it left off in the wake of a wildfire.

Crandell Mountain Campground, Waterton Lakes National Park

Another image in the series reveals the aftermath of the Kenow fire. Ignited by a lightning strike in late August of 2017, the fire burned three hundred and fifty square kilometers of land over the course of one month, including 39% of Waterton Lakes National Park. The fire was not classified as held until the third week of September, and finally under control at the beginning of October. The fire's extreme behaviour, as well as its timing late in the season, are historically atypical yet are becoming characteristics of a new norm. One year later, I noticed certain benefits of the wildfire within the park. Over eighty percent of the park's hiking trails were closed due to fire damage, as well as two scenic parkways. While a handful of trails had reopened prior to my visit, the parkways remained inaccessible to vehicular traffic. The consequential reduction in tourist traffic provided a quiet sanctuary for other-than-humans to graze on the regenerating foliage and berry crops. A park with habitat that supports a vast array of wildlife populations, it will not be surprising to see flora and fauna thrive in Waterton over the coming years in the wake of the Kenow fire.

Snowy Mountain Fire, Keremeos

The long, hot summers in the Okanagan provide ideal conditions for the winemaking industry and the cultivation of fruit and vegetables. These industries attract tourists and temporary foreign workers alike and represent a considerable economic revenue stream for the province. Sustainability and resilience have become key factors for agro-industries operating in a landscape increasingly affected by wildfire. While it is common knowledge that wildfire smoke poses a health risk, the exact scope of the effects of chronic exposure are dependent on a number of variables and are not adequately researched. Physical exertion during periods of poor air quality is discouraged by Health Canada, who have developed the Air Quality Health Index as a measure of risk assessment. On a scale of one through ten, it has become increasingly common for AQHI values to exceed twenty, and a record air quality value of forty-nine was recorded during the summer of 2017 in Kamloops (McElroy 2017). Not only does poor air quality affect workers, it is also a detriment to the tourism industry as recreational activities such as hiking, cycling and watersports are impacted as well (Beurteaux 2017). Recent research at The University of British Columbia 'underscores the immediate, harmful health effects of wildfire smoke and says there are concerning implications during the Covid-19 pandemic' (Canadian Press 2020), as smoke from wildfires threatens to exacerbate respiratory issues in people infected with Covid-19.

An aesthetic investigation of the aftermath and regeneration of areas affected by wildfire is one aspect of my research, however education and community outreach will play a critical role as well. Over the coming two years, I am collaborating with colleagues from various departments at UBC's Okanagan campus[1]. Our research under the collective title *Living with Wildfire*, will explore the ecological, cultural, and socio-economic dimensions of wildfire in the Okanagan, considering the regional landscape as a complex system, where human and ecological processes are linked across spatio-temporal scales (Parrott et al. 2012). My specific role is to connect scientific projections with landscapes impacted by wildfire through creative visual research. This will include before and after imagery of burned forests, which track regeneration over time. Our ambition is to provide a deeper understanding of fire risk, socio-cultural perceptions, and public understanding of wildfire dynamics.

1 Principal investigator Mathieu Bourbonnais, Assistant Professor, Earth, Environmental and Geographic Sciences. Collaborators: Dr. Lael Parrott, Professor, Sustainability, Dr. Greg Garrard, Associate Professor, Sustainability, Dr. Johannus (John) Janmaat, Associate Professor, Department of Economics, Philosophy and Political Science, and Dr. Kevin Hanna, Associate Professor, Department of Geography.

Kettle River Recreation Area [fireweed])

Projects such as *Living with Wildfire* will provide an alternative viewpoint to dominant discourses during periods of regional wildfire activity, yet our research will also supply critical avenues for discussion when fire is not regularly mentioned in the media. Going forward, it will be important to keep wildfire in our collective imagination as a significant modifier of the land on which we live. This process begins with recognition that the Okanagan region of British Columbia is one of the most fire-prone landscapes in Canada (Coops et al. 2018), whereby low to moderate intensity fires would occur at intervals anywhere between two to forty years. Small, frequent fires in this instance can provide an alternative to large severe fires. Cultural burning by Indigenous populations such as the Syilx dates back millennia, therefore the beautifully groomed forests that settlers considered to be old growth were in fact already managed forests. Methods such as cultural burning and adaptive management may present ways of working towards a future with fire. [1]

1 Term courtesy of Mathieu Bourbonnais, 2020

Christine Reid, Saul Herbert and Abi Bunker all work for the Woodland Trust promoting the protection, restoration and creation of native woodland for people and wildlife.

Learning from nature to achieve a resilient future forest

Christine Reid, Saul Herbert & Abi Bunker

Oak tree (image courtesy Woodland Trust)

Wild service (*Sorbus torminalis*) a tree associated with ancient woodland

Sanicle (*Sanicula europaea*) — an ancient herbal remedy and indicator species for ancient woodland (Both images: Christine Reid)

Learning from nature to achieve a resilient future forest

Christine Reid, Saul Herbert & Abi Bunker [Woodland Trust]

The foresters of the last four centuries could have had little idea how their actions would influence todays landscapes. Our predecessors could not second-guess the challenges, threats and pressures that would be facing woods and trees, nor the changing attitudes, values and responses of people many generations later. The wooded landscapes we see today are a product of both natural processes and the interventions of all the people and policies that have gone before.

Today, we have a lot more information, evidence and even predictive modelling that tells us about the current state of woods and trees, their present value to society, and what future conditions they may find themselves in. We know that our woods and landscapes need to be resilient to threats that could not have been imagined a hundred years ago when the Forestry Commission was created. We need to use our new knowledge wisely to help restore our forests and enable them to adapt to current and future threats.

Where are we today — the climate and biodiversity crises

Evidence of the size and pressing nature of the climate and biodiversity crises continues to mount. The 2020 report for the Intergovernmental Science-Policy Platform on Biodiversity and Ecosystem Services[1] offered a damning assessment of the state of global biodiversity, declaring a million species to be at risk of extinction. The Global Biodiversity Outlook 5[2] also set out a stark picture of nature in decline while the pressures driving losses continue to intensify. This holds major consequences not just for the natural world but for people, with biodiversity loss bringing consequent threats to the achievement of the UN's Sustainable Development Goals and undermining efforts to address climate change. The Inter-Governmental Panel on Climate Change have highlighted the need to limit warming to well below 2°C above pre-industrial levels if we are to keep large parts of our planet liveable for people.

In the UK, the Committee on Climate Change's recommendations for net zero by 2050[3] have shown the interconnectedness of climate and nature, recommending not only a rethinking of lifestyles but major land-use and widespread adoption of Nature Based Systems. In the UK, HM Treasury's review of the economics of biodiversity — the Dasgupta Review — published preliminary findings

1 https://ipbes.net/sites/default/files/2020-02/ipbes_global_assessment_report_summary_for_policymakers_en.pdf

2 https://www.cbd.int/gbo5

3 https://www.theccc.org.uk/uk-action-on-climate-change/reaching-net-zero-in-the-uk/

in April 2020[4]. This confirmed that the demands we are placing on nature massively outstrips its ability to supply the goods and services we rely on. This supply-demand imbalance requires us to 'reshape our understanding of sustainable economic growth'.

Woodland cover in the UK (now 13.2% of the land area) has more than doubled from the meagre remnants at the end of the First World War. Notwithstanding this relatively slow increase in woodland area, we have witnessed catastrophic declines in our biodiversity, including many species which are specifically associated with woodland habitats. Woodland butterfly species have declined by 41% on average since 1990, and woodland birds are down by 29% since 1970[5]. Alongside this nature emergency is the accelerating climate crisis, which is acting on woods, trees and landscapes already under huge pressure, amplifying the challenges faced by the people and wildlife reliant on them.

Policies which encouraged plantations of non-native trees on ancient woodland sites have been disastrous for most of our native woodland wildlife. Plantations on ancient woodland sites now cover around 38% of all ancient woodland[6]. In addition over the last century, traditional forms of woodland management, such as coppicing, have nearly been lost (for commercial production at least), capacity to process native hardwoods has fallen in the last 20 years and now 40% of our native woodland stands unmanaged (Forestry Commission 2018). Challenges have arisen as management has faltered, such as uncontrolled growth of deer populations and the spread of invasive plants such as rhododendron.

Some wildlife losses are a result of changes in surrounding agricultural landscapes, where the environmental consequences of large scale uniformity, simplification of systems, over-abstraction of water and use of agri-chemicals were largely unforeseen. For example 100% of woods in England receive damaging levels of nitrogen deposition (Rowe et al. 2020) from predominantly agricultural sources (Defra 2018), and, a recent study showed that across a swathe of eastern England over 80% of the field trees were lost from the landscape in the last 150 years[7]).

This same uniformity of structure and species composition found in farming systems became a characteristic of an increasing proportion of woodland cover too. From the mid-1980s, the Broadleaves Policy began to take account of the impacts of non-native conifers on native and ancient woodland, and grant rates were increased to encourage more planting of native woodland. Yet, in the last five years, only 45% of new woodland comprised broadleaved species[8].

The volume and diversity of plant material being shipped around the globe (whether as timber, horticulture products, or food) has increased exponentially, and with it have come hitch-hiking pests and diseases. In conjunction with

4 https://www.gov.uk/government/publications/interim-report-the-dasgupta-review-independent-review-on-the-economics-of-biodiversity

5 https://hub.jncc.gov.uk/assets/7162735c-9fa7-4962-aee7-709d242173f1

6 https://www.woodlandtrust.org.uk/media/1704/current-state-of-ancient-woodland-restoration.pdf

7 State of the UKs Woods and Trees 2021 — the Woodland Trust (in press)

8 https://www.gov.uk/government/statistics/forestry-facts-and-figures-2020

a warmer climate, the likelihood of damaging pathogens becoming established in the UK is rising — with at least 21 economically and ecologically damaging tree pests and diseases becoming widespread since 1990.

Where are we today — valuing the forest

Native trees and woods — alongside their intrinsic value as a natural habitat and home to a wide diversity of native flora and fauna — have enormous utility to people, as well as providing inspiration and emotional sustenance.

Ever since the 1600's and the push for more oak for ship's timbers, and wood for our great cathedrals, through coppicing for charcoal to fuel early industry, and onto modern conifer forestry, the products of woods and forests and how to grow and maintain them have become an evolving art and science of forestry, inseparable from the natural environment on which it's based.

Today the plethora of ecosystem services and consequent benefits to people provided by woods and trees, are being more widely recognised and quantified. For example, in terms of carbon storage, woodlands in Great Britain together hold 213 million tonnes of carbon (in their living trees) (Forest Research 2019). Trees can also help with adaptation to changes in the weather and climate by reducing the risk of downstream flooding. Urban woods and trees provide water management, pollution control, and temperature regulation in towns and cities where 80% of the UK population lives. The coronavirus pandemic and resulting lockdown of 2020 has brought into even sharper focus the importance of natural green space for recreation and wellbeing. However, we know that the number of people with easy access to woodland has declined since 2016. In 2020 just 16.2% of people in the UK have access to a wood of at least 2ha within 500m of their homes — down from 21.1% in 2016.[9]

What next for woods, trees and forestry?

The way we manage woods and trees, and the landscapes in which they sit, will need to deliver a more balanced and complex range of benefits to people and wildlife. The separation of woods from trees is an artificial construct; a consequence of societal changes and forestry systems and doesn't reflect how landscapes function. A more holistic view of stewardship and management of woods and trees in integrated ways and at landscape scale can bring multiple benefits, allowing us to realise benefits across the rural and urban landscapes.

We believe that by following nature's lead in our approach to creating and managing woods and trees, we will produce more resilient landscapes that have improved potential to adapt to future conditions. This means learning from, and making space for natural processes such as natural regeneration of native trees, and ensuring they are species and provenances well-adapted to local conditions. In existing woods, creating a varied age structure, and promoting species that support pollination, allowing natural seed dispersal and disturbance, creating a dynamic ecosystem, rather than imposing uniform structure on woodland. We need a renewed emphasis on protecting and restoring ancient woodlands, because of what these native ecosystems can teach us about

9 State of the UKs Woods and Trees 2021 — the Woodland Trust (in press)

resilience. And, we need to replace those lost individual trees which knit our landscapes together and enable wildlife dispersal and colonisation.

Woodland creation — expanding the cover of native woods and trees

It is vital to recognise the climate and biodiversity crises as being interconnected and not two separate challenges. To tackle these challenges and create more resilient landscapes, we need to not only protect what we have but also expand woodland and tree cover to support nature recovery and for carbon sequestration.

The government's response to climate change proposes a rapid increase in the rate of woodland creation as a key mechanism to lock up carbon in trees and soils, and provide an alternative to fossil fuel energy and resource-hungry building material; however, since the 1970s planting rates of new woodland have declined steadily. Over the last 5 years there has only been (on average) less than 10,000 hectares of new woodland created each year across the whole UK, despite ambitious government targets for new woodland calling for upwards of 30,000ha of new woodland annually. But there is an important dimension to this challenge — how do we ensure we expand our woods and trees and increase their quality and value to people and wildlife?

The significant change in land use that will be needed to achieve 30,000ha of new woodland each year across the UK, will require not only national targets that are translated into policies, funding and action, but also widespread support from landowners, local decision makers and the general public.

Success should not just be measured in timber volumes, but in the contribution to carbon sequestration, management of flood risk and water quality, provision of recreation and contribution to people's health and wellbeing, and critically to sustaining biodiversity and supporting nature's recovery. To deliver such a complex suite of outcomes under such challenging conditions forestry needs to adapt and change.

It matters what type of woodland we create; woodland creation needs to be based on the principles of ecological restoration. The characteristics of the land and landscape, existing features of conservation value and the land use and cultural history of the land need to be carefully considered. This assessment of the potential for restoring the ecological integrity of a site or landscape should underpin any creation of new woods and trees.

The potential for new exotic tree species and different provenances of our native trees to deliver resilience has been a recurring theme of the resilience debate. However, this approach carries risk. First and foremost the risk of introducing new pests and diseases is even more immediate and apparent than that posed by drought, fire, storm and flood. Looking overseas for a solution may in practice have many more risks than opportunities. It is no coincidence that there has been a significant increase in imported pests and diseases since 1990 when you consider that tree imports have increased from £6 million in 1990 to £93 million in 2019, that's a 1450% increase (Defra 2020). The industry's reliance on imports significantly increases the risk of further pest and disease introductions (Brasier 2008:792-808).

In addition, our native trees have a long history of co-evolution with other native species such as fungi, insects, birds, and mammals, and that because of this our native woodlands are richer and more diverse in wildlife. These associations cannot be replicated by exotic species. A recently published paper (Ennos et al. 2019:718-728) concluded that 'where conservation of biodiversity is an objective we find no support for introduction of new exotic species. Introduction of new exotics is likely to lead to an increase rather than a decrease in pest and disease problems, and to hinder rather than support the retention of threatened native tree species and their associated biodiversity.'

A clear illustration is provided by the loss of ash to dieback, estimated to cost the UK £15bn (Hill et al. 2019) in clean-up and replacement costs and in lost ecosystem services benefits. Over 900 species depend on ash trees, and will decline if ash is not replaced by other trees which can support the same species. The research findings published by Natural England and JNCC (Mitchell et al. 2014) identified that native trees are essential to support the species that depend on ash, and that some non-natives can play an important role where they display similar traits, like sycamore which has similarities in bark pH and heart rot.

Another recent report (Whittet et al. 2019) considered the value of introducing a wider range of genetic provenances of native tree species, yet concluded that 'native trees in the UK are shown to have a very high degree of genetic variability within their populations. So although we have a limited range of native trees and shrubs (about 40 species) they have an incredible genetic diversity, meaning they have great potential to respond and adapt to rapidly changing environmental conditions.' A key message from the report is that adaptation to site-specific conditions is more effectively promoted through stimulating successive rounds of natural regeneration through regular woodland management, than through attempts to introduce genetic strains from possible future climatic regions. This involves providing the space for successful regeneration and ensuring the effective management of deer and grey squirrel populations.

Managing existing woodland

An increase in well managed woods and trees is needed as part of a strategy to restore nature across our landscapes and stem the declines in biodiversity. Woods and trees will be impacted by climate change, as well as other threats and pressures. Whilst predicted average temperature rises may be within the adaptive limits of the majority of our native tree species and our woodland ecosystems, extreme events, such as more frequent and severe droughts, increased likelihood of storms and floods and a greater risk of wildfire, are likely to take their toll — and we are seeing the effects of this already — with forest fires in April in the north of Scotland, to shallow rooting trees like beech wilting in the south of England in the summer's drought in 2018.

These come on top of a familiar set of existing challenges of wooded landscapes such as fragmentation effects caused by development and changing agricultural practice, browsing by wild herbivores and livestock and the loss and degradation of ancient woodland to development, ammonia deposition, and non-native plantations. The important ecological effects of lost species such as beaver and pine marten are only now being appreciated following their return to limited parts of the UK.

Other existing threats are escalating in correlation with changes in the climate; an increase in tree pests and pathogens and growing pressure from invasive non-native species. The 2020 British Woodland Survey[10] asked over 1000 woodland owners and agents about what changes they were noticing in the woods they manage. 78% said they had noticed an increase in pathogen damage over the last five years, with increases in insect pests, mammal browsing, drought and wind damage also observed by more than half of respondents. There is clearly an observable need to increase the resilience of our woodlands.

A move away from even-aged monocultures, using clear-fell and restock systems, to a more diverse range of trees species and canopy structures, managed using low impact silvicultural systems is an important step to increase resilience of our existing woods. A lack of structure in woodland, as a result of management and made worse by deer browsing, has been clearly shown to be a key factor in the decline of specialist woodland birds (Fuller et al. 2016).

Management approaches which promote a diverse woodland structure are a good example of the complimentary delivery of conservation and utility outcomes, providing more habitat niches for wildlife, improved carbon capture and retention, protection of soils and better management of water quality and flood risk. For example ancient woodlands are the core sites for our woodland network — restoring ecological complexity to the 38% of ancient woodland whose ecology has been degraded by plantation forestry is critical.

Conclusion

Delivering resilient treescapes will require all woodland managers to look outwards, beyond their own woods and consider how they can integrate their aims and objectives with those of others. We will need a broader range of knowledge and skills; of ecology, hydrology, people management and collaborative working. Critically, it will require society and policy makers to start to attach meaningful value to all of the benefits that woods and trees provide for people and wildlife, and reward and incentivise landowners and managers for delivering these benefits. This needs policies, investments and markets which reflect the value of trees and woods. We must manage and expand forests so they contribute to resilient landscapes and habitats which store carbon, manage water, enhance biodiversity and provide space for people's physical and mental health to flourish.

It will require all those with knowledge, experience and those who care passionately for our woods and trees to continue to work together over the next 100 years to break down barriers, invest in science and evidence, inspire and engage people and find and implement solutions.

10 https://www.sylva.org.uk/bws

Kathryn Nelson is an artist and PhD student at Queens University Belfast. She has an MSc in Ecological Management and Conservation Biology and an MA in Arts in the Community. Her current trans-disciplinary research explores ecological knowledge dissemination through culture and visual art.

Roy Nelson is currently an Honorary Senior Lecturer at Queens University Belfast. He has a background in agriculture and plant science. His research interests are in decision-making and risk communication within a rural context.

Place, Patterns, Provenance & People: dynamic woodland biomes

Kathryn Nelson & Roy Nelson

Place, Patterns, Provenance and People: dynamic woodland biomes explored

Kathryn Nelson School of Arts, English and Languages, Queens University Belfast

Roy Nelson, School of Biological Sciences, Queens University Belfast

Introduction

Europe was once a forested continent with primeval trees harbouring a rich bio-diverse ecosystem yet now the continent is a mosaic of different landscapes: urban, moorland, intensively farmed, and scattered areas of forest remnants. This transformation of the once great forest began 8000 years ago when Neolithic agriculture began: yet there are two histories. The first is of the great northern boreal forest of conifers where human impact only became noticeable two thousand years ago and where much of the forest still remains intact. The second is of the mixed temperate forest where progressive impact from forest clearance and agriculture, some 6000 years ago, especially in northwest Europe decimated the forest biome.

Ireland was similarly affected, with forest clearance increasing in the 7th century. As the felling of trees continued, fragmented stands became vulnerable to the strong Atlantic gales and the loss of the once mighty forest became inevitable. Yet this narrative that our species was the only negative impact on the Irish forest does have its opponents. This is particularly so when considering changes in the climate and a summer cooling of 2° C before the Neolithic period caused an expansion of blanket bog in Ireland, Wales, and the southwest of England (Gallego-Sala et al. 2016). This caused waterlogging of soils, which in turn caused tree root death, and this predictably led to the loss of forest cover.

These changes in environmental conditions were also seen more noticeably at the end of the last ice age when much of Ireland was devoid of vegetation. The freezing temperatures were followed by a period of warming. This meant ecological succession could begin and the first to arrive were the arctic and alpine plants, followed by the grassland species that persisted until the temperature rose again which allowed the establishment of juniper woodland. This small evergreen was subsequently replaced by birch woodland, possibly due to a further oscillation in climate (Smith & Goddard 1991). The process of ecological succession continued with the arrival into Ireland of hazel, oak, and elm. These trees created the dense mixed primeval forest of Ireland.

The oscillation of the climate is a significant natural occurrence, and the subsequent changes in biodiversity provide evidence that species must disperse and colonise newly accessible habitat from refuges. These refuges are highly important since they can be relicts of past ecosystems, but they can also significantly mitigate against biodiversity loss. Ecological refuges are then vital for forest species survival.

◀ Oak at Coleridge, South Devon (photo: Richard Povall)

Place: habitat fragmentation and ecological refuges

Given current climate conditions Ireland would still be largely forested. Yet Northern Ireland tree cover is limited, with only 1% of semi-natural broadleaf woodland left (Cooper & McCann 2002). Habitat fragmentation can lead to biodiversity loss. Small patches of woodland might act as ecological refuges, but without habitat connectivity the forest species will not be able to disperse. Habitat connectivity is vital to safeguard forest biodiversity.

Nevertheless, the type of forest is also important when considering ecological refuges. For instance, most woodland in the British Isles can be divided into primary and secondary forests. Primary forest is an ecosystem that has had limited management and significantly trees that have never been harvested with a lineage back to the prehistoric forest. Secondary forest on the other hand is on land that was once cleared of trees but can still be considered 'ancient' if the land has been continually forested from 1600 (Rackham 1976). However, none of the semi-natural broadleaf woodland in Northern Ireland is ancient and unfortunately the secondary woodland that is left is fragmented. Hedgerows, which play a significant part in both acting as ecological refuges and in also connecting forest species communities, are in decline which is inevitably leading to a reduction in biodiversity refuges or 'reservoirs' (Schmitz et al. 2007).

Forest plant species have limited dispersal abilities. They are both restricted in the distance they can disperse and the time they take to colonise new patches of habitat. This has caused particular difficulties with natural colonisation and spread of herbaceous plants. This limitation is why woodland ground flora is often restricted to isolated ecological refuges, and why it is vital to maintain habitat connectivity to assist in the dispersal of forest herbs. This is particularly so when considering siting and planting a new woodland. Inevitably there will be some loss of biodiversity when grass is initially converted into woodland. Habitat corridors are therefore vital to encourage colonisation of woodland herbaceous species into these new habitats.

Pattern: colonisation of ground flora into newly planted broadleaf woodland

Little research has been completed on newly planted broadleaf woodland and the colonisation rates of their ground flora. It was recognised that research in this area was required (Nelson et al. 2021). Thirty study sites, between 11 to 21 years old, were selected throughout Northern Ireland. Before any fieldwork could be undertaken two groups of ground flora were identified. They are described below:

1) **Ancient woodland indicator species (AWIS)**

The ancient woodland indicator species are herbs that have been identified as growing in ancient woodland and are woodland specialists. Nine species were selected to represent the AWIS group and these were: bluebell, common dog violet, golden saxifrage, greater stitchwort, hart's tongue fern, primrose, ramson, wood anemone, and wood sorrel.

2) **Woodland indicator species (WIS)**

The woodland indicator species grow in shaded areas but are not commonly associated with ancient woodland. Four species were selected to represent the WIS group and these were: enchanter's nightshade, Jack-in-the-pulpit, herb bennet and male fern

The research hypothesis of the study was that ancient woodland indicator species would be slower to colonise new habitats than shade tolerant species. In addition, it was also hoped that the research would assist in providing information on how to improve colonisation rates of all woodland species.

After the two groups were selected for the study, the method of collecting the relevant information was devised. Study species that were found would be identified and their distance from the source population measured. A colonisation rate for each study species was then developed. The distance that each study species was away from their parent or source plant was used to calculate their maximum dispersal range (β) which was then divided by the age (A) of the newly planted wood. This gave the colonisation rate (φ).

$$\varphi = \beta / A$$

This colonisation rate was calculated for each individual plant's distance (m) from their source population. A novel 'fingerprint' analysis was devised using the calculated information (Fig.1 and 2). The 'fingerprints' clearly identified that each group were colonising the new habitats differently. Each fingerprint used the maximum rate of colonisation per species, per woodland site. The x and y axis show colonisation rate (m) from the origin (0,0) which represents the species colonisation source (parent plant). Each colour represents a different species.

A further investigation of the colonisation rates was completed by cluster analysis, which divided the data

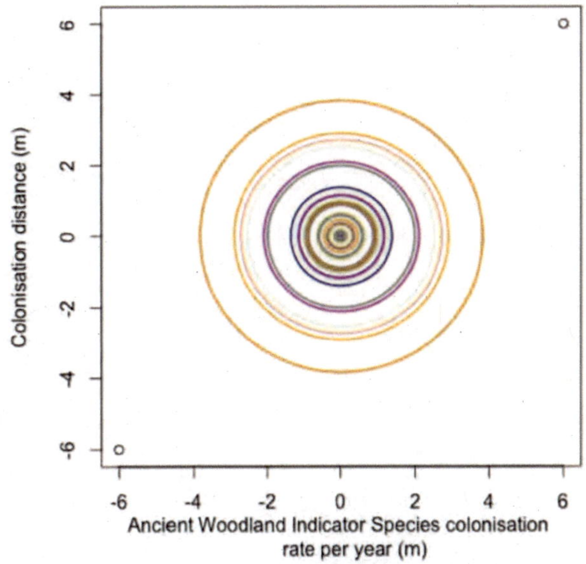

Fig. 1. Ancient woodland indicator species — showing that colonisation distance is to some degree limited and that there are restricted numbers of this group present in the new habitat.

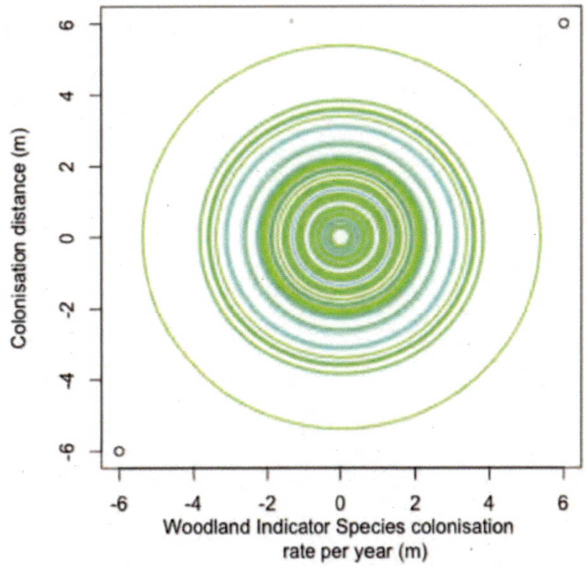

Fig 2. Woodland indicator species —showing that colonisation distance can be over 5m per year and that this group is reasonably plentiful in the new habitat.

into three groups instead of the original two. These new groups were named: Ancient Edge Huggers, Expansionists, and Woodland Dispersers. They too were analysed and presented by fingerprints (Fig. 3, 4, & 5). The Ancient Edge Huggers (a very slow dispersing group of species) and the Expansionists together were very similar to the ancient woodland indicator species. Likewise, the Woodland Dispersers are almost identical to the original shade tolerant group (WIS). The only difference is that enchanter's nightshade was placed in the Expansionist group.

The research concluded that the ancient woodland indicator species colonisation rates are slower and less frequent than the shade tolerant species. Nevertheless, the ancient woodland indicator species colonisation rates were significantly increased when the newly planted

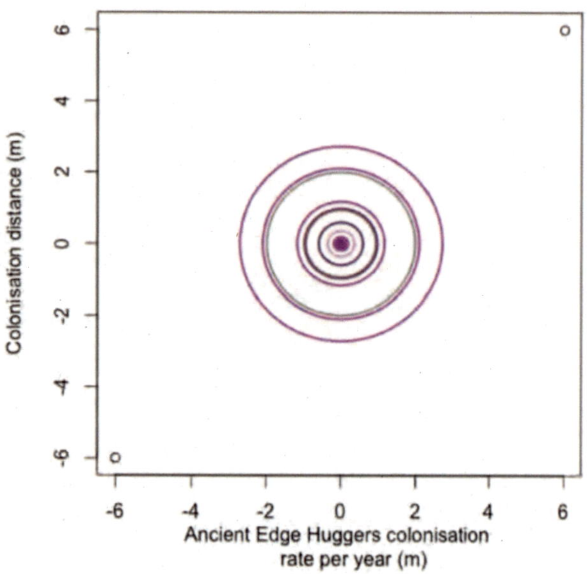

Fig. 3. Ancient Edge Huggers — (common dog violet, wood anemone and wood sorrel), showing both their limited colonisation distance and their restricted numbers present in the new habitat.

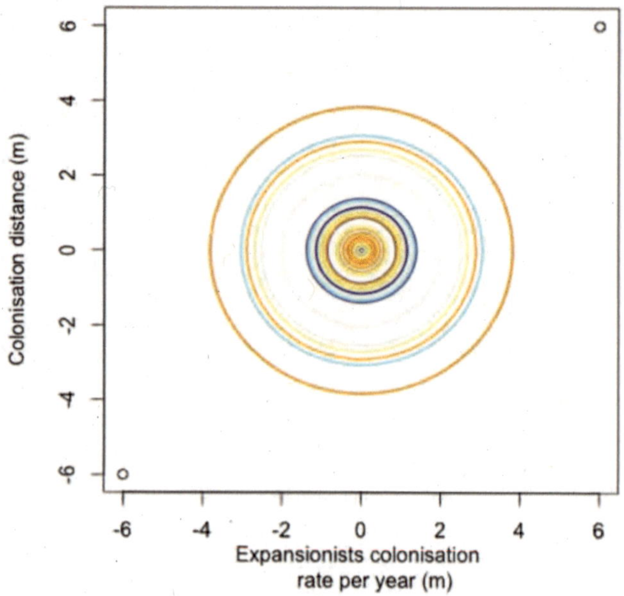

Fig. 4. Expansionists — (bluebell, enchanter's nightshade, golden saxifrage, greater stitchwort, hart's tongue fern, primrose and ramson), showing their restricted numbers in the new habitat.

broadleaf woodlands were close to a stream or river and at lower altitudes. The colonisation rates also improved when the newly planted broadleaf woodland were bordered by mature woodland or hedgerows that were species rich. These bordering lands improve the likelihood of source populations of parent plants being in the locality.

Provenance: local and exotic seed

Provenance of plant material is important and it has been shown that local tree populations have become adapted to their local habitat. An example of this is the hawthorn. Imported hawthorns can flower 5 weeks earlier than hawthorn that has local provenances. This has a knock-on effect since many birds and insects synchronise their

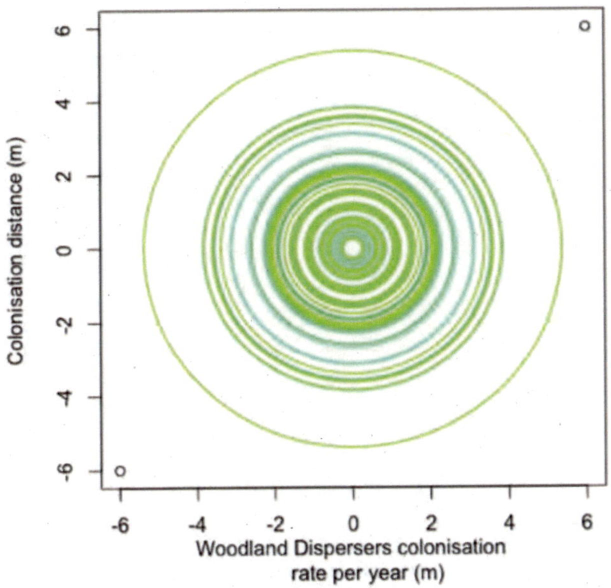

Fig. 5. Woodland Dispersers - (Jack-in-the-pulpit, herb bennet and male fern), showing that colonisation distance can be over 5m per year and that this group is reasonably plentiful in the new habitat.

breeding season to coincide with the hawthorns flowering period (Jones et al. 2001).

Local plants are key to improving both regional biodiversity and also maintaining a well-balanced ecosystem. Yet often plants are not well dispersed in the local environment and exist only in isolated refuges. As a result, it is vital that local refuges such as hedgerows, mature woodland and riparian zones are well managed. Research by Garbutt & Sparks (2002) showed that one Cambridgeshire hedge had a noticeable loss of ancient woodland flora, unexpectedly in an unmanaged section, away from intensive agriculture. It appears that to maintain biodiversity local refuges must be appropriately managed. This is particularly important when considering planting new broadleaf woodland when seed and plants can colonise from these refuges.

Sometimes colonisation from local sources may take too long, or the plant that is desired is locally extinct so the plant material may have to be collected elsewhere. In these situations, care must then be taken when sourcing plant materials to ensure that geographical and environmental features are similar to the planned location of the new wood. The use of non-local sources may have to be considered due to the pressures of on-going environmental changes. This can be regarded as 'assistant migration' and may involve planting native plants that are from more southerly areas to cope and survive future rises in temperature.

People: knowledge, attitudes and behaviour

At a local, regional and global level there is a need to change behaviour to ensure that people's actions promote vibrant, healthy, and diverse woodlands. People have three interrelated constructs or components of self: knowledge, attitudes, and behaviour, which are closely related, whereby a change in one can affect a change in another. Changing people's knowledge is the basis of many educational, and training programmes. However, longer-term changes in behaviour are usually aimed at changing attitudes, yet, the relationship between attitudes and behaviour does at times seem only loosely related which makes the outcome of how people make decisions often difficult to predict; does a developer of a new housing estate cut down a hedgerow or leave it standing? His positive attitude to the environment might suggest one type of behaviour, but his attitude towards financial gain might suggest another.

This type of decision-making requires a solution to be found for a specific problem. Decision-making can be a rational process, since it can follow a logical path as illustrated in probabilistic theories. Nonetheless, in everyday decision making the individual regularly follow their intuitions and avoid this type of rational thinking and instead use a set of 'rules' or heuristics (Tversky & Kahneman 1983). In these circumstances people regularly use mental short cuts that are 'fast and frugal' (Gigerenzerr 2000). This is when they tend to accept a choice that is 'good enough' (Simon 1956). There are several heuristics that may be used regularly in decision-making. We have selected two, to discuss.

1) **Availability**

People use this heuristic to judge an event if it is easy to imagine or recall and is affected by factors such as media coverage. This may result in a reliance on secondary information and small sample sizes. Significantly people regularly overlook aspects outside their given field of expertise. An example of this is that a person might not realise that picking some 'pretty' bluebells will damage woodland biodiversity. They remember collecting these when they were young, but they do not comprehend that they are trampling and damaging the existing woodland flora. They are unaware of the 'big picture'. They also do not realise that if everyone made the same decision, the woodland would be seriously damaged.

2) **Simulation**

The simulation heuristic is related to the availability heuristic and is described as a 'mental picture' of an event or issue (Bertini, et al. 2006). Imagery plays a prominent role in the interpretation of phenomena and is effective in developing appropriate responses in easy to imagined terms. This heuristic suggests that visual images may play a role in supporting positive environmental decisions; documentaries help people understand why tropical forests are important to the global biosphere. Perhaps visual images such as this should also endorse the woodland biomes closer to home, since they too provide biodiverse habitats and are places of beauty and wonder.

Integrating heuristics into communication programmes ensure that intended change can be managed to the benefit of all more effectively. Change can be understood as effective communication through some form of media, to an audience that improves their knowledge, or effects a change in their attitudes or behaviour. This concept of change through constructs or components of self may assist in our species appreciation and wonderment of our own native woodland, not just of the magnificent oaks, but of the complete biome; from the mycorrhizas of the soil, to the goshawks of the sky.

Conclusion

This chapter uses a transdisciplinary approach to argue that to maintain or/and to create a healthy woodland biome, certain key fundamentals have to be in position: well managed native bio-diverse refuges, good landscape connectivity, genetically rich biota and if possible plants of a local provenance (Fig. 6). In order to do this, it is important that dispersal and colonisation patterns are known. The fingerprint patterns exploit the simulation heuristic to visually show how the different ground flora colonise newly planted broadleaf woodland at different rates. When it comes to managing a situation with the aim of developing the concept of the 'evolving woodland' it is hoped these fingerprint patterns will be easier to recall thereby assisting in the decision-making process. After all if people have increased woodland knowledge, this will help policy makers, managers, and the general public to make positive and constructive decisions towards the woodland ecosystems.

Finally, our landscape is not natural, it has been farmed, altered, and shaped by our species over thousands of years. We are, after all, a keystone species and therefore what we do and how we do it matters to the environment. We have the power to destroy, or we can become guardians of our woodlands. Yet to grow and maintain their bio-diversity woodlands must be connected to the wider landscape through wildlife corridors, so that their biota can disperse and colonise new areas. Although our species has planted trees to form new woods, these trees are just living pillars in a monoculture of wasteland, since without herbaceous plants, insects, lichen, fungi, birds and mammals the rich ecological web of the forest can never truly exist. Places of diversity take time to grow and mature; but without care, patience and understanding they will never have the chance to fulfil their true potential. After all the establishment of woodlands only begins with the planting of trees. Woodlands enhance our lives and promote a sense of wellbeing and calm. Perhaps they should be understood as places of wonder and awe, since they are, after all, both our past and our future.

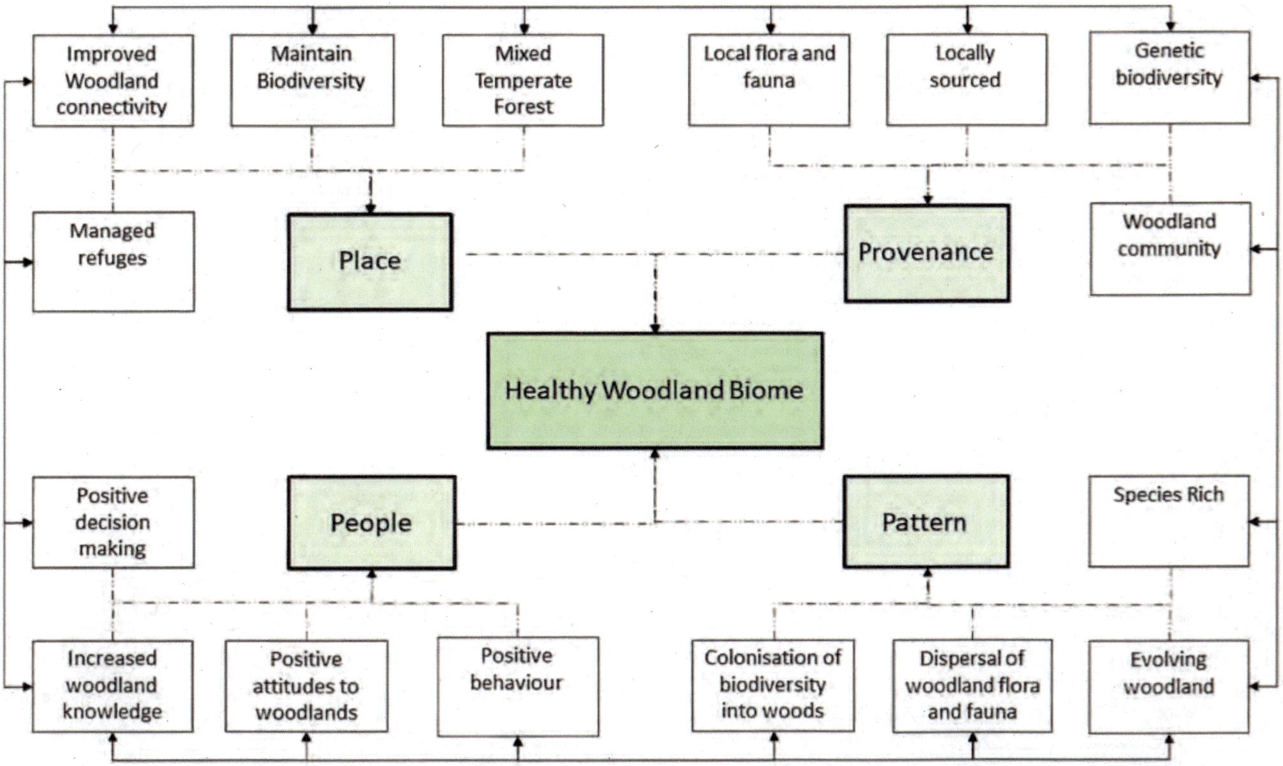

Fig. 6. The steps needed to create a healthy woodland biome

My career was with the Nature Conservancy Council and its successors (English Nature, Natural England) for 33 years as a woodland ecologist. In that time I was involved with various reviews of national forestry policy and strategies. Since retirement in 2012 I have returned to research in Oxford, looking particularly at long-term changes in vegetation. However I remain loosely involved with both government and voluntary forestry/ conservation organisations

photo: Richard Povall

Evolution or Revolution for Future Forestry

Keith Kirby

Evolution or revolution for future forestry?

Keith J. Kirby, Department of Plant Sciences, University of Oxford, South Parks Road, Oxford, OX1 3RB

Major changes to how we live and use resources are needed in Britain over the next fifty years, if we are to avoid major catastrophes. A new compact with trees and forests should be part of these changes.

Introduction

When our ancestors left the forest for open savanna the change in their environment contributed to the making of modern humans. However, we did not leave the trees behind completely. They continued to provide us with necessary commodities, enjoyment and inspiration, and helped to maintain the stability of the environment that is essential for individual and societal survival. However on all continents where trees exist, old-growth forests have been cleared, their wildlife destroyed, the structure and composition of the remaining forests simplified. In Britain we cannot agree on what the 'natural' structure and composition of our landscape might have looked like — largely dense, closed forest or more like open parkland — so completely has it been modified by human activity.

Our cavalier attitude to forests extends to the rest of the planet. Reports on progress with the Paris Accord on climate change suggest we have less than a generation to act if we are to hold the temperature rise below 2 degrees[1]. We seem to be on course to exceed several of the safe environmental planetary boundaries[2]. The world's increasing population cannot achieve and sustain the lifestyles and levels of consumption currently enjoyed by the richest, most developed countries.

Moving towards more sustainable lifestyles

Britain, along with other developed countries, has a disproportionately large environmental footprint per capita, yet we are not very clear or open enough about the consequences of our impact on forests overseas. We should fund mitigation measures elsewhere in the world, but we also need to address the basic problem that as a country we live well beyond our own wood supply. Perhaps the experience of Covid-19 will change the way that we view how we use our land to supply our food and fibre. We can seek to reduce wood use, but for some purposes such as construction it is better to increase it if the alternatives are brick and concrete. Where can we produce more of our tree consumption than we do at present?

We do not have to be totally self-sufficient at the GB level (which is not likely to be possible anyway); some issues are better viewed at larger European or world scales and on multi-annual cycles. Furthermore sustainability/self-sufficiency must not be judged just in material production terms but taking account of soil, water, wildlife and spiritual needs etc., through drawing on ecosystem services and natural capital thinking.

1 https://www.theguardian.com/environment/2018/oct/08/global-warming-must-not-exceed-15c-warns-landmark-un-report

2 https://www.stockholmresilience.org/research/planetary-boundaries/planetary-boundaries/about-the-research/the-nine-planetary-boundaries.html

Where does conservation fit in this?

At the global-scale many wild habitats and species are in decline — sometimes referred to as the sixth mass extinction. In Britain there are similar declines and losses on a local and national scale, largely through changes in land cover and use — the effects of intensification of agriculture, forestry and development[3] . For example, the transformation of ancient semi-natural woodland to conifer plantations, the impacts of increasing deer populations on woodland flora, the changes brought about by increased atmospheric pollution are all well-documented. Conservation successes — the return of red kites and beavers, the restoration of plantations on ancient woodland sites — have not been on a sufficient scale to turn around the overall pattern of decline. Even within protected sites species have been lost or declined in abundance.

We should care about these species losses because we have a moral duty to the rest of the planet and wildlife populations can often be a useful indicator that we are managing the natural world's resources responsibly (or not). More prosaically we do not know all the roles that different species play or might play in future and hence which might prove essential for our survival.

The environmental sector has argued strongly that industries (including farming and commercial forestry) should be adapting their methods and expectations to prepare for climate change, but on the whole conservation priorities still seem to me to be those drawn up in the 1970s. New, big measures are needed.

We may not have time for evolution, revolutions may be needed, bringing in new landscape patterns and priorities. Ideas are starting to emerge about what a future wild-life-rich countryside and urban environment might look like, for example in some of the debates about rewilding. However, even in these, there is often a reluctance to consider that this could involve species losses as well as gains; that future woodland may not be awash with flowering bluebells, new heaths may not be that heather-rich, but rather full of regenerating birch. Such messages can be difficult to sell to the millions of members who support wildlife- and landscape-orientated charities.

Who pays the piper?

Conservation in Britain over the last seventy years has been largely based around small sites with active management: it is likely to continue but it is something of a luxury activity — largely supported by government grants and voluntary donations. Very few protected sites, particularly woodland ones, can claim that they produce sufficient marketable goods to pay the full economic costs of their current management.

Protected sites do provide additional ecosystem services such as soil protection, water management and contribute to natural capital, but so do other forms of land cover and land use. The conservation sector must show that the *marginal* increase in the contribution to (say) soil protection, carbon sequestration, water regulation of a coppice-wood compared to a plantation outweighs the value of the greater timber production from a more productive high forest. I do not see the traditional conservation sector

3 https://nbn.org.uk/stateofnature2019/

Box 1: Moving forward with rewilding

- We must stop worrying and arguing over precisely what rewilding is; in practice it will take different forms in different places, but it is essentially about reducing the degree to which humans intervene in determining wildlife and conservation outcomes — let nature look after itself, within broad limits.
- We are unlikely to find anywhere in Britain where we can step back completely from intervention and there are indirect human impacts, some legacies of the past, some continuing, that will affect rewilding areas. We will still need to intervene in places, more in some cases than others, but we should be planning to reduce the need for intervention over time.
- The outcomes and benefits are uncertain; that is part of the difference to planned conservation management where we work towards promoting particular habitats and species. The conservation sector will need to get used to this. Some of the species we currently value may decline while others increase in rewilding areas. Short-term gains may disappear in the medium to long-term.
- Rewilding, ideally should be done on a large scale, but it must be done by consent, by owners and communities wishing to be part of such schemes, although large-scale withdrawal from farming could also lead to rewilding by default.
- Re-introductions might be part of some schemes, but some (wolf!) may be a step too far, for the foreseeable future.
- More tree cover is likely to be an outcome of rewilding in many situations, but not necessarily in all cases.
- Rewilding is not the only approach to conservation. Some rewilding projects may turn out not to 'work' for conservation as we see it today. However, existing approaches have not all been good value for money or delivered the conservation gains we would have liked.

being able to expand much beyond its current size in its current form, particularly with the escalating costs of the Covid-19 epidemic, our exit from the EU and possible economic recession.

Future conservation will depend largely, as it has through most of history, on how we combine it with the balance of other land-uses and at what scales we do that. For the last few decades, we have generally tried to merge conservation with production systems everywhere (land sharing), supported by agri-environmental schemes and forestry grants. This also appears to be the main focus for the new Environmental Land Management Scheme (ELMS). The approach works, but if government funding is limited (which it will be) it may not be the most effective use of those funds.

Land sparing

Some suggest that half the earth's surface should be devoted to nature[4] . I doubt that will happen but even in Britain not all land that is currently farmed may continue to be so. The Government's advisory Committee on Climate Change has suggested cuts of between a fifth and a half in beef and sheep production. This may gain further support from animal welfare arguments and pressures to go vegan. The economics of farming, particularly in marginal areas, could also be threatened by whatever new systems of tariffs and import patterns emerge, post-Brexit. If the Committee's estimate that 3-7 million hectares could become available for other uses, this could allow the space for more forests for wood production but also for big rewilding projects.

What could conservation achieve if say 10% (c.2 million hectares) of Britain were to be placed into some form of rewilding? The challenges of doing so would be big but need not be insurmountable (Box 1).

Rewilding should run alongside other more interventionist and targeted efforts to conserve habitats and species which will provide much of the source of species to move into the rewilded areas. Most of the British countryside would however still continue to be used primarily for a mix of food, fibre and energy production, recreation, or development, as now. The conservation sector needs to be ready to take advantage of the opportunities that such shifts in the balance of land-uses may open-up. This means being positive, strategic, holistic: i.e. prepared for some losses and to take risks in the short-term to achieve bigger, long-term gains; being sympathetic to and supportive of other land users and their objectives in order that they in turn will support ours.

What about production?

Tree cover may increase in the rewilding areas but any increased wood production from these, as from traditional protected sites, will be small in comparison to our overall wood-use. The bulk of ***our*** demand for wood products over the next 50 years is still likely to be conifer-based. The conservation sector should be more active in working with others to identify where this might be grown, rather than assuming it is someone else's job to come up with proposals to which the conservation sector will then (usually) object.

4 https://eowilsonfoundation.org/half-earth-our-planet-s-fight-for-life/

What is our competitive advantage in the world timber trade, given likely increases in competition to buy wood and wood products from China and other developing economies? Which markets — both for wood *and other services* — are best supplied by the limited home-grown resource, as opposed to what we will continue to have to import, assuming we can afford to and that we are not simply exporting our environmental debt off-shore?

For example, we cannot produce enough wood-chip to keep the DRAX power-stations going, but we should be able to produce enough barbeque charcoal from low-grade broadleaves. We cannot produce enough softwood to meet our total pulp and paper demands but could we produce enough construction-grade softwood to meet a big expansion of timber-framed housing? We can certainly improve our woodland cover's ability to take more visitors, as an alternative to overseas travel with the extra carbon footprint that entails.

Future forestry practice

In the twentieth century forestry, like agriculture followed the paths of increasing the scale of operations, mechanisation, a focus on a limited number of tree species, grown as single-species stands. Oliver Rackham compared plantations to just tall crops of wheat. However, the forest industry has taken on board many of the practices recommended by the conservation sector to improve the structure and composition of forests for wildlife.

Generally, the second-rotation crops in the big upland plantations are in somewhat smaller blocks and include, either through planting or self-sown introgression, a wider range of trees. There is a strong push towards Continuous Cover Forestry (CCF) as an alternative to clear-fells. The conservation sector has tended to welcome such moves but the evidence as to what sorts of species and assemblages will thrive under these regimes is still limited. We need more research to judge where the environmental gains are worth the increased costs involved, to decide how much of the current forest estate should go into CCF.

If there is to be a massive increase in tree cover, conservation micro-management such as we have developed over the last seventy years may not be the most cost-efficient way of getting the gains that we want, particularly in our changing environmental conditions. Rather than concentrating our broadleaved planting in purpose-designed native woods we could spread the same area out as a network of bands along waterways, paths and boundaries to provide functional connectivity for poor colonists. Then fill the lacunae with more productive species. If it takes (say) fifty years for ground flora to colonise some new sites because they are remote from sources of seed, we could do more introduction of the poorer-colonising species early on, as was done for the roadside belts in Milton Keynes. Rather than try to mould a Sitka spruce stand into some poor cousin of a native broadleaved wood, we could put more effort into building up the types of wildlife assemblages that occur in mature coniferous stands elsewhere in the temperate-boreal zone.

We need to embrace new mixed landscapes where trees, woods (at different scales) and open land function together both ecologically and productively. Perhaps the trend for increasing separation of forestry and farming over the last two hundred years can be reversed, as indicated by the very active, if still rather small agro-forestry movement in Britain.

Future governance

Forestry was never formally within the competence of the European Union (EU) but was heavily influenced by agricultural and environmental policies set at EU level. With our departure from the EU financial support for farming seems likely to decline, at least in the longer term. Forestry should be in a good position to benefit from Michael Gove's much lauded 'public money for public good' mantra, but it will be in competition with other land-uses. More work is needed on what the increase in benefits from shifting land into forestry is compared to existing or other alternative land uses at scales relevant to individual owners.

Devolution is likely to lead to greater differences between the countries in policy and support as we have seen in responses to Covid-19. However, we must avoid disharmonies or duplication of effort for example in research and biosecurity: the emerald ash borer, if it gets into England, is not going to stop at the border. In Wales and Scotland, the former Forestry Commission staff are now part of wider land-use departments/agencies. In England as well the trend is towards integrated land-use funding, but this requires more integrated visions of what sort of overall landscape we want to see, and such visions need public support.

Do we have the public on our side?

I think quite radical changes could take place in our countryside over the next few decades. We can try to shape those changes or leave ourselves open to be shaped by them. Social media is increasingly influential in terms of public opinion and government action. The whole forestry sector must build its expertise in this area, to respond positively and openly on challenges that arise and get the public on its side — to get more trees, in more places and for the right reasons.

For example, people may view proposals for a significant increase in tree cover as a return to blanket spruce afforestation; if that is not what is meant, foresters need to show this by deeds, not words. The public (and certainly the conservation organisations) will not countenance the free-for-all forestry expansion of the 1960s and 1970s.

The value of access to greenspace has been stressed during the last few months, which may increase pressure for a right-to-roam in all woodland in England and Wales. Many landowners may be unhappy with that, but their interests could be overruled. Making existing footpaths and rights of way through woods more welcoming might head off some of the pressure: at present private woods with a footpath through them are not counted in the Woodland Trust's measure of accessible woodland.

Game management has been a significant income generator for many lowland woods, but has also had recent bad publicity, including legal challenges around the large-scale release of pheasants. If lowland game management is restricted what will happen in woods where positive woodland management is currently supported by the shooting income. Conversely in the uplands if burning of grouse moors is restricted this could lead to more natural regeneration on to open ground.

There has been a well-orchestrated campaign against badger culling. Similar campaigns in future against deer and grey squirrel control would compromise much existing woodland management both for conservation and production. Culling will need organised and justified support from all parts of the forestry and conservation sector.

There have been moves in Scotland towards local community buy-outs; in England some woods have been divided up into small blocks and sold off separately (woodlotting). To date these have not changed the overall pattern of woodland ownership, but in future they might. This may require different approaches in terms of advice and funding to support the woodland management desired.

Conclusion

We need some big changes in how we live in the next few decades and there are good reasons why this should involve increasing tree and woodland cover for both for wood production and conservation. Large-scale landscape change can happen over such timescales — consider the National Forest in the English midlands, Kielder and Thetford Forests, or the scrubbing up of downland when the rabbits died off in the 1950s. If it is to happen again with some landscapes getting wilder, whereas other woods become more productive there needs to be open debate as to what balance of uses and objectives can be supplied from different parts of the country. This must involve particularly the landowners and managers who will implement the changes and the general public who are likely to have to pay for some of the new approaches.

Fig 1. *Von Siebold Tree: The Thinnest Line*; 100 x 75 cm, gouache and Conté chalk crayon on paper; 2018.
This is inspired by the *Zelkova Serrata* in the Botanic Gardens of Leiden.

Lilian Cooper is an artist focusing on nature and climate change. The fragility of the eco-system is central to her practice.

She was recently a visiting researcher to the State Herbarium of South Australia and is presently a visiting artist at Hortus Botanicus Leiden while also working with the botanic collections of Naturalis Biodiversity Center, Leiden. She is developing a deeper understanding of trees and while aiming to make botanic gardens and scientific research more accessible and comprehensible to the wider public.

The Life & Death of Trees

Lilian Cooper

Fig 2. *oak Altsasu*; gouache folding book; 23 x 100 cm; 2015.

The Life & Death of Trees

Lilian Cooper

A Good Tree

Trees form an essential part of my own urban experience; they are central to my practice as an artist. For many years I have been making drawings and portraits of trees. This came together in a single form six years ago when I began the *Xylotheque Unpacked: The Life and Death of Trees*. This umbrella project incorporates many different trees and allows me to explore the nature of trees within the parameters of a xylotheque.

The Xylotheque

The particular xylotheque-a library of trees- that inspired this project was from the late 18thC although as a concept they date back to the late 17th century. At the time it was made it was seen as the ultimate in contemporary research and a reference work to enhance and preserve our understanding of trees. It was an encyclopedic gift of knowledge, cataloguing trees of the Netherlands. These xylotheques were designed primarily as scientific reference instruments. Harnessing the same hunger for understanding, knowledge and research of the earlier xylotheque makers, my xylotheque uses present day scientific techniques, knowledge and ß. My inspiration was the xylotheque I encountered in Kasteel Groeneveld in Baarn, the Netherlands. It was made by Ferdinand Alexander von Schlümbach of Nüremberg and was originally presented to Leiden University by Louis Phillippe Napoleon (Napoleon III) in 1806. It was a panoply of tree specimens forming a collection of the trees of the Netherlands and it included leaves and seeds, laid on a bed of moss; the frontispiece was a text describing the tree and the entirety was bound as a book with the spine being made from the bark of each tree studied. There are presently 148 volumes in existence from this xylotheque.

Using this investigative approach, I made my own books in the same analytical visual language as the original: I produced a series of volumes of a xylotheque using contemporary science (I worked with electron microscopes to see the plants in detail). The physical realisation of these books was as cardboard book boxes containing folded drawings, these were created with the help of a bookbinder. They needed to be light and portable because I needed to transport them all over the world and they needed to be made of a material that would be allowed to cross international borders. Enhanced biosecurity measures to help eliminate plant disease mean that transportation in wooden boxes is not recommended.

Research

In the course of my research I spoke to botanists, plant pathologists, botanical gardeners and plant hunters and other scientific researchers on trees and their diseases. I have travelled frequently in the context of artist residencies or as a visiting researcher, visiting trees and creating portraits of them. I have been privileged to work in numerous laboratories and botanic gardens. I saw some diseases first-hand, others were the result of research. My xylotheque currently comprises 31 volumes and encompasses a series of tree portraits, details and tree diseases.

During my first visit to the plant pathology department of the Royal Botanic Garden Sydney in Australia I learnt of tree diseases first hand. What had been abstract ideas or articles read in a newspaper or journal became concrete through the microscope. It was the unexpected beauty of the viewfinder image that caught me by surprise.

Phytophthora cinnimoni causes Eucalyptus dieback; through the microscope it appears as a filigree network highlighted by what looks like bejeweled pods that grow ready to explode their contents and spread their spores further. This disease is deadly for eucalyptus, its spread is not fully documented — the botanic gardens only examine specimens sent to them from other parks not from the field. When travelling through the New South Wales bush I was shocked to discover how prevalent this disease was and the ravages it has caused.

By incorporating disease in the *Life and Death of Trees* project the aim is to recognize the whole tree: its seed beginning, its life and its demise. Making this visible gives a complete interpretation of all the characteristics of a tree. I bring the disease into the aesthetic realm; it is part of the entire project. I am working on a growing number of diseases within the xylotheque. A recent exhibition at museum Rijswijk in the Netherlands focused entirely on this aspect of the xylotheque, for me it is the entirety of the *Life and Death of Trees* project that is even more important because it covers so many aspects of trees. My aim is to make the public cognizant of the trees around them.

Fig 3. *Acer, Hortus Botanicus Leiden*; watercolour folding book; 23 x 100 cm; 2018

A wider perspective

There is nothing better than a good tree. Their sentinel forms often provide one of the few living plants in intensely urban surroundings. I have grown increasingly aware of the significant part trees play in my life and how they positively influence my sense of wellbeing. Being in close proximity to several trees recently has been a joy, while the circumstances of our times has intensified my own personal need for them. Their role in the urban landscape can be underestimated, overlooked, while the stillness of the present time has created space to appreciate them. Trees, plants and soil have a resonance like never before. By having a moment to stop I realized that what I needed most was to feel soil in my hands and to plant seeds. This is the most fundamental way I can relate to my environment and play a very small part in changing it for the better.

Fig 4 & 5. *Fusarium oxysporum*; watercolour drawing; 23 x 100 cm; 2016

Tree diseases make headlines; in the last few years increasing numbers of tree diseases have appeared in more virulent forms. It was fortuitous that I was already studying tree diseases as part of this project when the Covid-19 pandemic occurred because my work suddenly gained even more pertinence. The public is perceptibly more open to the concept that trees also suffer illness. Tree diseases are seemingly increasing, due in part to the prevalence of conventional farming techniques and the creation of monoculture tree plantations which mean that once one has succumbed to illness it is easier for the rest to follow. Equally young trees grown in one country with the aim of planting in another with the associated risk of diseases has proved to be an ill though-out idea. Additionally many commentators have suggested that the

Fig 6. *Keizersgracht tree*; pencil, watercolour, coloured pencil and wax crayon on paper; 28 x 76 cm; 2012

changing climate is helping exacerbate existing weaknesses in many plants and is making many more vulnerable. There seems to be a heightened awareness that we all live with the threat of diseases and viruses and the health of one individual can have a devastating impact on the collective whole.

The Von Siebold Tree

Under the auspices of the xylotheque I focus on individual trees; some become independent projects and one of these was the *Von Siebold Tree*. While working in the Hortus Botanicus Leiden I discovered a Japanese elm in their collection, brought by Frederich von Siebold from Japan to the Netherlands. Not only did von Siebold have an extensive collection of art and artefacts he also gathered a huge collection of plants. The *Zelkova serrata* tree was an example brought directly from Japan and planted in Leiden in 1830, and has been doing well ever since. It has

Fig 8. *Von Siebold Tree*: Triptych; gouache and Conté chalk crayon on paper 100 x 225 cm; 2018

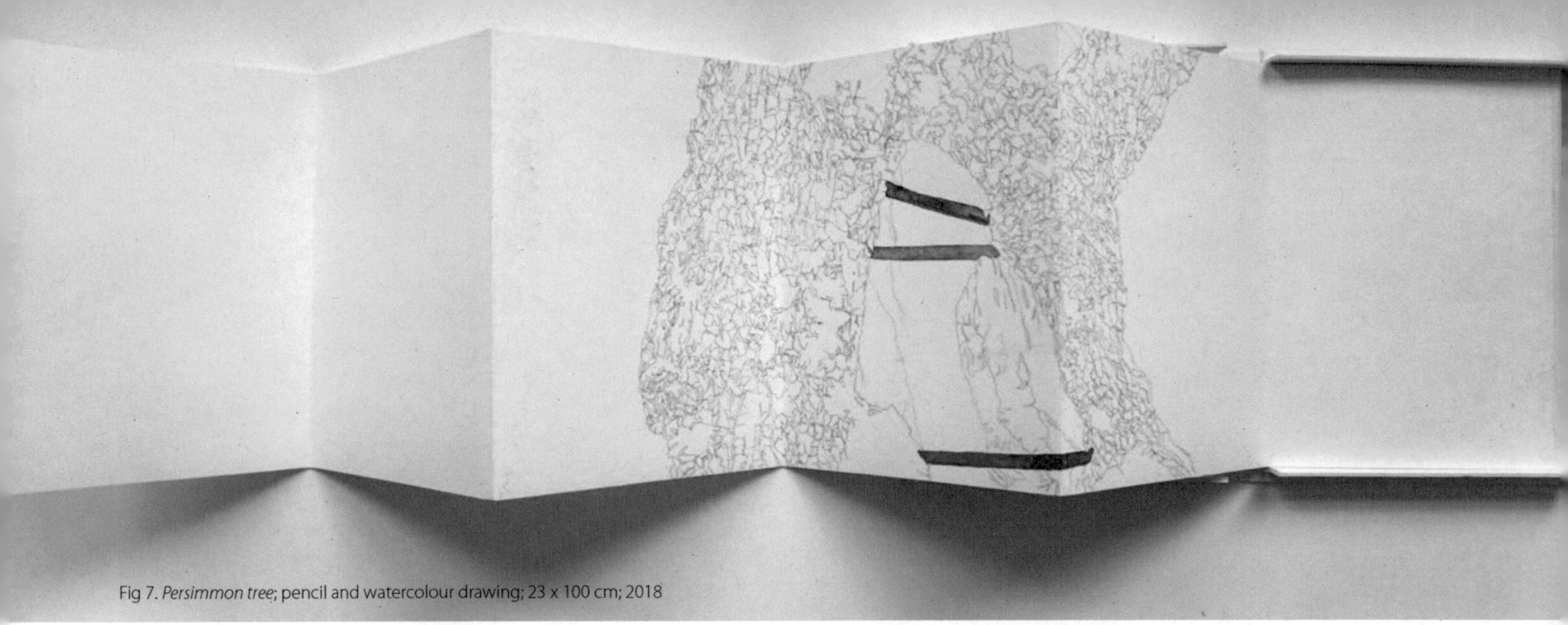

Fig 7. *Persimmon tree*; pencil and watercolour drawing; 23 x 100 cm; 2018

a characteristic multi-trunk form that looks like the nest shape formed by a human palm, with upturned finger trunks extending upwards. I became obsessed with the powerful form of the tree and the delicate patterning on the trunks. For over a year I drew this tree continually. It was the shape and how this worked in the space, as well as the infinite detail of the spiraling internal bark structure on massively solid trunks that fascinated me.

My von Siebold project was a vehicle for the understanding of a particular tree specimen, a recognition of its history and displacement from its origins and von Siebold's role as one of the foremost collectors of plants, whose collection continues to have contemporary relevance and be the subject of on-going research.

The story of a particular tree

Behind every tree in this project there is a story and a connection. The oak of Altasasu was one of these. It comes from a forest in the Basque mountains in the hinterland around San Sebastian in northern Spain. I was invited to work there because of my connection with the San Juan. The San Juan was a Basque whaling ship that set sail from Labrador to return back to Spain when it sank in the harbour in Canada. I had visited the location in Labrador and it was through this that I discovered the organisation Albaola in Basque Spain who planned to rebuild it. Albaola is based on the outskirts of San Sebastian, is an organisation dedicated to rebuilding the ship using the historical methods. On discovering my passion for trees they invited me to visit the forests where they harvested wood used in the reconstruction process.

These trees would be trained and grow into the various appropriate shapes needed for the sections of the ship's timbers. The wood for the ship would be planted at least 50 years in advance so that it would be the right size and girth when required. Often the tree would only be partially harvested and the rest would be allowed to grow further. The trees for the last cycle of planting became obsolete with the advent of steel ships. It meant that wood perfect for building was readily available for the San Juan II. It had

to a good tree.

been waiting for over a century. The forest itself was an extraordinary place. The oak trees were sculptural and well spaced out for easy access, it felt more like a landscape by Capability Brown than a working forest.

The wider role of the artist and trees

As an artist I see my role as facilitating dialogue between the public and those with a wealth of technical knowledge. My aim is to bring this expertise into a more approachable and accessible form. Moreover I care deeply for trees and I want to convey the beauty of tree forms, their strength and the seemingly infinite patterning of the bark. To truly understand the tree I need to draw it in detail.

It is the act of making visual that creates such an impact for both the Von Siebold Tree series and the xylotheque too. It seems in this very visual culture we belong to, talking about the diseases that affect trees has a less lasting effect than drawing them. Visual language helps us perceive these trees. The aesthetics of an arboreal environment lends itself to visual interpretation. More importantly the visual impact and the message behind the image can reach beyond, to work on a haunting subliminal level. My goal is to have a long-reaching effect, to subtly draw attention to the fragility of our tree landscapes to help make the wider public cognizant of their importance and beauty.

Scaring the public with dramatic headlines and terrifying bulletins will only work for so long, there is a longer lasting necessary message to spread. Trees are beautiful, omnipresent but more susceptible to disease than ever before, as our actions affect the climate and their habitat. We need to know and love our trees and protect our soils and planet to keep us all in harmony rather than discord with our environments, for the good of trees, for our own health and the longevity of our present societies.

Fig 10. *Californian cypress branch*; watercolour folding book; 23 x 100cm; 2017

Fig 9. *To a good tree* marker and gardening tape; extract from a text installation made during a residency in Weir Farm National Historic Site, Wilton, CT. USA; 2006

Fig 11. *Sycamore branch*; watercolour folding book; 23 x 100 cm; 2017

Fig 12. Weeping beech; gouache drawing as a folded book; 23 x 100 cm; 2016

explore it

Roderick Leslie joined the Forestry Commission in 1976 and after working in forest management posts became GB conservation officer just as the Flow Country dispute broke in 1985. He went on to be environment manager, regional director and chief executive of Forest Enterprise England, playing a central role in delivering the Commission's developing environmental and people policies. As head of policy for Forestry Commission England he leads the development of the Government's Woodfuel Policy

Fig 1. Dalby Visitor Centre (Roderick Leslie)

Transforming the Forestry Commission

Roderick Leslie

Fig 2. Ploughing in deep peat (Roderick Leslie)

Transforming the Forestry Commission

Born out of conflict, the Forestry Commission (FC) began life as a simple grower of pit props. 100 years on '*Evolving the Forest*' is a superb evocation of what the Public Forest Estate means today.

As Lord Clinton planted the first tree at Eggesford in Devon in November 1919 I wonder how the visionary group of landowners behind the Forestry Commission must have felt. Probably excitement, mixed with some trepidation.

Trepidation, because little was known about planting conifers on poor soils and the technology available was equally limited. But the fledgling Forestry Commission, having survived the first of many narrow escapes, the Geddes Axe of post-war cuts, set about its massive task with the commitment, determination and inventiveness that still characterises the organisation today. 100 years later its achievement is the largest planned land use change in British history, with England's woodland cover rising from just 4% to 10%.

The First Forests

Still controversial 100 years on, conifers were the focus of Forestry Commission planting because the straight, small stems of younger conifers were what the miners needed. The land available wasn't good enough for broadleaves and anyway conifers grow quicker.

What trees to plant, though? European larch and Douglas fir had been around long enough to grow big timber trees in Britain, but the Sitka spruce that came to dominate later planting was a gamble.

These early forests were different to what came later. Dalby Forest in North Yorkshire is typical: on good land for conifers, sixty years on the first generation Douglas fir produced stunning big timber. Early forests took a silvicultural approach, closely matching trees to soil to produce varied, attractive forests, including planted broadleaves. The best land was kept for forest worker smallholdings and the FC built forest villages for its workers and providing employment became an additional objective.

But afforestation is a big change and there were protests about the impact on landscape resulting in an agreement not to plant in the core of the Lake District. At the same time FC began welcoming people with the Argyll Forest Park launched just before WW2, a decade ahead of the first National Park.

Blanket Afforestation

The support of tree enthusiast Hugh Dalton, the first post-war Chancellor resulted in rapidly accelerating planting programmes which continued flat out through the 1950s and 1960s.

Two crucial factors meant these forests were very different to the pre-war planting: first, the post-war priority for agriculture forced forestry onto poorer and poorer land.

Second, with the nuclear age the Zuckerman report concluded future war would be short and sharp, meaning a strategic reserve was no longer relevant. Instead the Forestry Commission was given economic targets. The system of 'Nett Discounted Revenue' (NDR) required a 3%

return which was almost impossible to achieve because of forestry's long timescale. It pushed forestry to extremes — maximising the land planted and using more and more Sitka Spruce because it was so much more productive than other species on poor soils.

Planting such poor land became possible because the Forestry Commission had developed a potent relationship between researchers and deliverers and new technology was instantly applied. Caterpillar tractors with increasingly powerful ploughs and phosphate fertiliser were key tools in planting poor, wet soils. So the hated blankets of Sitka spruce came about.

NDR murdered broadleaves because they grew too slowly. Thousands of hectares were felled and replaced with conifers. In the East Midlands young oak were poisoned — cheaper than felling — to make way for conifers. Even at the time many foresters were unhappy with this vandalism.

The 1960s brought wind throw. When trees planted on wetter soils were thinned the stand blew over. Thinning was stopped but trees still blew well before maturity and foresters ended up chasing the wind as successive stands blew like ninepins.

Following the Forest Parks, the Forestry Commission took the radical decision to open public access to all its forests. By the 50th anniversary celebrations in 1969 Dalby Forest was laying on a whole range of activities and had developed car parks, picnic sites and way-marked walks, strung along the famous forest drive which became a second home for the day tripping people of Leeds. Those meadows kept back for smallholdings, now surrounded by maturing larch and Douglas fir were a lovely place to park and get out a folding chair and the Sunday paper.

By the 1970s Forestry Commission threshold signs were synonymous with open public access.

And the private sector joined the planting programme. Thanks to a neat tax dodge and the very high rate of income tax (up to 90%) investment in forestry became attractive and by the 1980s private planting was ahead of the Forestry Commission. Contrary to popular mythology private planting wasn't 'cheap and dirty' — Eskdalemuir Forest in the Scottish Borders became an exemplar, adopting new approaches to forest design ahead of the Forestry Commission. But the land available was getting worse for both state and private planters and the road to the Flow Country and the end of upland planting was set.

The Road to the Flow Country

The Flow Country is a vast, flat expanse of raised peat bog in the very far north east of Scotland, just below John O'Groats. Technology — wide apical track shoes — allowed caterpillar ploughing tractors to almost float over this sodden ground (Fig 2). What pushed forestry here was the prohibition of planting 'viable sheep farms' — a definition the Government had pushed way beyond anything even landowners supported. The discovery of the wildlife value — the best for moorland birds, like the iconic greenshank, in Britain — came later because conserva-tionists reasonably hadn't expected the area to be under threat. A ferocious and effective campaign by the RSPB and the Nature Conservancy Council stopped the planting and threatened the very future of forestry. Chancellor Nigel Lawson closed the tax loophole, planting stopped and the Forestry Commission was lucky to survive. But foresters realised that nothing short of a transformation would recover their reputation.

Transforming the Forestry Commission

It led directly to the movement that transformed the Forestry Commission. Responding to criticism, the Forestry Commission with consultant Dame Sylvia Crowe had developed a new approach to landscape resulting in big improvements, but only to special parts of the forest and led by landscape design. Foresters needed to take back control of their forests — both physically and in public opinion and that was how Restructuring was developed in Kielder Forest in the late 1970s. The key issue was to break up the huge single age plantings and that meant felling some areas early and, where trees wouldn't blow over, late to start producing a varied forest. It would also develop wind-resistant edges. There was an economic penalty — offset by future generations standing longer.

But restructuring went far further: conifers were pulled back from streamsides, sometime by ¼ of a mile in this big landscape, native broadleaves were planted, there was open space for deer lawns and harsh edges were re-designed.

The lesson that it is possible to completely change the way things are done has carried forward to this centenary. Restructuring was not about the sort of token gestures around the fringes that so often pass for environmental improvement: it was fundamental and engaged the productive forest first and foremost.

In 1985 David Clark MP, later, as Lord Clark of Windemere, Chairman of the Forestry Commission led a one line amendment to the Forestry Act requiring the Forestry Commissioners to balance economic and environmental aims. Seen by some as a threat to timber production, the Commissioners embraced their new duties enthusiastically. A seminal series of management guidelines tackled many of the justified complaints against 'blanket afforestation'. By the end of the decade re-structuring was the national norm.

Wildlife and People

Nature conservation had been seen very much as something separate from the timber forest but now the Commissioners agreed the policy that 'the whole forest has conservation value', justified by the wide range of species making the 'wildlife free' conifer forest their home — goshawk, red squirrel, nightjar and woodlark amongst many others.

1990 brought a new departure: the Dorset Heathland Project was launched to restore heathland by removing planted trees. The Forestry Commission is about planting trees, not removing them: in this spectacularly counter-cultural move it demonstrated just how far and fast it could change. It has gone on to restore more heathland than any other organisation, as well as other habitats including deep peat, limestone pavement and rivers.

But by far the biggest change was to broadleaved woodland. Since the coniferisation of so many woods the idea of ancient woodland had developed, led by Oliver Rackham and George Peterken. Far from being just broadleaves, ancient woods turned out to have extraordinary histories, with management by man stretching back a millennium at least. Not only that, but ancient woods have a very specific and special biodiversity. In response to a highly effective campaign led by the RSPB the Forestry Commission developed a revolutionary policy for all broadleaves woodland, not just its own, accompanied by a grant scheme which led to virtually all new planting after 1988 being of broadleaved trees.

In England the Forestry Commission set about restoring 35,000 hectares of its own woods. 5,000 hectares of the notoriously abused East Midlands forests were not just to be returned to broadleaves but also by natural regeneration. Before he died Oliver Rackham ceremoniously felled the last conifer in Chalkney Wood. Both Oliver and George Peterken recognised that ancient woods were recovering far better than anyone had expected.

The big problem for broadleaved woods was that small thinnings were virtually worthless. All that changed in 2007 with the well funded Government Woodfuel strategy. Aimed at 'small to medium' boilers for heat, there are now 6,000 boilers burning 1 million tonnes of wood a year and producing energy equivalent to half the output of Hinckley Point nuclear power station — and small hardwoods are worth ten times as much.

In 1999 the whole of the Public Forest Estate achieved the gold standard Forestry Stewardship Council certification, an independent assurance system covering every aspect of sustainability. Shortly afterwards WWF awarded the Forestry Commission a coveted 'Gift to the Earth' in recognition of it being the first national forest estate to be certified in its entirety in the world. Subsequently, the Forestry Commission in it's role as regulator produce the United Kingdom Forestry Standard which brought together all it's environmental policy into a baseline applying to both public and private sectors

There was a revolution in recreation, too. As the worn out first generation facilities were replaced, out went the earnest, informative visitor centres, and in came active woods: the day out in the car was on the way out, people wanted to be engaged and active. In Wales a keen mountain biking forester developed the first dedicated mountain biking trail, soon followed in all three countries. Old railway lines in the Forest of Dean were transformed into family cycling tracks and Go-Ape, thrilling high-wire courses through the tree tops, culminating in a terrifying zip wire, was a smash hit.

Art hit the forest. Grizedale Forest was the leader, including supporting early work by Andy Goldsworthy. The Forest of Dean Sculpture Trail, the first to commission works for specific sites, was designed for the appreciative few but soon had 50,000 visitors a year. At Moors Valley, Andy Frost combined art and play in a play trail featuring snakes, spiders and crocodiles and pulling in 800,000 visitors a year.

Amazingly, the revolution happened when low timber prices had left the Forestry Commission with no money to spend. From the EU Life programme for nature to Sport England for activity centres, the range of funding demonstrated the contemporary relevance of what the Forestry Commission was doing.

Four million pounds transformed ever-popular Dalby, with a new visitor centre and everything from gentle riverside walks and craft workshops to custom built mountain biking trails and Go-Ape. Employment in forestry had not gone as expected: every time the labour force should have risen technology intervened, first the chainsaw then the harvester, cut harvesting jobs by five times each and, of course, the big planting squads disappeared as new planting declined. Dalby's workforce dropped to 15. But, amazingly, now it is back to 60 again, doing very different things — catering, crafts work, manning Go-Ape and selling and maintaining bikes. And it has happened all over the estate. Alongside it has been a stealth privatisation. In 1970 80% of work in the forests was done by Forestry Commission labour and machines. Today 80% of the work is private, from multi-million pound harvesting companies to cafes and forest schools, an estimated 600 private businesses are associated with the forests.

In 2010 the Government announced it would sell the Public Forest Estate in England. The public outcry led to a dramatic U-turn by Prime Minister David Cameron. The FC had dramatically proved that it had won back public confidence.

Future Forests

As the new millennium dawned forestry was moving closer to the political agenda in two key areas: climate change and quality of life.

Foresters knew trees would be impacted by global warming, but the shock of a disastrous decade of new diseases wasn't expected. Disease has knocked out larch, Corsican pine and ash as forestry trees, and threatens others. Species selection, long thought a thing of the past is back. Most exciting has been the recognition that Europe as well as Britain is impoverished in tree species: a vastly greater range of species grew before the ice ages, recent in geological time, but were blocked from returning by the Mediterranean, Alps and Pyrenees. Who knows what the trees of the future forest will be?

The carbon benefits of trees are well established but resilience to increasingly violent weather has been brought home by annual flooding in the new millennium. Trees as part of a landscape approach should become key to flood management. In the New Forest a biodiversity inspired project to return rivers that had been straightened to their original course had a dramatic effect, drastically slowing the peak flows that do the damage. The Wild Ennerdale project in the North Lakes allowed the river Liza to spread into its natural flood plain. In this flood prone region only the Liza catchment didn't flood during the last event. In Pickering, the town closest to Dalby Forest, local people rejected a traditional concrete channel on the flood-prone Pickering Beck, controversially going for a landscape approach including tree planting and now beavers — which bred in Cropton Forest in 2020.

In 1995 the Forestry Commission began the restoration of the Nottinghamshire coalfield (Fig 3), turning 800 hectares of towering black coal tips into green, open access forests. The programme gathered speed when the Treasury awarded £10 million under the Capital Modernisation Fund (CMF), with land restored in the urban North West and the Thames Gateway, moving on to the South Yorkshire coalfield. Restoration was literally place-changing, transforming the environment from some of the worst to some of the best. Every wood is welcoming and open to local people and in CMF alone the Forestry Commission built 70 kilometres of wheelchair quality paths. The new woods are like doorstep National Parks and the Government's Natural Capital Committee has recommended 250,000 hectares of new public access woods, which it estimates would generate £500 million per annum in economic benefit. And that was before Covid which surely has rammed home the importance of local environments and access to people's quality of life.

So, from selling the forests in 2010 now in 2020 politicians are in a bidding war to promise planting ever more millions of trees.

The Forest Evolves

Just how many different things can go on in one forest at a time? And how can anyone comprehend that breadth? Few do and too often single interests argue as if the forest was theirs and theirs alone. That is why '*Evolving the Forest*' was so significant: organised by a forestry society, a forward looking timber business and an arts organisation it brought together people who might never normally have met, all bound by their own special love of trees and forests. Could there have been a better way to celebrate the Forestry Commission's first 100 years, and launch it into its second?

Fig 3. Sutton Manor colliery before reconstruction (Roderick Leslie)

Manan Bhan is an ecosystem scientist and Doctoral Researcher who lives in Vienna, Austria. His fascination with, and research on, forests goes back to his previous degrees at the Universities of Delhi and Oxford. His doctoral research tries to understand how societies engage with forests, and what that means for the carbon stored in these landscapes. Recently, he has started experimenting with how he expresses his thoughts on nature and the environment, and how science and art can intersect. He has written two poems on the memories associated with his immediate environment while growing up, and one poem on visualizing scientific research as theatre. He can always be found with a cup of chai in his hand.

Loss, Abandonment and Regrowth

Manan Bhan

Loss, Abandonment and Regrowth

I.

They had come one day
Man and Machine
Slashing, cutting, buzzing
Shaping their plunder
leaving behind an empty silence
Some had seen it before
Adjacent lands whispered
That same old story
Of wants, of greed, of loss

Once, every fruit that fell
Had a taker
Now the fruits fell for no one.
On the back of mammals big and small
Seeds would see the world
Now confined to sedentary lives.

Where once stood the *jamun*, the *shehtoot*, the *dhak*
Now the sun baked the Earth.
Predators prowl, preys' gossip, no longer.
Birds, reluctant to the foreign gaze
No longer punctuated the sky with calls.

They left burning wrecks
But Nature said, 'Smolder, go again!'

II.

Many years pass
Life sleeps, restive and underground
Reluctant to reveal itself, unable to forget.

Then one fine day
There is a release
Like a spring finally set free.
For they learned of opportunity in the city
At the altar of profit and globalization
Marginality was rewarded with a route back to Nature.

Awoken by surprise
Jolted into traces of community
Not new, but long forgotten.
A regeneration of potential and promise
Into dense and difficult landscapes.
Familiar sounds and,
Faint memories come charging back.

A solitary *Dhak* tree (affectionately known as the 'Flame of the Forest') stands in a wooded area near Delhi, India ◀

In the corner
It is the Mango
That stirs first.
She had been left standing
For shade, for product.
She knows this is unlike last year
Or the year before
She rises, her voice above the rest
Calm, warm and comforting
Like a grandparent with bedtime tales
Generational memory, even after all this time.

The importance of community: An uprooted tree rests delicately on another, deep inside a Himalayan forest.

III.

After the inertia, sprouts new beings
Although ashes still litter the wounded soil
They aspire to reach its lost potential
But never quite
Since the laws of biotic life have ravaged many such dawns.

There are friendships to be remade
For among the raucous noise of men and machines
Goodbyes last time remained incomplete.
Right now
The only companions are
Those that work tirelessly in the dark.

Soon the first shoots would emerge
Tender, they will jostle for light
And entangle excitedly in the breeze
Their leaves will get to see many moons
And their branches will shed much life in autumns
Several will join this rite of passage.

In this race, they will create their own personality
Their own niche
Many many moons like this
Slow, imperceptible.

IV.

They came again
This time not to disturb, but to count.
Overheard, their plans to shape our destinies
Smoothen our edges
Relational logics are assumed
Rhythms taken for granted.

Measuring our skin and bones
With a tape, or a tape recorder
Cameras peep through the clouds at our nascent canopies.
We stand naked, exposed
They come back again and again
Recognizing us as selves
In order to turn us into non-selves.

We are asked to 'hurry up'
Our ancestors long up in smoke
They have come back and asked for more
An outlet for their guilty conscience.

V.

In between, an order is passed somewhere
And a 'forest' is thus born again.
No longer a jungle, the maverick
Now a citizen, the responsible.
But what does it mean to be one?
To be tree-d, is that land's instinct,
Or a forefather's tale long internalized?

photo: Richard Povall

II: Reflection, Philosophy & Polemic

Jeremy Ralph is a forestry and timber expert with 20 years' experience in landscape-level forestry. In 2015, following a Nuffield Farming Scholarship and time at the Helsinki Wood School studying timber architecture, Jez set up Timber Strategies to work at the innovative future-facing face of forestry and timber. As well as working within the timber industry Jez regularly lectures at a number of Schools of Art and Architect on landscape and future vernaculars tying timber back to its landscape origins.

◀ Workshop during *Evolving the Forest*, Deer Park, Dartington Hall (photo: Oliver Raymond-Barker)

Forestry 2120

Jeremy Ralph

Forestry 2120

Jeremy Ralph, Timber Strategies

We face significant changes in the next century. Daunting, exciting, changes that can be viewed with pessimism or optimism, but changes that are inevitable. At what seems like a pivotal moment how do we, within the sphere of trees, respond to this. How do we look to 2120 to form a more equitable relationship with our woods?

The wooded landscape of the UK has been on a roller coaster ride since the retreat of the last glaciation. Natural spread with little interference from humanity gave way to small then much more significant interference as human population exploded and revolutions in agriculture and technology swept through society. In those early days of Neolithic transhumance wood was the primary building material, the forest a major source of food. With every new shelter and every hunting party some element of selection will have taken place. This selection started to alter the genetic make-up of the forest as straightness or strength were favoured. It would have started to alter the geography of our forests as easy-pickings were taken from close to home, close to habitations on accessible or defendable locations or close to crossing points or trade routes. By around 3000 BC agriculture overtakes woodland as the primary landscape feature; trees become relegated to those areas inefficient for food production. Looking up to Dartmoor from the *Evolving the Forest* conference it is difficult to imagine woodland cloaking the moors, hiding communities nestling within it, providing building material, food and warmth interspersed with field systems within forest clearings.

Stretches of unbroken wild forest will have hidden predators as well as life-giving (and affirming) products. It is easy to see how the mysticism of the forest began, how closely intertwined the relationship between safety and fear. The forest was both giver and taker. . As laws overtook tradition, as large forests became crown property, hunting and deer more controlled, the forest commoditised, folklore became an idyll of the past rather than an important passing down of forest lore.

Interspersed were peaks of effort to revitalise our forest and forest connection. The Charter of the Forest of 1217; the urgency of growing more ship timber for Henry VIII's expanding Navy; *Sylva* in 1664; The Forestry Commission in 1919; the move to naturalistic planting led by NGOs in the early 21st Century. There is no long continuum of forest protection, forest laws and forest culture here, instead we see boom and bust driven by resource needs.

In 1642 John Evelyn wrote in the introduction to Sylva:

> *'If to this there be any thing subjoyned here, which may a while bespeak the Patience of the Reader, it is only for the encouragement of an Industry, and worthy Labour, much in our days neglected, as haply reputed a Consideration of too sordid and vulgar a nature for Noble Persons, and Gentlemen to busie themselves withal, and who oftner find out occasions to Fell-down, and Destroy their Woods and Plantations, than either to repair or improve them.'*

This has left us, in 2020, with a resource that is easy to dismiss. In some areas a patchwork of woodlands reflecting our history rather than our future needs, in

◀ Douglas Barret & Katerie Gladdys *Eccentric Grids_Mapping the Managed Forest_Monetizing Trace* (photo: Oliver Raymond-Barker)

others a blanket of business-like forest hidden away in remote areas from prying eyes. The Civil Service arm responsible for that resource driven by political cycles so far removed from forestry time-frames.

Here, now, in 2020, we have a uniquely diverse resource that spans history in its age and continents in its species. It represents the best efforts of interested landowners and the results of intensely argued silviculture. Our woodlands have a renewed connection with our society whether that be a place to break the monotony of a life in front of a screen or impassioned protests on new developments. We have a framework, albeit patchy, to look forward to a new paradigm.

And a new paradigm is without question needed. For too long those of us in forestry have focussed our gaze inside the forest gate. The first words uttered to us as naïve young foresters at university by the esteemed professor was 'we are all in forestry because we prefer the company of trees to the company of people.' To me, this seemed far from the point of forestry then, and even further from it now. We seem to be on the cusp of step-change: there is the beginnings of an explosion of interest in wood for everything — the renewable material that takes carbon dioxide and turns it into oxygen and timber. In architecture, in materials, in pharmaceuticals, in health and wellbeing, in all walks of life society is turning to the forest, once again as a provider. In agriculture the benefits of breaking trees free from their constrained woodland boundaries are being realised on an exponential scale, the same in cities.

We are increasingly aware of the importance of the health of our woodlands as if it is a new idea from which we have been blinkered. We are re-finding knowledge of the above-ground ecosystems: the importance of symbiotic mycorrhizal fungi and the spread of indicator species between one woodland and the next forming connections. The health of the soil beneath our feet is everything: everything to the ecosystem, everything to quality timber, everything to a vibrant forest.

It feels like we are, at last, settling down to create a long-term silviculture of adaptive treescapes that can be healthy, resilient and productive through diversity.

Whither 2121

What will we be looking at in one hundred years? Will we be bathing in the glow of a deeply connected forest resource, diverse and healthy? or will our short attention spans have created the dystopian world of C S Lewis's poem *The Future of Forestry*:

> *How will the legend of the age of trees*
> *Feel, when the last tree falls in England?*

Such questions seem unanswerable, and all we can do now is seize the moment and decide where we want to be in in 2021. We are, thankfully, filling our ranks with scientists who can give us the processual tools to match climate and species; tools to help us understand soil health; to use timber more efficiently. As the forest resource expands so too will the number of people who want to engage with these questions. As markets increase and consumers want more, entrepreneurs and investment houses will turn their gaze on us. As the cost of flood relief and pollution mitigation schemes rise so too will the focus of politicians needing cost-effective bio-based mechanisms. Turning away from the confines of the gallery, artists will take us on personal journeys into our forests, adding a dimension to our forest culture that allows us to explore and connect.

But how do we deal with the 'whys'? Can we get to 2021 without proper consideration of why forestry matters, why we care, why we want to protect it? Why has a philosophical discourse on trees been so lacking until now and can we really progress without it? If there were no trees in Britain, would it matter? If there were 35% forest cover but no quality timber, would it matter? In either case wouldn't society merely move on, creating technological mechanisms to address our needs? How do we judge the precedence for ecological diversity over the needs of our grandchildren?

If we look to medicine and the deep conundrums that exist today we see everyone from the most junior staff to the most senior consultants actively involved in the ethics of their profession. To consider the ethics of our actions is to care; to care about those we are charged with protecting and to care about the future of how we protect them. Where is forestry's ethics committee? Where is the forum for properly considering, say, the implications of removal of woodland for development or the need to reduce productivity to increase soil health on either a site by site or national basis?

How do we address the irrelevance of government policy to real, substantial silviculture? Does anyone really expect a 20+ year government policy to last 25 years? And even if it did, what is 25 years to the time it will take to bring our soils back to vibrant life? Can a policy that expediently offers everything to everyone really make a difference, can it create substantive change without focus? How do we develop policy that has an influence over the next century, or two centuries?

If forestry is to be vibrant in 2120 I suggest that the physical mechanisms for getting us to that point will evolve, and must do so quickly. The explosion in agroforestry and soil health research in the past decade points to this, as does the fast-evolving technological revolution in modified timber products for construction. But none of this will help if we cannot deepen understanding of our connection to trees. Although it may seem old fashioned in our world of instant gratification and decision making, without a theoretical framework — a space to consider ethics and responsibility, policy and philosophy — I don't believe we will get to 2120 without re-shaping the rollercoaster ride of our past.

There is no time for navel-gazing. Climate, technology, and population are changing exponentially faster and we must respond to that. But we must respond in a thoughtful way that considers what is important in one hundred or two hundred years, not what seems is important now. Getting to that level of thinking requires us to draw together collaborative mechanisms that have the freedom and the bravery to speculate and to think. Mechanisms that work alongside the practicalities of the next 20 years but put them in a context of long-term health of our forests.

What these mechanisms are, who these people are, I'm afraid I can't answer on a rainy autumnal day in Devon. If you are looking for answers you have come to the wrong place. But isn't that the point? If we don't think and just respond we may hope to leave a humanistic legacy of vibrant treescapes in 2120, if we start thinking more and framing our actions we start down the road of forming a tree-human symbiosis that could, by 2120, be the defining paradigm of forestry.

Jude Allen has an MA in the Body and Representation and a PhD in Human/Animal Metamorphosis in Twentieth Century Literature. Since completing her PhD she has expanded her research interests into soils and narratives, and organised the literature element of the Soil Culture Forum at Falmouth University in 2014 – a project which explored ways in which the humanities could mediate the urgency of the degradation of our soils in a way that was more accessible to the non-scientific world. She recently convened a panel at the biennial ASLE conference at the university of Plymouth, titled: 'But they were quite normal. Bodies on the Frontline: Activists, Environmental Protest Narratives, and the Practice of Reading'. *She is currently heading a project called Soil Voices, looking at narratives and oral histories that reconnect us with the soil. @SoilVoices*

photo: Oliver Raymond-Barker

Tree Communication

Jude Allen

Alida Tree (photo: Jude Allen)

Talking Trees: Close Encounters of the Sylvan Kind

Jude Allen

In 1986, Prince Charles was famously and publicly lambasted and labelled 'potty' for talking to plants. Things have changed.

This article will briefly consider scientific understandings of tree communication and then consider the notion of anthropomorphism. I will then move on to briefly consider how tree communication has been represented in Literature as a fantasy-embedded in the magical and otherworldly. I will conclude with focus on a novel called *Pollard*, by Laura Beatty, and suggest that literary representations of trees might be changing — perhaps becoming more realistic. As a result of such literary re-evaluation, I ask if we might change our cultural imaginings of trees and thus enable a more productive relationship with them.

Recent research conducted into tree communication shows clear evidence that trees can both communicate and form relationships with other trees around them. Professor of Forest Ecology, Suzanne Simard likens the below-ground fungal network of mycorrhiza, through which trees communicate to the internet: a world-wide-web, this fungal network functions as a series of myriad biological pathways that allow communication between trees and thus enable the forest to behave as a single organism with a collective intelligence. According to Simard 'trees talk', in order to develop a community with an increased level of resilience. Trees are far better equipped for survival when in the company of others.

Similarly, in his book, *The Hidden Life of Trees*, the forester and ranger, Peter Wohlleben, sums up much of the current research to make the case that the forest is a social network. He says that trees are social beings that communicate with their own and other species of tree in a number of ways. For example, when grazed by giraffes on the African savannah, umbrella thorn acacias flood their foliage with a toxic substance that renders them unpalatable. The trees then give off a warning gas that indicates the presence of the impending threat to neighbouring trees. Furthermore, Wohlleben states that trees are also able to differentiate between the nature of attacks — for example, they can distinguish the difference between the bite of a deer and the cut of a pruning implement. In the first case, the tree is able to detect the saliva of a deer and as a result can then send out signals to produce toxicity, and in the latter, the tree will initiate a wound healing mechanism. This very specific information is then able to be communicated to neighbouring trees.

Examining research on brain equivalency, Wohlleben states that the 'root network is in charge of all chemical activity in the tree' and that trees contain brain-like structures in the tips of their roots. The Australian evolutionary ecologist, Monica Gagliano, finds that although 'plants may lack brains and neural tissues … they do possess a sophisticated calcium-based signalling network in their cells similar to animals' memory processes.' Botanist, Frantisek Baluska argues that the similarities his research has found 'between sensory-driven plant growth and animal memory, and the presence of offline behaviour in plants […] show[s] that under a wide, embodied interpretation of cognition, plants may well qualify as being cognitive.'

Such theories, however, are disputed by a significant number of scientists who suggest this is a provocative idea, and that,

> *'there is no evidence for structures such as neurons, synapses or a brain in plants. The fact that the term 'neuron' is derived from a Greek word describing a 'vegetable fiber' is not a compelling argument to reclaim this term for plant biology.'* (Alpi et al. 2007)

Although scientific attitudes have a significant impact on our individual perceptions of things, I suggest that cultural interpretations of such knowledge are equally, if not more important. Most people are far more likely to pick up a novel than to read a scientific journal paper — and it has been argued by scientists that 'new concepts and fields of research develop from the synthesis of creative thinking and cautious scientific analysis.' (*ibid.*) The 2019 BBC programme, *My Passion for Trees*, narrated by national treasure Judi Dench has contributed far more to our willingness to entertain the notion of talking trees than the inner workings of the Institute of Cellular and Molecular Biology in the University of Bonn.

I am interested in is how such a synthesis might be unpacked. What impact does our cultural perception of trees have on our willingness (or unwillingness) to accept them as possessing some level of cognition? — how might what we read about trees in the fictions of our time change our response towards them in real terms?

Wohllenben suggests a similarity between the 'vibrations in our own vocal chords… to the vibrations produced within a tree trunk when the flow of water to the leaves is interrupted.' Such thirsty plants get 'a bit riled up', their leaves are 'anxious' and they 'scream'. Such emotive language starts to lead us into the realms of anthropomorphism.

If we digress for a moment and look into the field of animal studies, we find that the notion of anthropomorphism has until very recently been 'usually applied as a term of reproach, both intellectual and moral' (Daston & Mitman 2005:2). However — in animal studies — there has been an increasing push to rewrite the rules of the ways in which humans apprehend other creatures. In *Thinking with Animals*, Lorraine Daston and Gregg Mitman, link the 'waning of anthropomorphic attitudes towards the natural world' with the 'rise of modern science'. Such resistance to anthropomorphism in the animal world, however, has lately been challenged both culturally and scientifically. Greg Garrard, in his book, *Ecocriticism*, discusses extensively the problems posed by anthropomorphism (Garrard 2011:136-159). Similarly to Daston, Garrard notes that 'until recently anthropomorphism has been used as a pejorative term' (*ibid.* p.154).

However, Garrard continues to argue that it is not so much anthropomorphism itself that is the problem, but rather the inability to 'distinguish between kinds of anthropomorphism'. He divides the practice of anthropomorphism into 'Crude anthropomorphism' and 'Critical anthropomorphism'. An example of crude anthropomorphism would be the reading of the smile of Ham - the first chimpanzee launched into space - as 'evidence of his enjoyment of the experience of space travel' confirming the desire to believe that Ham had a good time (Fudge 2010:26). However, chimpanzees do not bare their teeth as a sign of pleasure but rather as a 'gesture of aggression or even fear'. The anthropomorphic assumption that the chimpanzee is smiling is an assertion that enables and perpetuates the construction of the world in a human-centric manner.

Nevertheless, as Eileen Crist extensively claims, it is impossible not to be anthropomorphic. In the same way that

Thomas Nagel famously documents the impossibility of humans understanding what it is like to be a bat (Nagel), it is equally impossible for humans not to be human. Humans can only apprehend the world from a human perspective.

Depending on how it is mediated and the language that is used to describe the being in question, the encounter between a human and another being may be either empowering or disempowering to that being. Marc Bekoff suggests that '[b]ecause we have to use human languages and experiences to meaningfully describe and explain animal behaviour and animal feelings', anthropomorphism is 'unavoidable' (Bekoff 2006:26), however it does not have to be negative. Similarly to Garrard's suggestion of Critical Anthropomorphism above, Bekoff offers the notion of "biocentric anthropomorphism' to stress the point that we can indeed offer reliable explanations of pain, suffering and behaviour without losing our perspective of who animals are in their own world' (*ibid.*)

I suggest that we can apply a similar model to the way in which we understand trees. We need to adapt and to think about trees as if they are trees, although — like Nagel and his bats — we can only ever perceive of trees as humans imagining what it might be like to be a tree, such imaginations can be productive.

Pre-empting Thomas Nagel's arguments for different species' sensory experiences, the German biologist, Jakob von Uexküll tries to envisage how a tick could experience the world. He describes a beautiful rural scene — or rather the human perception of it — however, the tick does not see it.

The eyeless animal finds the way to her watchpost with the help of only her skin's general sensitivity to light. The approach of her prey becomes apparent to this blind and deaf bandit only through her sense of smell. The odour of butyric acid, which emanates from the sebaceous follicles of all mammals, works on the tick as a signal that causes her to abandon her post and fall blindly downward toward her prey. If she is fortunate enough to fall on something warm (which she perceives by means of an organ sensible to a precise temperature) then she has attained her prey, the warm blooded animal, and therefore needs only the help of her sense of touch to find the least hairy spot possible and embed herself up to her head in the coetaneous tissue of her prey. She can now slowly suck up a stream of warm blood.

The tick, as philosopher Giorgio Agamben notes, is:

> *[R]educed to only three carriers of significance […] (1)The odor of the butyric acid contained in the sweat of all mammals; (2) the temperature of thirty-seven degrees corresponding to that of the blood of mammals; (3) the typology of skin characteristic of mammals. […] Yet the tick is immediately united to these three elements in an intense and passionate relationship* (Agamben & Atell 2004:46).

The tick, according to Uexküll's assertions, experiences the world incorporating a set of relationships which include its own and other species as well as the world around it. Uexküll's tick, is the relationship between itself and its environment, which is apprehended as a series of relationships — a series of intra-actions shaped by that species being.

So let us turn to literary perceptions of trees — in the same way that talking animals are anthropomorphised, trees are too. The earlier notions Wohllenben describes of being 'a bit riled up', 'anxious' or 'screaming' is the only way we can actually conceive of how a tree might 'feel'. We have no other language to express this.

Like talking animals, talking trees often feature in Literature for children. Sometimes, they lack voices and instead either have a 'presence' or — like the trees in the sacred grove of Dodona where the rustling leaves are the voice of Zeus — animated by external forces. Their language is passive.

In the enchanted wood of Enid Blyton's *Faraway Tree* the trees speak softly to each other through their rustling 'wisha wisha wisha'.

In C S Lewis' *Magician's Nephew* in the Narnia series, the trees in the wood between the worlds, do not speak, but can be sensed — Digory can 'almost feel the trees growing'. It is a rich place he says — 'as rich as plumcake' it's a sort of in-between place 'not the sort of place where things happen — the trees just go on growing — that's all. In *The Lion the Witch and the Wardrobe* — the children need to be cautious of the trees — although mostly good, some are on the side of the white witch and may be listening'' always listening.

Sometimes the trees are more active and In Tolkien's *Lord of the Rings* trilogy, the trees outside of the safety of the Shire do not like strangers, *and* they watch you. In the daytime, sometimes the unfriendly ones may drop a branch, or stick a root out, or grasp at you with a long trailer. But at night they can be 'most alarming'. They 'whisper' to each other, passing news and plots along in an unintelligible language; and the branches sway…and grope…without any wind. They can even 'move, and can surround strangers and hem them in.'

In Tolkien's second book - *The Two Towers*, Treebeard/ Fangorn is said to be the oldest living thing that still walks beneath the Sun upon this Middle-Earth. He has been around so long that no one remembers where he came from. The language of Entish is 'unhasty' and the words are 'slow, sonorous, agglomerated, repetitive, and long-winded; formed of a multiplicity of vowel-shades and distinctions of tone and quantity. This is because each name for something includes its entire history. For example the word Treebeard uses for a particular hill is 'a-lalla-lalla-rumba-kamanda-lindor-burúme'. He tells Merry and Pippin that Entish is a 'lovely language, but it takes a very long time to say anything in it, because we do not say anything in it, unless it is worth taking a long time to say, and to listen to.'

However, each of these stories of trees is truly embedded in the realms of fiction. Each of the stories describe trees as rich and diverse and sentient beings, but the perception of such communicative wealth requires the reader to suspend their disbelief, asking them to enter and participate in worlds that are populated by the impossible and the fantastic. Tree sentience is firmly confined, therefore to the imagination.

I would like to turn now to the novel, *Pollard*, by Laura Beatty. Published in 2008, it tells the story of Anne, a fifteen-year-old girl who decided to live in the woods near to her house, making a home against the base of a pollard ash, in order to escape the chaos of family life.

The woods that provide relief and respite for Anne are significantly different than the fantasy worlds I have earlier discussed. These are real woods with real trees.

The trees in *Pollard*, do not speak words, but communicate within the world they inhabit — both as beings and holders of other beings. There is the same sort of 'plum-cake' richness that Digory describes in Narnia, and the lengthy concept of time that belongs to Tolkien's ents, however in *Pollard*, Anne does not have to enter into a magical kingdom to perceive this communication. Like the participants in Simard's community, although they are discrete beings, trees in the novel do not care for individuality. Although the 'The wood does see, its concern is with life, not the individual. It doesn't matter. There's always another time, for someone else if not for you.

Instead of individuality, there is a multiplicity of connections that link not only trees but also the other inhabitants of the wood. So much so, that sometimes it is hard to discern who or what is actually communicating. The 'Chorus of Trees' includes other beings too. There was 'room for everything to be themselves but still they fitted together, depended on each other even. Sometimes the fit was so tight , so interwound, it was difficult to sort it out.' (Beatty 2009:18) 'We are rooted, say the trees' and the collective narrative voice of 'growing roots' is described as 'a circle — that's all…a constant flux of up and down, and in and out, and wider and wider.'

The understanding of the wood/trees repeatedly extends to the birds that 'like leaves…rise and fall' in 'wide ellipses to clothe the branches and leave again'. The trees have 'necks' and hold 'fistfuls of leaves' and also 'whisper water.' The beech stand around like swimmers and have naked limbs (*ibid*. p.66) whilst the more modest oak covers up with moss and ferns. The buzzard's eye is related to the sun (*ibid*. p.245). The deer are the 'spirit of the wood; and it is their 'flickering presence' that is part of the queer ballet that makes the 'trees come alive — each of the deer carrying their own wood with them' Later the chorus of trees tells us 'the wind is our voice, should you wish to listen. And instructs us to 'pass it on'. The woods in *Pollard* are collective — Simard's notion of a 'single organism with a collective intelligence'.

Eventually, Anne too becomes part of the multiplicitous resonance of the woods. After a harsh winter, spring arrives and in response both Anne and the woods are 'greening all over in an agony of birth'. Something rages like fire or water under her skin … a force that is burnt and boiling … and stretching and straining …. As she watched, her fingers did burst and out from knuckle and fist and finger end pushed little leaves… Baby leaflets, delicately creased and furled, unfolding in front of her gaze until she was covered. All around her she heard the rustling of herself, a million leaves moving. And birds came and sat in her fingers until her arms ached with the weight of holding them all up so gently (*ibid*. p.93). As the weather warms is it the trees that 'hold' the summers in the same way they hold memories — not in the pinched rings of a hard season but in rings that are wide with growth (*ibid*. p.228).

She becomes part of the cycle as she swallows apple seeds whole, considering the notion that from where she shat, a grove would spring up — all with the flavour and stamp of herself, trees with her rhythm this time that carried the boom of her blood flow under their bark (*ibid*. p.169). Towards the end of the book, she is 'not much different from the moon … barely there, meandering back and forth at a loss' and 'almost erased by time' and in her confusion at the development, her mind becomes a 'tangling undergrowth' through which she can 'wander' (*ibid*. p.291).

Just like in the case of Uexküll's tick, the communication described is understood by Anne as a relationship between the tree, the woods, and its environment, which is apprehended as a series of relationships - a series of intra-actions shaped by that species being.

Beatty repeatedly draws on the phrase 'Tree Chorus'. If we look at the etymological roots of the word, the Latin origin takes us to 'a dance in a circle, the persons singing and dancing, the chorus of a tragedy,' from Greek khoros 'round dance; dancing-place; band of dancers; company of persons in a play, under a leader, who take part in dialogue with the actors and sing their sentiments at intervals.' [1] However, the Greek word is of uncertain origin. Because the original sense is unknown, and the suggestion is that perhaps it is from Π root *gher- (1) 'to grasp, enclose,' if the original sense of the Greek word is 'enclosed dancing floor,' or *gher- (2) 'to like, want,' if the original notion is 'to rejoice.'

Thinking about these definitions, the notion of chorus could be a very productive way in which we can apprehend tree communication — a way in which we can bring talking trees out of the pages of fantasy and into the real world. We might begin to accept that although a conventional response might be that we cannot understand trees — they cannot possibly talk, they have no grammar, there is a possibility of communication. It's just that tree 'talk' is different. Although, as Nagel says, we can only ever be human, we can also borrow from Uexküll and think about — as in *Pollard* — the interconnection, the journey, the cyclical exchanges and rejoicings of chorus that we too could be involved in.

David Abram argues:

> *While persons brought up within literate culture speak at great length about the earthly world, indigenous, oral peoples often speak directly to that world, and experience animals, plants, weather patterns, and landforms as expressive subjects with whom they sometimes find themselves in conversation. Obviously, these other beings do not speak with a human tongue; they do not, that is, speak in words. They may speak in song, like numerous birds, or in rhythm, like the crickets and the ocean waves. They may speak a language of movements, of gestures or slowly shifting shadows.* (Abram 1997)

Language, for traditionally oral peoples, is not a uniquely human possession, but rather a property of the animate earth, in which we humans participate. Ultimately it is not we who speak, but rather the earth that speaks through us, and through the countless other styles of existence that buzz, whistle, and howl across its surface. (Abram 1997)

If we return to *Pollard* — towards the end of the novel the town begins to intrude into the woods and a concrete footpath is built. Anne is almost unable to walk properly on the path — it is 'clean and very hard'. A passer-by greets her saying: "What a privilege it is to be in the woods on such a beautiful morning". Struggling to move and 'walking funny' (Beatty 2009:240), Anne says "Yes", absently, but then thinks about the word 'in'. This isn't IN anything — this is ON. We need to stop being ON, and get back to being IN.

1 https://www.etymonline.com/word/chorus

Ecological artist, David Haley PhD HonFCIWEM, believes our ability to survive climate change is the enactment of a complex evolutionary narrative — the dance of creation and destruction demands new opportunities and meanings for the other side of collapse.

He is a Visiting Professor at Zhongyuan University of Technology. He is Vice Chair of the CIWEM Art & Environment Network, Advisor/Mentor (founder) of Future's Venture Foundation, a Trustee of Chrysalis Arts Development and Art Gene. Haley publishes, educates and makes artworks, internationally, on questions of climate change, species extinction, urban development and 'capable futures'.

Trees of Grace

David Haley

Trees of Grace: ode to the last ash

and then in the night
awake thinking about trees
when the time will come

a matter of time
it's just a matter of time
just matter and time

future's on the line
dream beyond the horizon
it's a long way off

all in good time then
what we can learn from this tree
focus attention

atmosphere transformed
unintended consequence
fuel for the fire

as rain keeps falling
unescapable values
the fires keep burning

prospects diminished
appropriated future
fate predetermined

lost in a moment
clouds pass between the branches
witness the passing

ode to the last ash
what will green beetles eat now?
dieback and evolve

and in the morning
stark black against sulphur skies
when the crows fly out

the energy coast
under the cover of trees
a razor-wired fence

no choice between rocks
under nuclear duress
seeking a hard place

radioactive
waste not, want not, refuse not
trade with open arms

absurd is the norm
and paradox is the game
return to chaos

migrants flee their homes
disasters risk reduction
events of control

questions to be asked
critical recovery
matters over time

the silence silent
civil-military dreams
the stuff of nightmares

tourists at the feast
when we were once innocent
was it ever so?

♦

and then at midday
sitting on a bench nearby
rivers meet to dance

this naked landscape
Fells by name felled by culture
trees fallen from place

weathering the storms
ash clinging to its viewpoint
floods cleared the deadwood

lose ground, gain wisdom
rhythm of adaptation
emerging with hope

with ears that listen
with an open mind to all
with eyes wide open

how big this place is
how long our now could become
who is with us now

passing time passes
one thing leads to another
time and time again

and when the time comes
as the rivers find their way
seeking their freedom

our viewpoint has changed
confluence defines itself
the last ash lives on

♦

and in the evening
playing on a thermal breeze
when the crows fly in

living in context
turn to look, see what could be
forests of meaning

cities as forests
settlements within forests
forests as cities

air, water and food
habitat and energy
metabolism

casting a green net
to reimagine landscape
keys to the future

mutate to evolve
symbiotic relations
planting the future

forest transpiring
carbon, water, nutrients
cycles that respire

the most moral acts
as fundamental culture
life to move onwards

Earth sighed, desire gone
another revolution
seeing trees of grace

David Haley November 2020
Dedicated to Helen Mayer Harrison (1927–2018)

How to hygge a tree (when you can’t hug a tree)

Karen Price, Susanna Bayliss, Alison Cobb & Ben Oliver

Karen Price is Community Coordinator at Westonbirt Arboretum, Forestry England. Co-authors Susanna Bayliss, Alison Cobb and Ben Oliver also work at Westonbirt.

Westonbirt, The National Arboretum is cared for by Forestry England. Located in Gloucestershire, today it is one of the best collections of temperate trees in the world as well as a Grade 1 listed historic garden of national significance. Opened to the public for the first time in the early 1960s, it is a highly successful visitor attraction receiving over 500,000 visits annually.

Funded through the Heritage Lottery Fund (HLF) the community programme was a new venture for the arboretum. Designed to change the way the arboretum works with and is perceived by the local community, as a means of augmenting the site’s existing reputation as a world leading tree collection and major visitor attraction. The programme was designed to specifically support harder to reach and often marginalised / excluded audiences to help fulfil the arboretum’s mission ‘to connect with trees to improve the quality of life.’

◀ Dartington Hall gardens during *Evolving the Forest* (photo: Oliver Raymond-Barker)

How to hygge a tree (when you can't hug a tree): connecting with nature during Covid

Karen Price, Susanna Bayliss, Alison Cobb and Ben Oliver

Westonbirt, The National Arboretum

Hygge: a deep sense of place and wellbeing; a feeling of friendship, warmth, contentment and peace with your immediate surroundings.' (danishweb.wordpress.com)

Photo: Ian Lishman

Nature, togetherness, creativity, sharing, simplicity & the here and now

Introduction

In June 2019, a group of people wandered mindfully through the gardens of Dartington Hall, towards a copse of trees set within a clover field. Here we lit a campfire, toasted marshmallows, made botanical bunting and discussed how the Scandinavian concept of Hygge can be used to create wellbeing moments to support better mental, physical and emotional health in a woodland environment. The workshop was based on *How to Hygge a Tree — Wellbeing at Westonbirt Arboretum*, a book outlining the lessons learnt over four years of running community programmes at the National Arboretum in Gloucestershire.

In recent years, there has been a growth in research and recognition into how spending time amongst trees and nature is good for our wellbeing. This has been highlighted in the Defra 25 Year Environment Plan published in 2018.

> *'Spending time in the natural environment — as a resident or a visitor — improves our mental health and feelings of wellbeing. It can reduce stress, fatigue, anxiety and depression. It can help boost immune systems, encourage physical activity and may reduce the risk of chronic diseases such as asthma. It can combat loneliness and bind communities together.'*

We know this to be true from our own personal experiences. How many of us, when we feel worn down and burnt out, head to the hills, the beach or the forest? Whether for peace, solitude, perspective, grounding, or a deeper-rooted connection with an ancestral belonging, being in the natural world sooths the soul.

However, how do we connect with trees and nature when we cannot physically visit them?

During the latter part of March 2020 as the coronavirus pandemic spread around the world and lockdown hit, Westonbirt Arboretum like many outdoor sites suddenly closed to the public. For lots of people, access to trees was restricted to only those few growing in gardens or local neighbourhoods that could be visited within the daily exercise allowance. For many of our Community Programme participants, living in houses without gardens, in care homes closed to visitors, or shielding due to health, access to trees and their healing properties, became even harder.

The following pages explore how Hygge can be used to connect people with trees and green spaces when physical access is restricted. We reflect on our initial, online offer to maintain a connection with our audience whilst the arboretum was closed and how this offer changed to support people to reconnect with trees, others and themselves as lockdown restrictions eased. Finally, it explores how we can use digital technology to enhance and deepen our offer to vulnerable groups in the future.

Nature

We know that spending time in nature improves our mental and physical health. In her book *The Art of Rest* Claudia Hammond (2019) explores the Top 10 activities people do to unwind, calm their minds and recharge their bodies. Based on the results of a global survey of 18,000 people across 135 countries, spending time in nature came out strong at number two.

However, there has also been growing research exploring how simply looking at images of nature can lower our stress levels. Researchers at Vrije University Medical Centre (van den Berg 2015) in the Netherlands found that visual access to green space provides readily available micro-restorative opportunities and suggest viewing green scenes may be particularly effective in supporting relaxation and recovery after experiencing a stressful period.

2020 has definitely created many stressful periods.

Good Morning, Good Night

Social media enabled us to maintain a sense of community and connection with our regular visitors. Using still images and video clips captured by staff, people were able to visit the arboretum from their mobiles and laptops to watch spring unfurl. Each post was accompanied with a supportive message to reassure readers that they were not alone and to start and end each day with a positive feeling.

Westonbirt Arboretum - Forestry England
April 30

Good morning,

deep breaths, steady steps, it's alright to wobble, it's ok to stumble, and even fall. We're apart, but we're still together in this, and we can help pick each other up.

#stayhomestaysafe

125 9 comments 17 shares

Comments from members of the public include:

> *'I am loving all these beautiful posts — hopefully we will be able to get back there soon x'*
>
> *'How beautiful to wake up to this'*
>
> *'I love your little posts...Brightens the day'*

Creativity

There is a secret to engaging non-traditional visitors with a botanical garden of trees: fire, food, and something to make to take home. The latter is useful as it not only creates a safe space for participants (if everyone is focused on what they are making then they cannot be focusing on you), it also enables participants to make and keep a tangible memory of their connection with the trees.

Hygge is very much about being in the moment. It is a time to escape the problems of the wider world for a short while and focus on nurturing our own wellbeing. Creative activities are a great way to do this. They enable us to cultivate flow, a concept identified in the 1970s by psychologist and happiness researcher Mihaly Csikszentmihalyi[1] which describes those moments when we are completely absorbed in a challenging but do-able task. If our mind is focused on the creative task, then it cannot be worrying about everything else.

Creative activities also enable us to experience success, learn new skills and test our abilities in a safe manner. Failure may happen, sometimes quite often, but the result of this is little more than passing frustration and a potential masterpiece relegated to the recycling pile.

1 https://positivepsychology.com/mihaly-csikszentmihalyi-father-of-flow/

Creativitree

Trees have inspired generations of artists and storytellers from all over the world. They have the power to take our minds wandering off into the depths of our imagination; and even those of us who don't consider ourselves artists can't help but be inspired when we are surrounded by trees.

During lockdown, we wanted to continue our creative connection with people and encourage people to get creative themselves. We reignited a previous onsite offer and took it into the digital realm by suggesting a new creative activity, linked to nature, every day for 52 days.

Sharing

As part of the Westonbirt Community Programme, we offer a six-week outreach project to care homes and dementia groups. This includes a visit by Forestry England staff to the

care home and the loan of a box of multi-sensory activities and resources for activity co-ordinators to run their own tree themed sessions. With Covid-19 and the closure of care homes to visitors, we were unable to provide these activities. Given the crisis faced by care homes during the pandemic this may seem insignificant; however a study by the University of Exeter found that just one hour a week of social interaction can improve the quality of life for dementia patients in care homes. Unfortunately the average amount of social interaction for people with dementia was just two minutes a day. We could not secure them more resources or better PPE, help connect with family members or take away the fear of infection. What we could do, in our own small way, was provide opportunities to share memories, stories and laughter with each other.

Westonbirt Community Wellbeing Activities

Several free online activity packs were created and shared through local community networking groups. Each contained ideas to help residents connect with trees and nature in their gardens or through the window. Packs were also created for families with children with additional

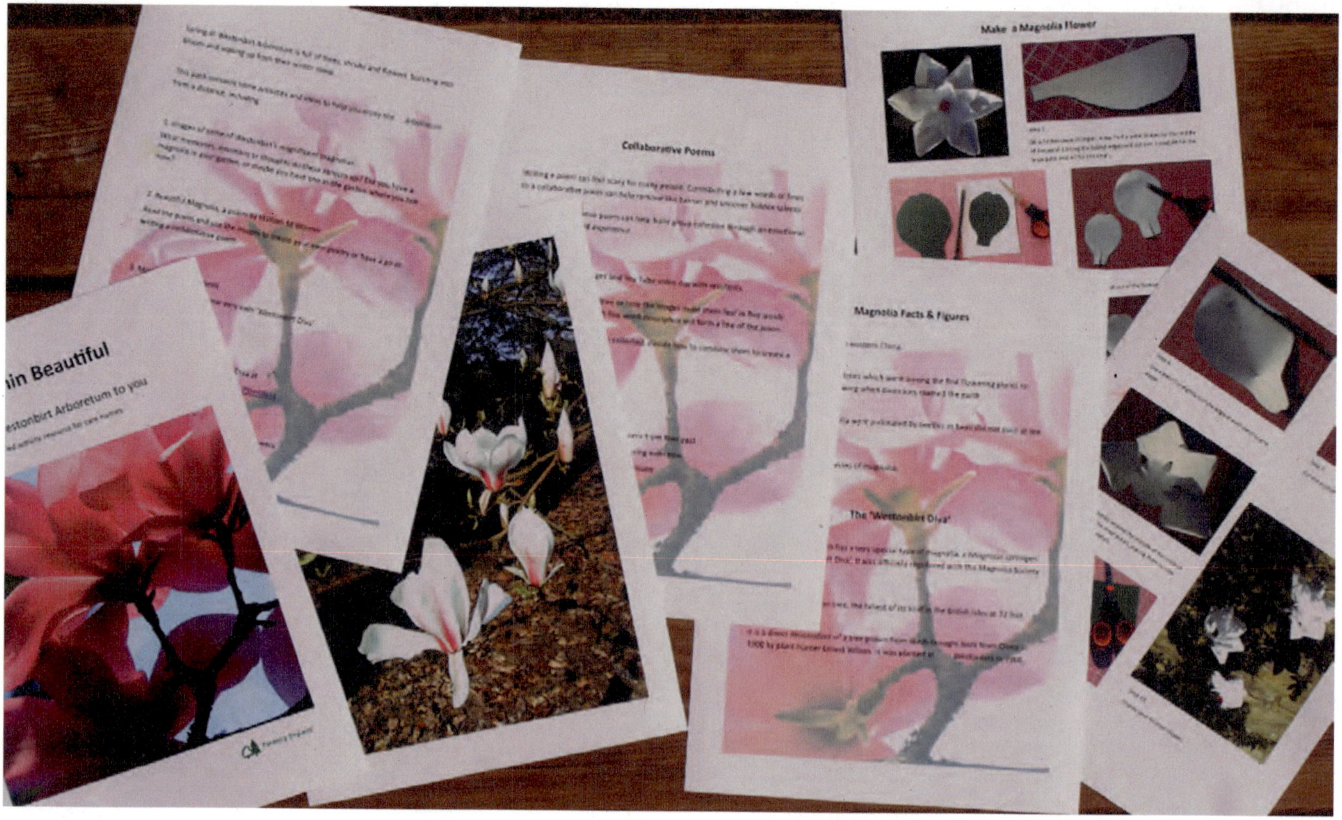

needs who were also finding leaving the house too difficult.

What we discovered later was that by creating bespoke resources for specific 'often overlooked' audiences, we reminded those same audiences that they had not been forgotten as the world closed down around them.

> *'Thank you for thinking of us, looking forward to when we will be able to visit.'* — Care home activity co-ordinator

> *'Most families are not currently wanting to venture out, however, the fact that they have been thought about makes them feel valued and included.'* — from a charity supporting families and children with additional needs.

Togetherness

Togetherness is an integral building block of the Westonbirt Community Programme. We thrive best when connected with others and we spend a lot of time and energy as facilitators creating opportunities that enable participants to build relationships with us, their support workers and each other. Togetherness is about being a part of a group with whom we can share our worries and concerns, our discoveries and achievements; they become our allies in whom we entrust our physical and emotional wellbeing.

As Meik Wiking, the author of *The Little Book of Hygge* (2017) puts it

> *'Time spent with others creates an atmosphere that is warm, relaxed. . . snug and welcoming. In many ways, it is like a good hug — but without the physical contact.'*

...quite apt for the current pandemic!

Reconnect at Westonbirt

As restrictions eased and parks and gardens reopened their gates, Westonbirt was well placed to enable friends and families the opportunity to spend time with each other in a relaxed and safe environment. We purposefully chose not to set a traditional trail, recognising people would be feeling overwhelmed after weeks of home schooling and coronavirus information overload. Instead we opted for a series of informal invitations, to be discovered by chance and prompting the reader to spend a few moments reconnecting with themselves, each other, and nature.

The here and now

Hygge is about slowing down and taking time to enjoy the moment. It is easy to become caught up in a never-ending stream of 'must do' lists and tasks. Even in the initial lockdown period, when a large proportion of us were being

told to 'stay home, stay safe', there was still a slight feeling of guilt if we were not using the time constructively to landscape the garden or redecorate the living room. With restrictions lifted and people returning to work, there has been a need to play catch up on missed time, despite all our resolutions not to go back to how it was before.

But it is important that we savour the moment for what it is. Taking a short a break from daily concerns and by being present in the here and now, we limit the urge to re-live past conversations or predict future catastrophes. Focusing on ourselves also stops us looking on social media at all the 'productive' hobbies and jobs others have been doing during lockdown and feeling inadequate. 2020 has been a year when it has been incredibly easy to do all three of these.

2020 has also been a very busy year for our woodland sites. It has been amazing to see so many people turning to the nation's forests for their own solace, but it has also meant an increase in work and pressure for our staff. Following a couple of in house blogs about the importance photography has played for some colleagues over the previous months, a staff mindful photography group was established to encourage others to press pause for a short while and enjoy being in the moment.

A mindful photography journey

By encouraging people to slow down, and relook at the natural world around us, mindful photography can open the door to the secret, hidden and amazing world of the unnoticeable.

Each journey is framed around one or more themes and the task is to take a photograph that represents each theme. There are no real rules to worry about and no particular photography skill is required beyond the very basics. You are not setting out on a hike; distance travelled is not the purpose, but a slow wander to savour the landscape and let the unnoticed take centre stage.

(image: Johnny Hathahway)

Maybe you won't capture all of the themes, it isn't a competition. Maybe you will only find two before being distracted by buzzards soaring overhead or a patch of wild garlic. It doesn't matter; you've achieved the purpose just by slowing down taking notice and looking again.

Here are some themes to try:

▲ *Shades of Green*

◀ *Water*

▶ *Nature Takes Over*

Keep it simple

Hygge is not about trying to wow people with extravagance or professional / corporate polish — but about creating a warm and supportive environment in which people can grow in confidence and self-esteem.

We don't know how long the current pandemic and its ramifications will last. As the months pass, we may adapt to a new normal or struggle long term under the weight of worry, most likely a mixture of both. So why add to the pressure by setting ourselves impossible targets to deliver an activity with all the bells and whistles attached? This can also leave the recipient feeling under-skilled and under-qualified to take part. If the ultimate aim is to support people to have better mental health through a connection with trees, then we don't need to teach them how to paint a masterpiece when creating a junk mail woodland collage will do just as well. And during those early weeks of lockdown, junk mail and a stick of glue were sometimes the only resources we all had to hand.

What we do know about the future is that trees, woods and forests will continue to play an essential role in our wellbeing. Covid has shown us how we turn to nature in times of emotional need and we need to harness this. Unfortunately, despite our best efforts, Westonbirt Arboretum will still be inaccessible for some whether through distance, transport, health, economics etc. Projects like the Westonbirt Community Programme can only feasibly work with a finite number of people. However, there are still opportunities to grow.

We can continue to grow our online and virtual offer, enabling new audiences to enjoy the wonders of Westonbirt from their own homes, enhance their own organisations' activities or make resources available to non-targeted groups. Feedback from an adult mental health support group commented how some of their service users had enjoyed using the online activity packs with their children. The packs were not aimed at adults living with mental health conditions, but we hadn't considered those adults were also parents.

One colleague has been walking many of the 17 miles of path at the arboretum to capture video footage of each journey, enabling people to take a virtual tour if they are unable to visit in person. In addition, these also enable potential new audiences with specific requirements to assess surface conditions, distances, and bench locations etc to plan their day out in advance and continue to grow our audience diversity.

We can continue to grow strong partnerships with other organisations. Sharing ideas, working collaboratively, and ensuring as many barriers as possible are removed to enable people to benefit from the therapeutic properties of trees.

Shane Finan is an artist from Sligo, Ireland. His work is interdisciplinary, including traditional artistic media, contemporary technologies, dialogical processes, event management, curation, and writing. His work is about networks, blending fields from ecology to technology to philosophy. His work on mycorrhizal networks forms part of a project called 'The Wood Wide Web,' partly completed in collaboration with Visual Arts in Rural Communities (VARC), UK, and Northumberland Wildlife Trust, UK. https://shanefinan.org

We, the mycorrhizae

Shane Finan

We, the mycorrhizae

Shane Finan

1 Forest

Peeling off a layer of loose soil with our fingers, we find a multitude. Hordes of lichen and fungi greet us, reacting in imperceptible ways to the introduction of light from our careless disturbances. These protected areas of growth run deep, and are abundant. We too are just as much a hoard of life. The ecosystems in our body support thousands of microscopic lifeforms, all forming part of an interconnected network that forms us, forms you, forms me.

Foraging for mushrooms in the autumn is still a common practice in many countries, where an excited collector's rustle can be heard among the papery leaves. In Ireland, despite a long tradition of living from the land, foraging mushrooms today is often considered either too dangerous or a symbol of poverty. Nonetheless, I began rooting around for mushrooms a few years ago, guided only by books and caution, and now eagerly look forward to the rich diversity of flavour in the autumn season of abundance every year.

Scouring the forest floor for the autumnal treats made me start to think about these organisms in more detail.

Mushrooms are the fruit. Just as an apple grows on a tree to spread its seeds, a mushroom surfaces to distribute spores and encourage new generations of fungus. Fungi are extraordinary organisms that are neither plant nor animal, and so justify an entire specialist vocabulary of their own. Under the soil, fungi exist as often massive lifeforms (*mycelia*) that are made up of a chaotic tartan of intertwined fungal thread (*hyphae*), surrounded by protective coating (*glomalin*), often forming close, collaborative relationships with green plants (*mycorrhizae*).

It is the last of these that I find most fascinating. Mycorrhizal networks challenge our sense of what an organism is. These networks are made from fungi and green plants that work together. The fungi below the ground find and extract water and nutrients from deep soil, and 'exchange' this with the trees above for carbohydrates that the fungi cannot produce themselves.

I have deliberately placed the word 'exchange' above in inverted commas. There is a danger, when writing about the non-human, to anthropomorphise. The idea of exchange implies a happy, peaceful to-and-fro. This may be the case, but one microbiologist that I met described the relationship instead as 'reciprocal parasitism'. Both organisms benefit from the arrangement of the network, but he believes we should not see this as altruistic organisms working in tandem.

This description opens a broader question about how we perceive this exchange, and what we see as 'value'. Is this an exchange or parasitism? Is it collaboration or competition? Do species work together for the benefit of all, or fight for the scarce resources that are available? Much of 20th Century western theory would suggest the latter is the key to all survival. But perhaps this is only a perspective, one that matches ideological beliefs about markets and ownership, which has often been challenged.

The only reason I am able to digest food at all is because of the complex microbiome in my gut (Yong 2016). I do not consciously thank these micro-biotic helpers, and I do not remember signing a contract and agreeing to terms, but

all photos in this chapter: Shane Finan

still we work together. Perhaps we are mutually parasitic upon one another. Whether we are or not, without this relationship neither of us could survive.

There are fossil records of tree-fungi relationships that date back hundreds of thousands of years. In western science, mycorrhizal networks were first discovered in 1885, at a time when the idea of symbiosis was still controversial among scientific communities (Frank 2005: 267-275). While Alexander von Humboldt had identified the interconnectedness of species, environments and weather systems in his *Naturgemälde* — his 'nature painting', 1807, referenced and reprinted in full in Wulf (2015). By 1879 the idea of collaboration between plants was still contentious, as exemplified when Anton de Bary coined the term 'symbiosis' and was rebuffed by the scientific community for its ridiculousness (Sheldrake 2020). At this time lichen were thought to be one organism — they were soon found to be at least two (a fungus and a green plant) but in recent studies we have learned that each lichen is made of hundreds of different organisms. While organisms do of course compete for resources, the landscape is more complicated than that.

In 1997, Professor Suzanne Simard (Simard et al. 1997: 579-582) uncovered a fascinating symbiosis in mycorrhizal networks during an experiment investigating relationships between trees (*ibid*). In an accidental finding typical of great discoveries, Simard was studying the movement of carbon between trees when she realised that neighbouring trees communicate with one another, under the soil, using fungi as a channel through which to send signals. If a tree is infected, for example, it can warn its neighbours to put out defences. This complex finding in mycorrhizal networks was dubbed the 'Wood-Wide Web' by *Nature* magazine in 1998 (Helgason 1998: 431)). It was a significant discovery, which has since continued to influence thinking on forestry.

Of course, the trees and fungi always knew this. It just took us some time to catch up.

Soil is the transmitter in mycorrhizal networks. Water moves through it, is absorbed by fungi and passed back up to the roots of trees in exchange for food. But as a transmitter, soil can also absorb and distribute harmful materials. In the 1960s, scientist Rachel Carson (1962) published the danger of pesticides by demonstrating the permeation of toxins from pesticides through soil (*ibid.*). Creatures like earthworms, who can survive these toxins, are able to surface and provide food for birds or animals; these animals in turn build up high levels of toxicity by eating many such creatures and eventually die from the dosage. Some of the most vivid descriptions in Carson's work include birdwatchers aghast at the birds falling out of the sky in areas where pesticides were sprayed sometimes months before.

The soil, the fungi, the micro-organisms and all the lifeforms work as part of an intricately entwined system.

When I find an edible mushroom, the feeling is like being a child again. Out in the woods, fingers damp from scratching the earth, nose and toes cold, the findings give off an excitement that is both ancestral satisfaction and modern satiation. But now, I never consider the mushroom as a single organism — it is a part of a network. I picture how it is wrapped to the roots of the Scots pine or birch tree that forms a canopy overhead. By lifting it from its growing place, I spread its spores. When I pick it, I not only thank the mycelium underground, but I thank the nearby trees, the soil, the insects. The complexity of this network makes it possible for me to find this little bit of joy on autumn afternoons. I am grateful to this mesh network,

from the fungus to the books and writers that led me foraging, from the mushrooms to the trees.

Trees that were alive during the first nuclear tests carry the mark of the beginning of the atomic age. Trees that are alive now carry the burden of the abundance of carbon in our atmosphere. These living records entomb past events in their rings, which are only revealed when we unfortunately kill them. As carbon sinks they pull in the toxins that would eventually kill humans, and instead help us to survive. The record of global events form part of how trees record our interconnected existence. And simultaneously, they keep us alive, and the fungi in the soil keep them alive. Trees also keep the fungi alive, and we help by planting new trees. Oaks rely on jays to spread their acorns, while each fig tree species has a single wasp species that has evolved to pollinate it. Nettles grow where human structures once stood. Hedgehogs inhabit hedgerows. Lichen break down rocks to create soil for growth, and provide soft beds for cattle to rest on. Bacteria break down grass in the cow's stomach. Humans drink its milk and feed it grain in leaner months.

Somewhere within this complexity, we eke out an existence.

2 Technology

Digging in with a spade, we unearth sharp soft slops of congealed clay. The spade is the technology, the aide that we have built, that is an extension to our body. Somewhere in that soil there is also the microscopic evidence of human existence: carbon stores and microplastics — obvious to those who know how to look. Our bodies are a multitude of self-contained organisms, and we extend that body with our technologies. The spade is a body extension, enabling our body to perform tasks more efficiently. Arguably, such a technology is potentially a cognitive extension, changing how we behave with soil.

The argument of where a body ends and a technology begins is complex. A radical paper published in 2017 by Hilton F. Japyassú & Kevin N. Laland (2017:375-395) (and which has been repeatedly refuted, defended, and debated since) provides a good platform for considering this question. In his previous work, Japyassú had argued that the spiderweb is not only a tool created by a spider, but also an extension of its body. In this more recent theory, he and Laland suggest that spiders can 'think' through the web in what is called *extended cognition*; The extended web creates mental calculations and reactions by the spider based on the changeable circumstances of a web (Laland). While controversial, the idea resonates with the idea of multi-species communication as put forward by Simard, and also with (human) philosophy of extended cognition (Latour 1986: 1-40) and the concept of 'posthumanism' (Braidotti 2016:13-32), both of which ideas create arguments that suggest the non-human is at least a relevant controlling factor in the behaviour of a body, if not sometimes entirely in control.

Like the spade, paper is a technology, and one that has real importance in human development. Today, paper is produced from tree pulp, usually from trees that have been pulled down, washed, bleached, and repurposed. Paper was predated by the invention of writing, which can be done on stone, wood, or any other medium. Paper simplified this process, just as the spade simplified digging, or the world wide web simplified sending messages to distant corners of the earth.

✦ ✦ ✦

While paper is the source of such wealth of information, it has also been used to enforce laws and ideologies that can oppress and individualise. The recently deceased philosopher Bernard Stiegler (1998) argued that first we invent our technologies, then they change our behaviour (Stiegler). The technology of paper has ensured the longevity of peace treaties, of stories, of law and religion. It has been involved in the formation of nations, in the genocide of millions, and in the salvation of millions more. It is the material embodiment of bureaucratic nightmares. And it has dictated the structure of our current western society, with maps and deeds that demarcate the ownership of the earth under our feet, the division of soil from one person to another.

A newspaper is a mode of communication that is referred to as 'centralised': a central source creates and spreads the information, and controls what is printed. An alternative, decentralised information, is that which spreads from node to node without a central authority. Ham radio broadcasts were seen as a decentralised communication technology. The internet was built to work this way, and in its early days it was thought to herald a new form of decentralised communication, but this has slowly changed.

I first encountered the internet in the late 1990s, on a Gateway machine running Windows that my father used for work. At that time, the hungry signal monopolised the phone-line, leaving a choice between the telephone or the internet — one form of telephony or another. As a teenager, the chatrooms and online game spaces provided both an escape and a community, but little in the way of critique or review. I remember the fresh excitement of online identities, of becoming someone other to a new audience. The technologies were fresh but quickly became natural, and as online platforms became more 'user friendly', my behaviours changed to suit the media.

Our global network of interconnectivity has become so important in a short space of time that there are calls to list internet access as a human right (Reglitz 2020: 314-331, La Rue 2011). Like all complex inventions, there were many contributing parts to its story. Paper is one. Telephony is another, where we learned to connect via threads — like fungal hyphae — transmitting messages across oceans in milliseconds.

And in this story of technological development, we do not always end up at the destination that we set out to find. It is unlikely that Ada Lovelace foresaw the structure of today's computing systems when she wrote what is regarded as the first computer program in 1843.

Some of the main building blocks for what would become the world wide web developed from work at CERN in the 1980s and 90s, and include publicly funded military or university programmes for connectivity, such as ARPA's contributions to connectivity protocols from the 1960s onward. The invention of the transistor in the late 1940s brought what is now a key component in all modern computing, and makes small devices like smartphones possible. And looking back, just a few years before the invention of the transistor, wartime cryptography helped shape the modes and models of encrypted messaging that gave vision to a possible future internet.

When written out like this, it seems like there may have been a clear, hereditary (or patrilineal) logic to technological development. *Paper begot word processors. Telephony begot the internet*. But this simplified history doesn't take into account the chaotic ecosystem of research and development on different possible communications technologies, much of which is now either forgotten or embedded somewhere deep in the code of our modern computing. On top of this, there are many alternative technologies that do not form part of this equation. It is as difficult to precisely map technological development as it is to know that this development is even the best that we could possibly have.

Digital communications work using binary, or two numbers together. Binary communications need everything to work in blocks that multiply by two (such as 2, 4, 8, 16, 32, etc.). Our system of counting in base-10, whereby we batch our numbers together in groups of ten, happened solely because we have ten fingers. If we had twelve, or eight, our base system and all of our mathematics would be formulated differently — the 'father of computing' Alan Turing refused to use base-10 in his early computing experiments. This questions whether our bodies have unintentionally inhibited our technological development, or at least have inhibited one popular form of technological development (binary computing) (Parker 2014:16-25).

Other complex computations have been performed by clockwork devices, magnets or sunlight. The extraordinary *Antikythera* mechanism is the oldest known example we have of an analogue computer, dating from around 2,000 years ago. This machine was lost in a shipwreck (perhaps ironically, as it is believed that the mechanism was designed to predict sea storms). It offers a clockwork, mechanical type of computing that is not organised around binary numbers. The website random.org uses wind and weather systems to generate random numbers with more 'randomness' than a binary computer is capable of, which may not seem important if picking lottery numbers, but can be very important in unpredictability mapping (Haahr). Another possible form of technology that is getting a lot of attention these days is biocomputing, which can include making calculations using living material like DNA strands, moulds, fungi or lichen (Church et al. 2012).

All this leads to a question: do we actually have the best possible technologies that our human minds can conceive? As the 21st Century progresses, we have seen the antisocial nature of many parts of the purportedly social internet. This presents at least a challenge to anyone who would argue that technological progress should move in only one direction.

The technology of paper has given us modes of communication that we could not imagine. Even with subsequent inventions, paper remains a key medium of communication after 2,000-odd years. Internet technologies use print and keyboard layout similar to past technologies, combined with the messaging speed of telephony. The words used are crucial. They form cyphers and keys that unlock ideas, or that imprison them. As the young technology grows older, we can see how it brings people together, and how it pulls them apart. The intertwined networks of social groups, collaborating through technology, exist because of a history of coincidence and circumstance.

Complex technology grows and changes like a living organism, but the paths that we choose for its growth are not random. We have a responsibility to choose how we allow technologies to grow, as sooner or later they will influence our behaviour.

3 Community

Into the soil we place a seed, one at a time, evenly spaced. This will one day be a forest, or a hedgerow, or a stand of fruiting apple trees. We can decide that ourselves. But for now we have only soil, and a little hope for a future that is made of connections, from us to the soil, to the fungi and the trees, to the pipes and the machines, and to one another.

When I stand on the peak of mountains in western Europe, it is the demarcation of land that is visually pronounced. As the wind drowns out all other sounds and the clouds threaten rain in the distance, the landscape below emerges as a network of places, each one neighbouring another, all nodes in a large system. From a mountaintop, the irony of this is also clear, as the blades of grass or mounds of bog around attest to the durability of place, and to how its identity and association is all created.

The demarcated landscape is an illusion. When a pandemic circulates or a pattern of severe weather hits, it does not affect one area and leave the other alone. The boundaries, whether physical (in walls and hedgerows) or invisible (in county or country borders) only highlight societal rules about land. The soil will still carry water from one farm to another. The pollen and spores will sweep through the air, happily ignoring boundary walls and rows of hedge or fence. If you ask the mountain who owns it, I expect the answer will be vague and distracted (if, as Wittgenstein argued about the lion, the mountain could even understand our bizarre concepts of ownership at all). The concept of ownership implies that there is always an 'other' — someone or something that doesn't own or isn't owned. So demarcations let us know where one place ends and another begins.

Ownership is generally agreed on paper — deeds and contracts assign a right to use and modify a landscape. Ownership can extend beneath the soil, to valuable resources, or can stay on the surface, depending on national or local laws or customs. Commodities mined or farmed from the landscape are bought and sold, sometimes at speeds that defy reason in high frequency trading stations, thousands of miles from where resources are mined.

Something is missing from this story. There, underneath the soil, there is something more. A relationship. The paper writ, the human connection, is only one part of the story. The roots and fungi, the soil and insects, tell another competing one. When one material, such as the wood, is taken away to make paper, the fungi that rely on that tree for sustenance also go. What seems a simple gesture can be disruptive in unimaginable ways.

With all of our technologies to communicate and demarcate, we try to distance ourselves from these species, these places, these 'others' that we see as unlike ourselves. And yet, time and again, we fail in this distancing. The assumption remains that if we disturb one element, the others will remain intact.

Creating a sense of identity for a place might be as simple as experiencing it through walking, gaining a sense of the phenomenon of a place — how it feels underfoot, what it smells like, the coldness of the air. Sometimes we create places. This often involves using objects or events to invent memories or experiences, such as with public art or festivals. This creation of experience is at the root of technology as an extension of ourselves: *tekhne* in ancient Greek translates as *art or craft*. It is the creation of tools to better ourselves.

Of course, human beings have always attached to places, whether nomadic or grounded. We often see a human influence on place as negative, but this may be a relatively recent phenomenon. The landscape architect Sylvia Crowe (1958) worried in the mid-20th Century that markers of human influence on the countryside were becoming too pronounced. She argued with a bias of what she believed a countryside should look like, but simultaneously presented ways through which landscapes of industry and electricity can be beautiful when they intertwine with the unbuilt world around them.

As with the happy accidents of discovery and invention, perhaps we need a happy accident of growth in ourselves. Somewhere in our capabilities of understanding, we can make room for a complexity that we try so often not to see. The trees, the paper, the mycelia, the cables, the wild, the tame: a coexisting mass of interconnected networks of everything we know is part of us.

We, the mycorrhizae.

Liz O'Brien is head of a dynamic Social and Economic Research Group at Forest Research that focuses on understanding the complex relationships between forestry, the environment and society. Her research explores well-being, social and cultural values, and the cultural ecosystem benefits of trees and woodlands including a strong focus on the health benefits of engagement with trees and woodlands – physical, mental and social. She has researched groups that are excluded and disadvantaged and their engagement with woodlands and wider nature. She has been involved in a large number of evaluations of projects and programmes and has collaborated with a range of countries in her research including Norway, USA, New Zealand, Sweden, and Australia.

Time to reflect on trees, woods & wonder

Liz O'Brien

Time to reflect on trees, woods and wonder

Liz O'Brien, Social and Economic Research Group, Forest Research

Evolving the forest

As head of the Social and Economic Research Group at Forest Research[1]. I want to reflect on our exploration of human-treescapes relationships over the past few years and explore through a recent project whether the Covid-19 crisis is changing our relationship with treescapes and wider nature.

There has been much research in the past twenty years focused on the health and wellbeing benefits of treescapes and wider nature (see for example: ten Brink et al. 2016, Bratman et al. 2019, Sallmannshofer et al. 2019) from benefits associated with being in woodland, to viewing trees from indoors or while walking or driving along roads, from trees in people's gardens and communal spaces. What people do in treescapes is important from accessing woods for walking, running or cycling; to sitting under a tree in the park, to active hands on engagement through foraging, conservation volunteering, or citizen science data gathering. Understanding the value of these benefits has become increasingly important and ways to elicit these values through approaches that can feed into natural capital accounting are developing. A key aim of much of this work is to identify monetary values associated with the service or benefit, and this narrows the range of values reported on, as not all of them can be expressed in monetary terms. There are also strong ethical and justice issues for not monetising all aspects of nature.

How we have researched human-treescapes relationships

We have been researching human-treescape relationships for twenty years. In that time terminologies, frameworks and definitions changed. When I started at Forest Research, we were talking about the non-market values of forestry. There was a strong focus on monetary values for nature — with a particular focus on recreation (Willis et al. 2000). We had moved on to talk about post-productivist forestry with a focus on wider environmental and social benefits rather than a sole focus on timber production (Mather 2001). Social forestry encompassed community and stakeholder engagement, recreation and access, and quality of life. In recent times we have moved on to talk about ecosystem stocks, flows, services and benefits. A key driver behind this is the desire to raise the profile of treescapes and their importance as part of the country's critical infrastructure alongside roads, rail, and building infrastructure. This creates frustrations about the values that cannot be easily articulated through a single metric such as money, and the tendency for those values that are not captured in such approaches to be left out in decision-making processes. Appreciation of these values sometimes arise through conflict. For example, the removal of street trees in Sheffield in 2018 and the consultation proposing the 'sell off' of the public forest estate in England in 2011 (Kenter et

◀ Photo: R Menzies-Gow (from Hall et al. 2019, *Tribute to Trees* project)

1 Forest Research is Britain's principal organisation for forestry and tree related research.

Photo: I Smyth (From Hall et al. 2019, *Tribute to Trees* project)

al. 2015), these illustrated that not understanding or appreciating the values people hold for treescapes can lead to large scale protests. Bujis and Lawrence (2013) highlight that emotions are important components of treescape related conflicts and values. They argue that forestry professionals focusing on rational debates about forestry can often dismiss emotions as irrational and therefore not to be taken into account in decision-making or valuations.

My initial research involved exploring the social and cultural values of treescapes. An initial review of literature (O'Brien 2003) led to research on urban and rural areas in northwest and southeast England (O'Brien 2005). I wanted to hear about how people spoke about treescapes from trees in the street or park through to woodlands. Those in the urban areas I was exploring raised issues that did not come up in the rural discussions. A couple of women talked about being 'flashed' at by men on Southampton common, in Liverpool someone highlighted how it was easy to identify poorer areas in the city as they had fewer street trees. The urban groups expressed greater concerns about the loss of greenspace to housing or business development and highlighted more concerns about personal safety as some of the urban woods had evidence of abuse such as litter, detritus from drug taking, and evidence of fire setting. Since those initial studies our group within Forest Research has grown and we have explored many different human-treescapes relationships including research on children, education and learning (O'Brien and Murray 2007; O'Brien 2009), woodland focused interventions for young people excluded from school, motivations and benefits of conservation volunteering, the impact of NHS greenspace in Scotland for staff, urban health and treescapes, and how physical activity or mental health interventions can work for different groups within society (Williams et al. 2013, O'Brien 2018 and 2019).

We brought together work from over thirty projects to explore the distribution of wellbeing benefits gained from treescapes in Britain. We found that quantitative survey work identified a narrower range of benefits than the qualitative approaches which gave space for people to express more freely their relationships with treescapes (O'Brien and Morris 2013). The disabled, lower socio-economic groups

Photo: P. O'Neill (From Hall et al. 2019, *Tribute to trees* project)

and BAME[2] groups were less likely to benefit from engagement with treescapes unless there were targeted interventions that specifically sought to support them in that connection. These projects and interventions, however, were time bounded and although they often identified many benefits for participants it was not clear what the medium- and longer-term impacts would be once the projects ended. Would participants have the confidence to carry on engaging with the woodlands without support or specific organised activities?

Why using a range of research methods matters

Focus groups, interviews and surveys have been a staple of much of our research and have been effective ways of understanding what people are doing in relation to treescapes and why, how it makes them feel, how it fits into their lives, and what it means to them. We have also used a range of other methods such as photo elicitation in a project focused on Lyme disease and another on peri-urban treescapes. We got participants to take photographs of anything in the wood that they felt was positive or negative. While the majority of pictures were of the treescapes or individual trees participants also took pictures

2 Black, Asian and minority ethnic groups

of paths to highlight that this enabled people to access the woodland, and of a lake which added variety to the scene (O'Brien et al. 2012). Negative aspects were confined to photos of rubbish and an abandoned vehicle on the edge of the wood. Someone took a picture of her friend in the wood to highlight people she liked to socialise with, another person took photos of families enjoying the woodland as she enjoyed watching others have a pleasant time.

In the past decade we have undertaken more in situ data gathering which has involved 'being and doing' with people who are taking part, often, in targeted interventions. Part of the Westonbirt Community Project was targeted at people less likely to visit the arboretum and who had drug/alcohol problems, mental health problems and young people with behavioural problems and autism (O'Brien 2018). The adults and young people spent a day at the site undertaking a variety of conservation, creative and practical activities. In evaluating the project we felt that spending time with participants, carrying out participant observation along with short interviews and informal chats would be the most appropriate ways of understanding, how participants were getting involved, what they were doing and what their experiences were. The project itself was inspiring in terms of the approach Forestry England had taken to engage participants, the care taken to encourage and support them so that they gained a sense of achievement, and the community shelter area created in the arboretum where the participants would undertake or begin their sessions. The shelter area had a cob oven and fire pit allowing participants to make pizza for lunch, toast marshmallows on the fire, make tea, and chop more wood for the fire. The participants talked about finding the arboretum to be atmospheric — a calm and peaceful place, where they felt less judged as someone with a problem and more treated as a person.

Photo: Paul Tabbush. Cooking round the fire (From O'Brien, 2018, Westonbirt Community Project)

An ongoing project focuses on encouraging physical activity in the forest, through a targeted progamme called Active Forests, it includes a mixed methods approach including 'in situ being and doing' of activities with participants. Joining Nordic walking sessions, a mountain bike weekly class for women, a bootcamp, duathlon, buggy fit and parkrun and undertaking the activity with participants has allowed us to get an idea of the dynamics of the group, how the person leading the activity supports the participants, and how the session works overall. This provides a basis for then sitting down with participants after their exercise and running a focus group to explore how people got involved in their activity, what motivates them to keep it up, what benefits they feel they gain from participating, and what challenges they face (O'Brien 2019 and 2020).

We also recently got involved in analysing the data from Forestry England's Tribute to Trees project. (Hall et al. 2019).

A webpage was set up and specifically asked people to contribute their stories, poems, prose or photos that illustrated anything about their connections to treescapes. From the analysis we found people expressed many emotional and sensory experiences and these were linked to the types of treescapes they interacted with in specific places, the activities they were doing and often the people they were enjoying the experience with. (Hall et al. 2019).

What are we finding about our relationship with treescapes during the Covid-19 restrictions in 2020?

The Covid-19 pandemic in its initial phase led to the lockdown of many of the activities that people normally undertake as part of their everyday life. There was closure of shops (except for food), schools, hospitality and leisure venues and people were only allowed out in the first few weeks once a day for an hour. This unprecedented curtailment of people's normal activities led to a strong media focus and advice from a range of public bodies on how to cope with the lockdown and what could be done within the constraints. There was a lot of encouragement on social media for people to access local nature spaces and enjoy their gardens if they had one. Environment sector organisations developed a raft of communications to provide advice and ideas of how people might engage with nature.

Photo: Liz O'Brien. Buggyfit session (From O'Brien, 2019, Active Forests project)

We wanted to explore the impact of Covid-19 and engagement with nature on people who were generally already well connected to nature. We developed an online survey and selected a sample of people from the survey to interview to find out in some more detail people's experiences. We got over 2,100 responses to the survey and undertook 25 interviews

What we found were some key reasons that enabled people to sustain or increase their connection with nature and treescapes, these included time saved due to some participants being furloughed, or not commuting. Coupled with time saved was the lack of opportunity for people to undertake many of their usual leisure activities. The initial lockdown phase when people were only allowed out for one hour a day coincided with spring and improvements in the weather. Furthermore, people were not allowed to meet with others outside of their household. Those who had more time and fewer of their usual activities to occupy them spent part of it connecting with nature from tending to their gardens, to appreciating trees in the streets, to exploring their local area and finding new routes and footpaths not previously used. People felt their happiness increased when in nature and they appreciated nature more than ever.

Photo: R. Gutsell (From Hall et al. 2019, Tribute to Trees project)

Are we seeing a change in people's relationships with treescapes and will any changes last?

It is clear from our research on engaging with nature before and during Covid-19 that many people who were working at home, retired, or home schooling children took more time to explore their local areas and nature spaces whether they lived in urban or rural areas. They spoke about enjoying and growing things in their gardens, taking time to appreciate treescapes and wider nature, noticing flora and fauna, as well as the changes brought about by spring. A number of important themes came through.

Immersive experiences

For those who are very connected to nature and prefer to avoid others, there were some opportunities for immersive forest experiences, finding remoter spaces and spending quiet time away from others and distractions, if they were fortunate enough to have a forest nearby.

> *I think that's because I was going right deep into the forest and wasn't seeing anybody. I even on a number of occasions put my hammock in the panniers on the bike and went right, right, right in — places I'd never seen before — and hung the hammock and took a jet boil to make a cup of tea*

and a book, and I'd be up there for the afternoon with the dog asleep next to me and then cycle back again. So, yes, definitely. (Female, self-employed, peri-urban)

Exploration — discovering the new

The initial lockdown restrictions of only leaving the house for one hour of exercise a day meant many people could not visit their usual nature spaces and had to explore and discover what their local area had to offer and became more adventurous sometimes when restrictions eased.

> *Yes. It surprises me that I've explored it but I've always gone to the same paths and the same places and never really veered off what I didn't know, so it was quite nice… because I downloaded an app as well of certain trails and now I just go and think I'll try that walk today and I'll try different areas and I've seen things that I've never even seen before in walking distance from where I live.* (Female studying peri-urban)

Appreciation of nature

The disruption of Covid-19 to people's everyday lives allowed some time for reflection on and appreciation for nature, even for those who are already strongly connected.

> *I think you tend to take for granted what you've got and it's more special when you actually step back and we have more time to appreciate what we're seeing rather than just taking it for granted.* (Female, working, peri-urban)

> *It pushed me into looking at everything a little bit more deeply and a little bit more closely.* (Female, retired, urban)

Nature — Solace from stress

Covid-19 has created a lot of concern and anxiety for a whole range of reasons from concerns about employment, worries about health, relatives, concerns about social distancing and many others. Connection with treescapes can help support people at these times.

> *I've suffered from really bad stress through this. We're going through redundancy at the moment, my husband's being made redundant and it's all part of what's happened with Covid. So it really has been my sanctuary to be able to get out at times to find them and a lot of them are in forests and woods, so we do actually spend a lot of our time with our hobby (geocaching) in forests and woods.* (Female, working, peri-urban)

Importance of a sense of freedom

A small number were concerned about the loss of freedom and how the restrictions constrained their lives giving rise to some anxiety and concerns.

> *Yes, the way I kept describing it to friends and stuff is, although the restrictions and life didn't feel like it changed very much, what I felt was like a low level anxiety. Not like stressful every day or anything but it was just that little bit undercurrent all the time because you know you don't have the freedom that you had before.* (Female, working rural)

Treescapes for reflection, support, longevity, and resilience

Many people have become more connected to nature due to the Covid-19 pandemic. Our lives are played out mainly indoors but many of us have found time for some exploration amidst the anxiety of Covid-19. Evidence shows that treescapes can help us to reflect on what is meaningful to us, and what we care about, they can provide a sense of atmosphere and natural grandeur not easily mirrored by many other types of green space. The sensory aspects of treescapes provide a sense of grounding, immersive engagement, and connection with the natural world. They provide markers of seasonal change and the passage of time as well as providing a connection to natural cycles, with old and large trees acting as a reference point to gain perspective on our lives — linking the past and the future.

Our research highlights the importance of connection to nature from childhood and how this can lead to familiarity and an interest in engaging with nature throughout life. Through long-term engagement and familiarity treescapes can become places of solace as well as places to experience excitement and adventure. The evolving forest is the relationships between people and treescapes, and people need to experience this for themselves through embodied experiences. At present however, the wellbeing benefits, and the barriers people face in accessing treescapes is unequally distributed across society. Inequalities in proximity, amount, quality, size of spaces, and access to treescapes needs to be addressed. There is a strong government focus on the need to create and expand treescapes across Britain and an opportunity to consider how to address some of these inequalities. These are social and environmental justice issues that can be improved through investment in nature-based interventions that reach out to those currently underserved by the current resource. Targeted approaches need to be long-term in order to lead to sustained change and provide people with the confidence to engage. With the climate and biodiversity crisis and the concerns about people's lack of connection to nature, there has never been a better time to reflect on the role and wonder of treescapes in our lives and the potential for enthusing and engaging younger generations and all spectrums of society to appreciate and understand how caring for treescapes matters.

◀ Photo: Liz O'Brien, Micheldever Woods, Hampshire

Why Trees Matter

Fiona Stafford

Fiona Stafford is the author of The Long, Long Life of Trees and The Brief Life of Flowers. She is Professor of English at Somerville College, Oxford, and a Fellow of the British Academy and the Royal Society of Edinburgh. Her research interests include Romantic period literature, Place and Nature Writing, Literature and the Visual Arts, Scottish and Irish Literature. She regularly contributes to natural history programmes on BBC Radio and has written and delivered Radio series on trees, flowers, beaches, composers and their dogs. Recent books include Jane Austen, Local Attachments, Reading Romantic Poetry. *Her play* The Dimlight Hours *was performed in Edinburgh in 2019. She has also written for* The Financial Times, The Sunday Times, The Observer *and* The TLS.

photo: Fiona Stafford

The Tour de France tree in Harrogate

Why Trees Matter

Fiona Stafford

When I visited Harrogate last summer, I was struck by what an open, green town it is, full of healthy trees. Two especially caught my eye. The first was a young lime growing by the well-kept lawn beside the War Memorial, the second, the stump of an elm. A neat plaque told me that the lime was planted in June 1994 to commemorate the 50th anniversary of D Day. The nearby elm, older and fatter, looked like a kind of totem pole, carved with a wooden relief of a cyclist pedalling hard uphill or taking off into the sky. On the sliced stump branching from the trunk was a wooden model of the Eiffel Tower. The tree, carved by Mick Burns, recalled the first stage of the 2014 Tour de France, which started in Leeds and finished in Harrogate.

Both are memorial trees — one to the dead, one to the living, the former growing and flourishing, the latter leafless, but with a strange new life of its own. It made me wonder how others saw them, whether many people still pause to read the 25-year-old notice beneath the lime and whether the tree prompts thoughts of D-Day throughout the year, or just in June? Or perhaps in November when

The D-Day Lime in Harrogate

the War Memorial is adorned in red wreaths? And what about the Tour de France tree — is it seen as a stump or a sculpture? Does it proudly record a single memorable day in Harrogate's long history or is it a public monument to lasting international connection? A dead elm might just as easily recall the loss of an entire species of tree, once common across the country. Perhaps people who live in the town still see the tree as it once was, as the towering stump stirs private memories of days gone by? Since it's now such a familiar part of Montpelier Hill, those hurrying to work or school or the station may no longer see it at all. But if either the Tour de France elm or the D-Day lime were suddenly brought down by a gale or a chainsaw, the people of Harrogate would see them anew, spot-lit against the dark shadows of disappearance.

Everyone knows that trees matter. And yet, if asked why, many of us would be hard pressed to come up with a simple answer, or indeed, a single one. Human-arboreal relationships are too various for easy explanations. When the Woodland Trust invited people to write about the trees that meant something to them in 2017, they received c60,000 different responses. Foresters, ecologists, conservationists, craftsmen, artists, writers, ramblers, teachers, druids, dog-walkers, birdwatchers, teenagers, parents, pensioners — people of every age and walk of life — offered personal stories as rich and varied as ancient woodland. In *The Tree Line*, a collection of verse compiled at the same time by Michael Mckimm (2017), contemporary poets reflected on their own arboreal attachments, writing on alders and ashes, hawthorns and horse chestnuts, stands of poplars and saplings standing in retail parks. Freshly observed or rooted in memory, their trees ranged from Cornwall to Cumberland, Mallow to Manchester and teemed with beetles, birds, owls, acorns, atmosphere, sadness, scents, mystery, reverence and gratitude. The rich variety brings to light how deeply trees matter to people — and how differently people see trees.

Poets and artists see trees in their own special way, but their work can often distil what many are feeling, startling what's lying silent, even dormant, into consciousness. A well-made poem, a fine drawing, a photograph, a film, a song or a good story, can each strike familiar chords with audiences or open people's eyes to seeing trees in new ways. When Philip Larkin listened to trees in the spring, he saw green buds opening 'like something almost being said'. By the end of the short lyric poem, he was able to share what that might be, 'Last year is dead, they seem to say, /Begin afresh, afresh, afresh.' Although we might not hear or see the same trees Larkin knew, his poem still offers everyone a way of understanding why trees matter.

Philip Larkin was not in the habit of expressing hope in his poetry, which makes *Trees* all the more striking. The poet-artist William Blake, who as a child saw trees filled with angels in Peckham Rye, was far more open to the visionary potential of the every day. But he was also well aware that others saw the world quite differently: 'not every one sees alike' he wrote to his friend John Trusler, 'the tree that moves some to tears of joy is in the eyes of others only a green thing in the way.' Profoundly contrasting perspectives on the world still prevent the meeting of minds between workmen tasked with felling mature trees and protesters horrified by the loss of their local greenery. When the Sheffield City Council engaged contractors to manage their street trees, many residents were surprised to discover just how much trees mattered to them personally. Suddenly the tall trees marked for felling were understood to be living companions, whose disappearance seemed unbearable. Although skilled arboreal management is essential to the overall health of a street, as it is to a park or wood, the distress in Sheffield over the needless destruction of many flourishing trees demonstrates their importance to communities for reasons that are not merely practical or economic.

Arguments against felling urban trees often rely on practical issues, such as the beneficial effects of trees on air quality, traffic noise, light pollution and urban heat; or for birds, insects, urban wildlife and children's understanding of nature. Among the Sheffield trees marked for removal was a healthy, mature elm, rare in itself and host to the large white-letter hairstreak butterfly, a high priority species for conservation. Rare species have intrinsic scientific significance, but thoughts of extinction are profoundly unsettling to everyone, especially if what's under threat is as beautiful, fragile and defenseless as a butterfly.

The arguments for tree-felling also tend to be practical, as the claims of increased light, unimpeded drains, safer pavements, easier access for large vehicles and emergency services, and savings in tight budgets are brought to the table. Councils are routinely faced with hard choices over spending priorities. And yet, the logical arguments marshalled in favour of preserving or felling are often driven as much by emotion as reason — by fear, anger, anxiety, attachment, sorrow, pride, dislike, or hope. Conflicts over planning decisions usually arise from competing visions of a better future. While the rational arguments are clear enough, the underlying reactions to felling, planting and preservation are just as important. It is the less quantifiable, emotional, psychological, ecological and aesthetic perceptions of trees that may bring us closer to understanding why trees matter.

Like the D-Day lime in Harrogate, trees are often planted as memorials — to young lives cut off long before their time. What's planted in a spirit of commemoration also looks forward to future generations growing up with the new tree. A new tree is a pledge of faith in the future, which is why foresters and gardeners are agents of hope. Our memories are bound up with what was once someone else's dream. We are the heirs of earlier plans, plantings, pollardings and purges — something that's more obvious in the tree-lined streets of a carefully designed Garden City, or among the matching planes of a London square, or on a country estate marked by chestnut avenues, walnut clumps and oak-scattered parkland, than in old, mixed woodlands where trees of every age jostle together. The well-known designs of Capability Brown, John Nash or Ebenezer Howard are duly admired, while the names of thousands of men and women who also planted acorns, grafted apples, set saplings or just allowed trees to seed naturally are now lost, even though their legacy continues to flourish. A mature tree is a link to earlier lives. An old apple tree can take us back to World War II; a two hundred and fifty-year-old oak to the reign of George III; an ancient yew might predate the arrival of the Saxons and even the Romans.

In the pursuit of why — and how — trees matter, the past is very illuminating. During the eighteenth century, for example, competing attitudes to trees were just as prevalent as today, but for the first time, powerful, arboreally-related feelings were being consciously articulated. The cultural history of the time therefore has much to tell us. It was an era of rapid rural change, with trees being cleared and planted on a grand scale. The gradual reform of agricultural practices, such as experimental crop rotation and selective breeding, facilitated by new ploughs, mechanised drills and better transport systems, demanded wholesale change in land use. Bigger fields often meant clearing wooded areas and enclosing common land, while miles of hedges and boundary trees marked expanding farms. At the same time, the invention of steam engines and the onset of widescale industrialisation increased demand for timber — pit props for mines, charcoal for smelting, oak bark for tanning, planks for wagons and barges, beams for mills and factories, towers, bridges. Global trade meant an increase in the number and size of ships, which in turn meant the rapid felling of mature trees.

The demand for oak timber in the early 1700s registers in Alexander Pope's great poem, *Windsor Forest*. His celebration of the Royal Forest sweeps across centuries of invasion, war and blood sports, before reaching the contemporary age of 'Peace and Plenty', sustained by international trade. To achieve universal harmony, Pope imagined the great trees leaving the forest to 'rush into' the sea as ocean-going ships. *Windsor Forest* was published in 1713 to mark the end of a major European war, but it is haunted by a longer history of violent, internal conflict. As symbols of strength, stability and togetherness, oak trees held strong appeal in an age where thoughts of Queen Anne, now ageing and heirless, raised the spectre of Civil War as readily as the prospect of peace and plenty. An old oak forest included trees that had been growing peacefully in the same spot for centuries — offering solid, living reassurance of natural continuity and healthy growth. The Royal oak, popularised by Charles II on his restoration to the throne after the Civil War, meant far more to his subjects and their successors than mere raw material.

Charles II's reign had seen tree-planting on a grand scale: John Evelyn's wonderful book on trees and arboriculture, *Sylva*, was published in 1664, just four years after the Restoration. Although oak trees became rooted in the national psyche, a major impetus to planting new oak trees was the need for more ships — for the Navy as well as trading vessels. Despite Pope's hopeful vision of peace, competition between expanding European powers for rich colonial prizes provoked a series of conflicts, culminating in the cataclysmic Napoleonic wars. Pride in oak trees as Britain's 'wooden walls' flourished throughout the century, the great era of planting and appreciation of forests, woods and trees. Since the construction of a single ship of the line required 2,000 mature oak trees, demand for timber remained buoyant. Tree planting became a patriotic duty, though dependent on very long-term thinking: the time taken from acorn to armament makes the production of a modern aircraft carrier seem surprisingly quick. Charles II's obsession with oak, however, meant that there were many mature trees when the invasion threat from Napoleon was at its height at the turn of the nineteenth century.

Alexander Pope, who spent his teens at Binfield, in those days still surrounded by the Royal Forest of Windsor, was a keen gardener as well as a poet. His serious botanical interests were sustained by contemporary trade and exploration, also facilitated by oak-built ships. The famous weeping willows in Pope's garden at Twickenham were among the first to arrive in Britain from Turkey. In the Age of Enlightenment, of Newton and Leibniz, Hooke and Linnaeus, the urge to discover the workings of the Universe inspired extensive study of the flora and fauna of the Earth. With the discovery of Continents new to Europeans came a huge interest in plants of every kind. Unfamiliar trees were arriving in Britain from all over the globe: weeping willows from the Levant, magnolia trees from America and China, cypress trees from every continent. The first Eucalyptus seeds came back from Australia with Captain Cook to be raised at the new Royal Botanic Gardens at Kew. With this vast expansion of knowledge, plants were being reimagined as objects of astonishing wonder and beauty. Imagine seeing a *Magnolia grandiflora*

for the first time? Reports of exotic trees were sent to London from around the world and when the seeds and saplings arrived, excitement mounted over what might grow in Britain. Pineapples were regarded as the fruit of the gods — or at least the wealthy — as hothouses were modified to include manure-warmed pineapple pits like those that have been restored at the Lost Gardens of Heligan. By the end of the eighteenth century, plant gatherers and botanists like Joseph Banks were being honoured as national heroes.

The new readiness to wonder at botanical discoveries stimulated fresh interest in native plants, too. John Evelyn's classic guide to native trees was reissued in 1776, with beautiful engravings by John Miller. *Sylva* was a work of art as well as information, encouraging wonder as much as practical enquiry. Even trees that had failed to impress Evelyn were now displayed in glory. The sycamore (left), for example, unfolded from the handsome quarto to reveal leaves and samaras as finely formed as tropical vegetation:

The new edition included copious notes by Alexander Hunter, reflecting recent decades of botanical knowledge and advances in forestry. Trees such as the larch and the chinquapin, unknown in the British landscape when Evelyn wrote his classic account, featured in the footnotes, along with extensive advice on improving soils, observing climate and raising seeds.

Up-to-date knowledge of trees was essential to the effective management of land. Mature woods were major assets, which helps explain Elizabeth Bennett's admiration for Mr Darcy's fine woods when she visits Pemberley for the first time in Jane Austen's *Pride and Prejudice*. Fine trees, like the tall, solid oak tree that rises above Mr and Mrs Andrews in Thomas Gainsborough's famous painting, were signs of a well-run, productive estate. The tree where Mrs Andrews is sitting, with her husband leaning proprietorially with his hand on the back of the seat and his gundog at his feet, signals wealth, respectability and security. The mature tree leads the viewer to the mature woods in the background, affirming a long-established bond with the land, which will continue for centuries to come. Gainsborough was a pioneer of a new, realistic style of landscape painting, but his choice of setting also recalls the more traditional iconography of the family tree, a well-known metaphor for linking blood relations through proliferating generations.

Thomas Gainsborough: *Mr and Mrs Andrews* (courtesy National Gallery)

Although trees provided attractive, meaningful backdrops, they were increasingly celebrated as subjects in their own right. Paul Sandby's striking portrait of an old ash pollard in Luton Park is one of the earliest depictions of a tree as tree — neither background nor framing device for figures, but right at the centre of the canvas, commanding full attention with its strange mass of smooth trunks, springing from a single stool. Luton Park was owned by the keen botanist, Prime Minister and first Director of Kew Gardens, John Stuart, Third Earl of Bute. Sandby's tree portrait is a fine example of how practical arborealism, aesthetics and personal pride could all come together. Traditional techniques of forest management, such as coppicing and pollarding, which entailed cutting through the trunk to encourage the regrowth of multiple shoots and a sustainable supply of poles, posts and cattle feed, contributed to the growth of very distinctive ancient trees. If a pollarded tree was left to grow, its numerous shoots thickened into a distinctive, multi-trunked form, as appealing to artists and writers as to builders, shipwrights or furniture makers. Such flourishing ancient trees were metaphors for a thriving family, while maintaining their own unique character as a living individuals. Practical methods of harvesting wood and foliage also prolonged the tree's life: some surviving ash and lime pollards in ancient woodlands are hundreds of years old and now seem even more remarkable than they did to Bute and his contemporaries.

Since ancient trees were valued like old family treasures or relics of classical antiquity, it was important to get them right. The accurate drawings made by artists such as Jacob Strutt now offer a valuable record of particular trees as they were two centuries ago, offering illuminating comparisons with their current state. The pictures also shed light on how trees mattered to those who owned them at the time — and their contemporaries. Old trees were valuable treasures and status symbols, but also offered silent comment on human pride, on those who regarded themselves as

Jacob Strutt: *Great oak at Fredville*

owners of organisms whose lifespan far exceeded their own.

Many ancient trees were not the exclusive property of the landowning classes and had been central to local communities for centuries. Distinctive trees — taller, fatter, older, or somehow deformed — are obvious natural landmarks, easily recognised as meeting points, party venues, or places of prayer. In the eighteenth century, as people woke up to the widespread social and antiquarian importance of trees, writers such as Thomas Pennant, Gilbert White, William Gilpin and Hayman Rooke started to record the special trees valued by different communities and the stories hidden in their abundant branches. This means that in addition to specially commissioned tree portraits, there are also surviving records of the names, measurements and local traditions of many ancient trees, such as the Major oak in Sherwood Forest, the Fortingall yew in Perthshire, or the Ankerwyke yew at Runnymede. Evidence of how trees were regarded in the past may complicate or reinforce 21st century assumptions of why they matter. If we are less likely to rely on trees for healing sick cattle, we can still wonder at their beauty and antiquity and feel a dim sense of connection with earlier generations who gathered there.

While certain trees were being recognised and even revered as special living features, however, many were being felled on a massive scale. This was not merely on account of their value to timber merchants, but also because of prevailing fashions. The era of tree-appreciation was also that of the grand garden makeover, as designers such as Lancelot 'Capability' Brown, Humphrey Repton, ordered new lakes, sweeping approaches and open prospects, with new plantations and parkland. In the process, whole woods, avenues and even villages were removed to enhance the view. If such state-of-the art landscaping was a matter of pride for fashionable landowners, it often provoked deep dismay among artists and poets. William Cowper was profoundly distressed by the fate of local trees, felled merely for the sake of fashion. Landscape gardening brought out his deep sympathy for the trees that failed to fit the design, 'Ye fallen avenues, once more I mourn your fate unmerited', he wrote in *The Task*, a long meditative poem on the state of the nation in the 1780s. Cowper was even more dismayed by the loss of trees along his favourite riverside walk, 'The Poplars are felled, 'Farewell to the shade and the whispering sound of the cool colonnade.' For the sensitive, troubled poet, trees were an emblem of his own mortality: 'My fugitive years are all hasting away, /And I must ere long lie as lowly as they'. Although a rather reclusive character, living quietly in the Northamptonshire market town of Olney, the enormous popularity of his poems meant that across the country, readers were responding to his touching expressions of dismay over the destruction of familiar trees.

Cowper was greatly admired by William and Dorothy Wordsworth, whose own feelings about arboreal fashion victims were startled into life during a holiday in Scotland. They were deeply shocked by what had happened to the ancient woods along the banks of the River Tweed near Neidpath Castle. William Douglas, 4th Duke of Queensberry, who had followed the trend for opening out prospects, had the dubious privilege of being immortalised by a very angry, and increasingly famous, visiting poet. Wordsworth's poem begins with a memorable exclamation, 'Degenerate Douglas! Oh the unworthy Lord!' before taking the Duke to task for his 'love of havoc' and careless order.

To level with the dust a noble horde,
A brotherhood of venerable Trees,
Leaving an ancient Dome, and Towers like these,
Beggared and outraged!

The publication of Wordsworth's sonnet ensured that the Duke, already famous for his enormous wealth, became equally well known for his destructive behaviour. Wordsworth's outrage over the loss of the 'brotherhood of venerable Trees' was intensified by his sense of how the loss had affected the local community — 'Many hearts deplor'd /The fate of those old Trees'. This was not just an aesthetic offence, but a human one, all the more unpalatable when those distressed had so much less in the way of material possessions and public agency than the proud, unthinking landowner. A few years later, Wordsworth would denounce the mass planting of larch trees in the Lake District for similar reasons.

Poets were as adept at drawing attention to tree-planting as to felling. Robert Burns, less successful as a farmer than a poet, encouraged more sensitive tree-planting in Perthshire by adopting the perspective of the River Bruar, which ran through the Duke of Atholl's estate. Burns appealed to the Duke's chivalric nature, by giving the river a female voice and pointing out her embarrassment over the lack of a decent covering. The Duke duly took heed and planted trees all along the riverbanks. Poetry was so popular at this time that as poets woke up to trees and their disappearance, so did vast numbers of readers.

All too often, however, ordinary people felt powerless to halt the tides of fashion, economics and industry. The poet John Clare, though far from ordinary, was an agricultural worker, deeply conscious of contemporary changes in the landscape, to which he was inadvertently contributing. His writings are full of detail about collecting wood, planting saplings, birds nests, old trees and associated stories. Trees also prompt deeply personal comments on the changes forced on his home:

Took a walk in the fields saw an old woodstile
taken away from a favourite spot which it had
occupied all my life the posts were overgrown
with ivy and it seemed so akin to nature and the
spot where it stood as tho it had taken on lease
for an undisturbed existence it hurt me to see it
was gone for my affections claim a friendship with
such things but nothing is lasting in this world
last year Langly bush was destroyed an old white
thorn that had stood for more than a century full
of fame the Gipseys shepherds and Herd men all
had their tales of its history and it will be long ere
its memory is forgotten

Clare, who worked on the land from the age of ten, was very much part of the transformation taking place in the village he had known all his life — and deeply unsettled by what was happening. Poems such as *To a Fallen Elm* convey an acute sense of loss over the felling of his favourite old elm and the pained realisation of its importance as a lifelong, personal friend, 'Thou ownd a language by which hearts are stirred /Deeper than by the attribute of words /Thine spoke a feeling known in every tongue'.

As in 21st-century Sheffield, it is often unexpected and unstoppable loss that makes people see familiar trees, as if for the first time. The process by which something commonplace is magnified by disappearance is powerfully articulated in a poem by the First World War writer, Edward Thomas. The effect of seeing a workman clearing the last remaining tree in a local copse prompted unexpected feelings, as the poem states with great clarity: 'I never had noticed it until /'Twas gone'. Although he had passed it every day, it was only the sight and sound of the last of the willows being removed that brought them to life — too late.

The sense of loss prompted by tree-felling has been echoing through British culture for centuries. There's nothing new about passionate protests in response over new building projects, new roads, High Speed rail, or indeed, plant pathogens, though climate change has intensified their urgency. The impulse to defend the environment, to stand up for ancient rights and save trees for future generations is — and has long been — widely felt. And it is partly because of earlier protesters that we still have green spaces even in areas most under pressure from development. Often the fear of losing trees unites local people, heightening a sense of shared identity. Communities on the eastern side of greater London, for example, still define themselves through Epping Forest. The little bookshop in Loughton sells books and pamphlets about the people's forest and the historic battle for its future, once pressure from Victorian London, the expanding centre of a wealthy, industrialised nation, threatened the survival of the ancient treescape. Local people rose to defend their trees and after a long campaign, the Epping Forest Act was passed in 1878, saving the forest from excessive development and helping to secure a distinct local identity which continues to flourish even within the enormous conurbation of 21st century London.

The long history of feeling that their trees were under threat has inspired writers such as Tricia Moxey (2013) to celebrate *Loughton and its Trees*. At the heart of the story is a very clear articulation of 'Why Trees Matter', which lists the numerous arboreal benefits to the local environment in terms of creative inspiration, improved health and quality of life, enjoyment of urban wildlife, the reduction of sounds, smog, air pollution, carbon, and increase in supplies of sustainable fuel, oxygen and property values; as well as enabling community activity in the form of planting, which in turn 'leaves a lasting legacy'. It is a fairly comprehensive summary, but the impulse to quantify springs from a heartfelt attachment to a special place and alarm at any suggestion that its defining character might not matter.

The London Tube map is haunted by the ghosts of earlier places: Burnt oak, Gospel oak, Poplar. The names carry dim recollections of the world beneath the underground network, of the poplars that once flourished on the banks of the Thames, of the remnants of the great Forest of Middlesex, of the great oak on the parish boundary of St Pancras and Hampstead, which became an outdoor church for non-conformist preachers and their vast congregations. Seven Sisters is named after the circle of seven elm trees that grew there from the seventeenth to the twentieth century — a local history that has risen to consciousness again thanks to the efforts of the Tottenham Trees community group.

Cities with a history of submerged local identities and lost woodlands are often especially conscious of benefits of trees. The villages of Willen, originally a place of willow trees, and Great Linford, named after the maple trees on the Ouse are now both part of Milton Keynes, their old identities somewhat swamped by development since the 1960s. When Milton Keynes celebrated its 50th anniversary in 2017, the Council highlighted its proud history of tree planting, with websites identifying 50 trees and a map of the urban canopy. It is a strikingly green city with a great

photo: Fiona Stafford ▶

variety of thriving trees, though the great oak that was left to continue growing inside the Midsummer Centre gave up its struggle for life quite quickly, once encased in chain stores and fast-food outlets. The general effort to maintain trees in the midst of a thriving modern economy is admirable nevertheless.

There is no single answer to why trees matter. Trees are alive and growing, and so human relationships with trees grow too. Trees mattered to the earth before human beings evolved, they have mattered to human society from its prehistoric beginnings and through every age since. They matter now and they matter for the future. The growing awareness of climate change is prompting more urgent and often horrifying speculation about what the Earth may be like in the centuries ahead. But the ever-evolving story of trees can offer more hopeful prospects, because of their long history of resilience. Some of the biggest challenges of the 21st century can be mitigated by imaginative approaches to trees — carbon emissions, climate change, air pollution, flooding, urban heat islands, land contamination, plastic waste, fossil fuels, depleted resources, declining wildlife and extinction, as well as the more individual miseries of depression, mental illness, loneliness, obesity. Many of these growing problems can all be alleviated through the protection and planting of trees — if only everyone recognized their power. And this is where art, literature and history can help.

For writers, artists, poets and visionaries, even the most ordinary trees can offer a sudden glimpse of truths that have somehow been lost. Whether we recall little William Blake seeing angels in the Peckham trees or Vincent Van Gogh seized with the urge to paint the trees of Provence in brilliant, seething colour, their special perception of the extraordinary in the everyday is unmistakeable — and uplifting. After the traumatic experience of the First World War, Paul Nash returned to the visionary trees of his childhood and Stanley Spencer saw the fields around his family home at Cookham transfigured in divine light. David Hockney's remarkable Yorkshire trees affected thousands of astonished admirers when arrayed around the walls of the Royal Academy in 2011. Poets such as William Cowper, John Clare, Robert Burns and William Wordsworth, all helped their contemporaries see the true importance of trees. Their startling perceptions have been affirmed and reaffirmed by writers ever since — from Thomas Hardy in rural Dorset to Robert Frost in New Hampshire, from Seamus Heaney in Ireland to Kathleen Jamie and John Burnside in Scotland. Philip Larkin's unexpected celebration may have been inspired by the same trees that Hockney saw and loved and shared in his spring paintings.

What art and literature can do is to startle us all into seeing familiar trees before it's too late. History can enhance understandings of trees and their deep-rooted entanglement with human society and local identity. Art can waken the dormant feeling that bursts into anxious life with the sound of saws and axes, before favourite trees are under threat. Poetry can enable people to see their trees — and so to nurture, manage and grow to love them. There is no need to miss out on the profound pleasure, the heartening thereness of trees, by not noticing them until they are gone. Most trees need no explanation or justification: they are just there every day of the year, defining the endless sky. Lucky the human being who stops to look.

Sarah Abbott *is a Doctor of Social Sciences candidate (ABD) at Royal Roads University, and associate professor in the Department of Film at the University of Regina. Her interdisciplinary doctorate research explores the sentient relationality of trees through public ethnography, Indigenous research methodologies, plant science, philosophies associated with the non-human turn, film, and interspecies communication. Sarah is a recipient of a Vanier Canada Graduate Scholarship (2014-2017), the Saskatchewan Lieutenant Governor's Arts Award for Arts and Learning (2012), and the City of Regina's Mayor's Arts and Business Award for Innovation in the Arts (2009). www.sarahabbott.ca*

Simon Leadbeater *has degrees from Oxford Brookes and Oxford Universities, the London School of Economics and the Open University. After a career in local government and the third sector he now divides his time between restoring the PAWS woodland, Priors Wood near Welwyn, Hertfordshire, purchased with this wife Toni in 1999, and running Priors Environmental Ltd., an environmental, health and safety consultancy specialising in the waste management and forestry sectors. Simon has written for the Royal Forestry Society's* Quarterly Journal of Forestry *and is a trustee of BANC, the British Association of Nature Conservationists, which publishes ECOS. He can be contacted at simon.leadbeater@priorsenvironmental.co.uk, and www.priorsenvironmental.com.*

If a Tree Falls…
Perspectives on Sentience

Sarah Abbott & Simon Leadbeater

If a Tree Falls... Perspectives on Sentience

Sarah Abbott and Simon Leadbeater

We begin our chapter by acknowledging the land, in and of itself, for our relations with it, and for all that it provides, has provided and will provide for all life throughout the past, present and future.

Summary

Through a lens of perspectives for and against accepting the sentience of trees, this chapter reflects on different understandings of trees and woodlands as alive or inert; deforestation and climate change; the role of forestry in its relationship with woodlands; thought patterns; and concepts of interconnection.

The Domesday oak, Kings Waldenbury Estate, near Hitchen, Herts (photo: Simon Leadbeater)

Introduction

The idea for this jointly written chapter germinated at *Evolving the Forest*, an interdisciplinary symposium held at Dartington estate, Devon, in June 2019. The conference's eclectic dynamic of tree and forest considerations was energising and unnerving territory into which we authors stepped, met, and wondered how our presentations on the controversial topic of tree sentience would be received, even as 'delegates were encouraged to move outside their comfort zone' (Bladon 2019:11). Here, we reflect on some of our understandings of how perspectives in favour and against sentience impact the world humans create, sustain, and live in. We know it is extremely difficult for most people to accept the possibility that trees are sentient. Although *Evolving the Forest* took place a while ago, we reference it because historically it was a progressive symposium that, as a microcosm, reflected worldwide understandings of and approaches to trees and forests.

The idea of trees having sentience intrigues and polarises people. 'The precise meaning of sentience,' Hobson-West and Davies (2017:673) write, 'is contested in science and in philosophy but could be summarised as the ability to experience pleasure and pain' (see Brown 2015). For Mancuso and Viola (2015:78), sentience means 'capable of perceiving,' much like Ryder's (2012) indication that sentience entails the ability to experience sensation. Marino (2010:132) defines sentience as 'a multidimensional subjective phenomenon that refers to the depth of awareness an individual possesses.' Sentience is usually regarded as an aspect of consciousness, along with intelligence, and self-awareness (Brown 2015).

For us, trees are individual, agentic beings with sentience, intelligence, perception, and consciousness. We subscribe to the concept of 'biosocial becoming' (Ingold and Pálsson 2013:1-21) wherein all life, human and non-human, evolves equally and intrinsically through both social and biological influences. Our beliefs are based in tree and plant science, ethnographic research, Western and Indigenous worldviews, and personal experiences. For us, trees, just as humans, are conative; 'deeply embedded in their own life force, purpose, and interconnections with the environment(s) they interact with as home and community' (Abbott 2020:224). To move in the world with an understanding of trees in this way is vital to transcending the human-centered treatment of the Earth and all its inhabitants at a time when environmental, climate and ecocide crises are dire. To begin to move in the world with an awareness that trees have sentience cannot help but challenge, and change, the way a person lives their life.

Neither of us authors were consciously alert to the sentience of trees until recently. Like most people, we had been educated to think of trees and their functions in a biomechanical sense. At the start of an article outlining current scientific thinking on plant sentience, Simon acknowledges that when he and his partner purchased their 'woodland nearly twenty years ago I thought of trees principally for the habitat they provided and little much else. Haltingly at first, then through intermittent jolts, a companion world began to form, although initially my distrust defied belief' (Leadbeater 2019:1). As it turns out, we authors are in synch with the non-human turn that has been gaining momentum academically in the social sciences and humanities since the last decades of the twentieth century, 'decentering the human in favor of a turn toward and concern for the non-human' (Grusin 2015:vii). In our writing, we capitalise species' names in recognition of their non-human agentic individuality.

In the lead-up to our conference presentations, we encountered a range of responses from other delegates upon hearing of our topic. Some had similar awareness of tree sentience and/or were excitedly curious to hear our talks. One man shared an experience of a tree offering to teach him about the wind when he was aged twenty. For other people, there was doubt, resistance, and derision, including the comment that there is more sentience in a person's belly than in a tree. When Sarah met Sir Harry Studholme, then Chair of the Forestry Commission, on the first afternoon, Sir Harry seemed disturbed by the idea of tree sentience. Yet he came to the *Ethics and Sentience* session with an open mind, saying 'it's part of my education,' and afterwards seemed pensively sparked by what he encountered. Forest ecologist Keith Kirby reflected that the session was perhaps the most difficult of the conference for him because it challenged conventional thinking. Approximately seventy people attended the session, apparently almost triple the audience for a concurrent session on the direction of UK forestry over the next one hundred years. Delegates wanted to hear about tree sentience. The energy in the *Ethics and Sentience* room was viscerally electric, open, and stirred with emotions of joy, confirmation, remorse, excitement, and connection.

Impacts of Instrumentalism

Over millennia, thickening anthropocentric viewpoints and activities have increased people's indifference to the suffering of animals and other non-humans, including vegetal life (see Kopnina 2016). Beginning with Plato and Aristotle (see Innis 1949; Marder 2013; Pierotti 2011), this human-centred outlook evolved from 'animistic, relational' sensibilities with 'explicit recognition of kinship between [all] living things' (Hall 2011:17 & 18), to a solipsism that has severely limited our ability to perceive any reality other than our own. By extension, we have lost empathy for non-human realities because we have learned to innately fail to acknowledge them. The complex, oppressive history informing our separation from kinship with nature is based in hierarchical, patriarchal, 'positivist, reductionist, and consumer stances [that have been] embedded in intention, lack of attention, political power, religion, science, education,' (Abbott 2020:225), colonialism, materialism, and insecurity. Vandana Shiva (2014, para. 25) refers to its modern version as the 'fossilised mindset of the fossil fuel era' that separated us from the consequences of instrumentalism and continues to disconnect us from a holistic knowing of nature.

Our resulting vainglory from treating nature as inert material for consumption and economic obsession has become 'the bane of us, the humans' (Oliver 2016:7). As we watch, 'with each advance in climate science, the news keeps getting worse: …the world is carbonising at an unprecedented rate' (Hamilton, 2010:1 & 5). The statistics, accelerating rates and impacts of deforestation in the picture of our planet's transformation are overwhelming and horrifying (see Kniver 2019; see Butler 2019; Dalton 2019). Agricultural conversion, livestock ranching, logging, infrastructure growth, and human overpopulation are the five main, intertwined drivers of mass deforestation (Lam 2019), which contributes to dangerous changes in nature overall, and is a major cause of accounted for species decline and extinction (IPBES 2019). By 2010, deforestation accounted for 12 to 25 percent of human-produced CO_2 emissions on Earth (Hamilton 2010) — more CO_2 than is produced by the total number 'of cars and trucks on the world's roads' (EarthTalk 2012:1). Over the 300 years leading to 2011 there was a global loss of 17 million square kilometers of wilderness to agriculture (Hall 2011). Between 2014 and 2018, 'on average, an area of tree cover the size of the United Kingdom was lost every year. Tropical forest loss accounts for more than 90% of global deforestation' (Kniver 2019, paras. 8 & 9; see Climate Home News 2019). To add to this devastating picture, Hamilton, writing in 2010, indicates that the effectiveness of the terrestrial biosphere, a natural sink 'at removing carbon dioxide from the atmosphere, has declined by 5 percent over the last 50 years, and the decline will continue [due to the] detrimental effects of climate change on the absorption of CO_2' (p. 10). Additionally, the warming of the planet 'is expected to cause more deforestation through droughts, fires, and high temperatures inhibiting plant growth' (p. 10).

When trees are harvested, the animals, plants, birds, and insects who make them their home inevitably perish. Research on Norwegian Spruce felled for Christmas has revealed that as many as 25,000 individual organisms live on a single tree (Adnanes 2012). oak trees host potentially over 400 different organisms (Alexander, Butler, and Green 2006; for the scale of individuals lost when trees are felled see Stork, Hammond, Russell and Hadwen 2011). In his audio recordings of natural soundscapes that began in the 1960s, sound ecologist Bernie Krause (2013) observed that 'now because of global warming, resource extraction, and human noise, among other factors, … fully 50 percent of my archive comes from habitats so radically altered that they're either altogether silent or can no longer be heard in their original form' (03:11). For his TedTalk, Krause uses a visual sound graph and accompanying audio clip to illustrate the alarming difference in a forest's soundscape before and after a year of selective logging, while his identical before and after photographs of the forest show no signs of intrusion. Forests, the World Wildlife Fund states, 'are so much more than a collection of trees. Forests are home to 80 percent of the world's terrestrial biodiversity' (2019, para. 2). Joseph Settele, co-chair of the IPBES Assessment (2019, para. 11), succinctly observes that 'the essential, interconnected web of life on Earth is getting smaller and increasingly frayed. … This loss is a direct result of human activity and constitutes a direct threat to human wellbeing in all regions of the world.'

Disrupting Patterns

As the commissioners of the Truth and Reconciliation Commission of Canada state, 'Indigenous laws stress that humans must journey through life in conversation and negotiation with all creation' (2015:18). Over those aforementioned millennia, while Western worldviews moved towards instrumentalism, the deep understanding of natural law held by Indigenous peoples was sustained. Based in a nonlinear understanding of nature (see Cajete 2000; Pierotti 2011), natural law is composed of knowledge systems embedded with ancient covenants and strict protocols to honour kinship systems and interconnection among all species, the land, and the elements (Brass 2020). By repeatedly breaking natural law, humans have directly and indirectly interfered 'with the natural carbon cycle [to the extent that] the effects of carbon we emit now will last longer than that of nuclear waste created today' (Hamilton 2010:11 & 9). The 'original instructions' that humans were born with to guide our responsibility for the Earth have been suppressed by 'many non-Indians…because they view [these instructions] as detrimental to progress' (Lyons 1984:6).

In the 1970s, a wide range of holistic thinkers recognised that the new concept of pattern language, 'a framework for describing good design practices within a field of expertise, [provides] a powerful tool to solve all kinds of problems' (Brock 2017, p. xxi; see Alexander 1977) — by revealing and working with patterns as well as disrupting them. Giving mindful attention, intention, and courage to recognise and change patterns and comfort zones has the potential to make significant impacts on the pressure humans are putting on the Earth. As Stone (1972) knows, until we step out of our human solipsism, there will always be resistance to making changes until the new and unknown things 'can be seen and valued for [themselves]' (p. 456).

We authors may never know how our presentations on sentience ultimately impacted Sir Harry back in the summer of 2019. We are not disrespectfully singling him out, but as a person of high profile in the forestry industry, we were delighted to read in an autumn 2019 interview that he is thinking about forestry in terms of pattern language. He recognises that 'a lot of how we talk about trees is tied up with a methodology' (Agyepong-Parsons 2019 para. 22). Rather than taking the dominant anthropocentric view, in which trees are, to borrow from William Blake (1799), only green things, Sir Harry goes on to say 'there is an inherent, deeper connection with us, as animals and beings, with forests' (para. 22).

Trees are not inert. Far from being static and unmoving, trees swell and contract as they go about their lives (O'Connor 2019), have a pulse, and exhibit alternate states of waking and resting (Żlinszky, Molnár and Barfod 2017; see also Coghlan 2018). Their sensing and communication mechanisms manage many of the same challenges animals have (Karban 2018). Trees communicate and co-operate through the wood-wide-web; as Macfarlane (2019) observed, we are likely to encounter such a powerful, awakening insight only once or twice in our lifetime. Increasingly, scientific evidence is radically shifting our preconceptions of trees and plants, contesting age-old opinion that the activities of vegetal beings are just 'unthinking, bio-mechanical actions devoid of subjectivity' (Reber 2019:203; see also Baker 2017; Sample 2019). There is a growing canon of research indicating that plants can feel and exercise volition (see Gagliano 2018; Mancuso 2018; Mancuso and Viola 2015; Trewavas 2014). As Karban (2018) writes, 'plants perceive their own state and many aspects of their surroundings and adjust numerous traits depending on these conditions' (p. 3; see also Karban 2015). Examination of old and current plant research led plant scientists Calvo, Sahi and Trewavas to a newly 'more agnostic position' (2017:1) on plant sentience. As Gagliano asserts,

> *if we think we already know how things are and fail to continuously question our own assumptions, but construct our claims on a system of beliefs we are dearly attached to, then we are in deep trouble and miss the opportunity for true scientific discovery to occur. (Sample 2019, para. 12)*

As a 'science of planting and taking care of large areas of trees' (Forestry 2019), forestry could move to different patterns of language and questions when seeking solutions, to disrupt and transcend its usual assumptions that centralise human (more specifically, market-led) demands, and to shift from Shiva's (2014) fossilised mindset toward more holistic stewardship. Forestry could take a stand for 'the unthinkable' (Stone, 1972:456): the rights and value of forests in and for themselves, and it could follow Sir Harry's acknowledgement that 'we do need to learn to allow the magic of nature to happen' (Agyepong-Parsons 2019, para. 9). There are many systems that offer the opportunity for intentional disruption. As Kopnina (2016) succinctly explains Aldo Leopold's (1949) 'land ethic,'

> *something is right when it preserves the integrity, stability, and beauty of biotic communities and wrong when it does otherwise. Leopold's land ethic highlighted the value of restoring natural processes, not just for the sake of humans but also because nature has intrinsic value.* (Kopnina 2016:227)

In considering interrelations with nature and stewardship in support of the rights and moral standing of forests, Stone (1972) writes,

> *it is not inevitable, nor is it wise, that natural objects should have no rights to seek redress in their own behalf. It is no answer to say that streams and forests cannot have standing because streams and forests cannot speak. Corporations cannot speak either; nor can states, estates, infants, incompetents, municipalities or universities. (p. 464)*

Conclusion: If a Tree Falls...

Given their dedication to trees, forests, and land, no host representatives from *Evolving the Forest*, and only a few delegates, expressly acknowledged or expressly gave thanks to trees, forests, or the land as part of formal conference proceedings. This was disappointing and ironic considering the majority of people presenting at and/or attending the conference make their living in various ways with or from trees, forests, and the land. Between the two of us authors, we took in many of the sixty or so conference events and noticed only three gestures of acknowledgement by presenters.

When Sarah began her presentation for the *Ethics and Sentience* session, she explicitly offered acknowledgement of the land, for itself, and drew people's attention to gratitude for our relationship with it and for the ways it sustains all life. An immediate, palpable ripple through the room shifted the energy in the space. Some people in attendance commented on this afterwards. It is vital that we humans recognize our 'reciprocal interactions' with all aspects of the environment (Hauge 2007; Whitinui 2014), beyond the moment some of us may take to give thanks before dinner. Despite being taught otherwise, people raised in a Western education system are an inextricable part of the reality of interrelations.

The literal answer to modernist philosopher Bishop George Berkeley's question of perception, 'if a tree falls in the forest, does anybody hear it?' is always; with infinite, complex conative ripples that we humans can never be fully privy to. Berkeley's question makes the erroneous assumption that 'anybody' and perception are only in the domain of humans. The Indigenous phrase 'all my relations' profoundly acknowledges a beginningless and endless interrelation of all things. As Wagamese (2013, para. 2) explains, to understand this phrase is 'to come to understand that you are alive because everything else is.'

Sunrise over pastures green, Priors Wood in Hertfordshire. Photo: Simon Leadbeater

Myc Riggulsford MCIoJ
is a science and environment journalist.

The Charter of the Forest and our Lost Commons Rights

Myc Riggulsford

The Charter of the Forest and our lost Commons Rights

by Myc Riggulsford, with illustrations based on mediaeval manuscript marginalia

Your electricity bill may be illegal, according to the Charter of the Forest, the 800 year old law which gives us our rights as common people in Britain today. Many people think our legal protections stem from Magna Carta, which simply stopped the Norman barons from being taxed and imprisoned by King John in 1215. But it wasn't until some double dealing barons, and a revolt by the people of Dartmoor, Exmoor, and other royal hunting forests in 1217 that destitute commoners were granted rights such as pannage, estovers and agistment, known now as Commons Rights in the former royal hunting forests. These are rights which all of us may still share today — rights to food, shelter, clothing, heat, light and the chance to earn a living from our own efforts, all without being taxed or charged for access to these basic needs, but which we have forgotten about in the eight centuries since.

Until the Norman Conquest much of the land in Britain was held and managed by the community or tribe which lived there, not owned 'privately' as we think of property today. The Charter of the Forest first returned some lands which had been seized by the Crown — at one time Exmoor was ten times larger than today's National Park, and with Dartmoor as a 'forest' as well, royal hunting grounds covered half of Devon. The Charter then lists various things that Commoners are allowed to do, things which had been banned under previous Norman laws, displacing entire villages and throwing people into poverty. Which also made them unable to pay their taxes.

Turbary

Turbary is the right to cut turf for fuel, as crofters still do in Ireland and Scotland today, slicing out patches of the peat and stacking them to dry in the air. The right belonged to the house, not the land, which was held in common. Turbary was widespread and later a source of wealth for the mediaeval monasteries which industrialised the scale of the process. Is the ancient right to harvest peat something that should be commuted to a payment in lieu, so that we can warm ourselves with a more environmentally friendly source created from renewable energy instead?

Piscary

Commons rights are usually described in terms of the rights to get food for the table such as piscary, the right to take fish, from lakes, rivers and the seashore. 'Fish' includes rabbits of course if you're Catholic. Pope Gregory I declared them a marine species in the Middle Ages around the year 500, so suitable to eat during the 180 fast days of monasteries, which often had warrens. This ruling was a myth, but it was so widely believed that even in my youth, nearly 750 years later, rabbit was still sold in fishmongers rather than butchers' shops.

Hawks, Herons, & Honey (and Herbs)

I was surprised to discover that peasants in the 13th century were allowed to take from the eyries of hawks, sparrowhawks, falcons, eagles, and herons found in the woods. I had assumed that social class, with the nobler birds being reserved for persons of higher rank and so on down, had existed for a very long time, but it seems that when the Charter of the Forest was sealed we could all have a hawk. In the days before firearms Commoners could take chicks from the nests of hunting birds and train them to collect pigeons and other birds for the table.

Honey was the only widely available source of sugar before the development of sugar cane plantations and locally grown sugar beet, so was desired by nobles and common folk alike, in spite of the difficulty and danger of getting it from wild bee colonies which had made their hives in hollow trees. It's also an important preservative if you want to keep some of your soft fruit crop to eat during the long winter months, and is commonly still used as an antibiotic to treat wounds around the world today.

The Common of Herbage, the right to forage for wild herbs could be regarded as the ancestor of our National Health Service, since it didn't just give people the right to collect leafy greens such as wild garlic from the forest to eat, it also gave them access to medicinal herbs such as meadowsweet, from which aspirin was first isolated.

Pannage

The ancient rights enshrined in the Charter of the Forest include pannage, which means allowing pigs into the woodland pastures to eat acorns and other nuts. The New Forest pannage season usually begins around September 11th and runs for a month, but can be extended when the oak trees have produced a particularly heavy crop of acorns. The pannage has two particular uses, pigs destined for the winter dinner table are fattened up and finished off, and in addition, acorns are such a rich food that in large quantities they are poisonous to the herds of ponies which roam the commons on Exmoor, Dartmoor, and in the New Forest. But pigs can eat them with impunity, so the pannage season helps to clean the ground up, making it safe for livestock such as sheep and cattle to graze through winter.

Acorns would have provided a good high protein food for people as well as their animals, and could be stored to eat through the winter months. The liquid that you get from leaching out the tannins can be used in curing leather, along with steeped oak bark which is also very rich in them, and was the traditional way of curing skins and making waterproof leather for shoes and clothes.

Agistment

Agistment is the right to graze livestock, but pasture was in short supply, so the number of animals needed to be controlled by special officials called agisters. Grazing was one of the most important rights returned to commoners under the Charter of the Forest, since it meant that they could feed their sheep and cattle, which in turn provided wool for clothing and bedding, and milk and meat for the family, and mutton fat was used to make rushlights, giving the family some light in the evenings. As well as larger animals agistment included pasturing geese, goats, and ponies.

Estovers

Today Commoners in many of the National Parks have the right to pick up sticks for firewood, but the right of estovers meant that households could make all the tools and objects they needed for their everyday domestic and work chores. Small tree limbs could be taken for essential house repairs. The trunk of oaks and other timber trees were usually owned by the lord of the manor, but underwood was used every day. People made their own farm implements, hurdles to keep livestock in, or out of vegetable patches and crops. Fallen wood was used for cooking fuel, bracken and heather to stuff beds, and alder to make clog soles. Hazel and willow were used for almost every task that today would be made in metal or plastic, such as chairs and baskets, and other woods made spoons, plates, and drop spindles.

Underwood was worth perhaps ten times as much as the timber value of an area of woodland or coppice, and what we think of as 'woodland' or indeed 'forest' would have looked very different then. Old coppices, worked over centuries where the right size tree of the right species was chosen and felled for a particular job, or shoots harvested from the coppice stool during the normal rotation, have a patchwork of different species, heights and ages, interspersed with clearings, providing a much wider range of woodland habitats and supporting many species of animals, plants, fungi, and work for human woodlanders.

Common of Marl

Amongst our most important ancient rights was free use of clay, another plastic of its time, which could be stamped down into an impermeable layer to form a pond, used to make cooking pots, plates, drinking vessels, or ovens to bake bread. Even more importantly, mixed with small stones and straw, it was used to build cob walls, so you could build a house, or it could form the infill material, daub, and flung onto wattles of split laths as the panels between the main posts in a timber framed building, or make interior walls and partitions. Other types of stone, sand, and even coal could be collected and used or sold in small quantities under this right, so it could provide income as well as shelter.

What about Water?

Strangely, to our modern minds, the Charter of the Forest does not mention the right of Commoners to access fresh clean water for drinking or livestock. It does say at Article 12: 'Every free man may henceforth without being prosecuted make in his wood or in land he has in the forest a mill, a preserve, a pond, a marl-pit, a ditch, or arable outside the covert in arable land, on condition that it does not harm any neighbour'. This seems like a jumble of disconnected ideas, but what is being discussed is a schedule of major water works which most landowners today would hesitate to allow the dispossessed poor to undertake on their property.

The list starts with a mill, which usually meant a water mill, so the King was allowing Commoners to excavate a wheel pit, divert water through a sluice, and build a major construction on land they didn't own, and then run a business, all without hindrance, fees or taxes, because that must have been common practice across the country at the time. The second item, a preserve, follows logically since it can also refer to a water feature, as at the time a preserve meant a fish pond, providing food for the table.

The next item, a pond, is self-evident, and differs from a trout pool in that it will provide drinking water for the family when the stream is low, and more importantly a pond was a drinking trough for livestock in the fields and pastures. If you dig a hole in clay, a marl pit, it will quickly fill up with water as a dewpond in most of Britain, or could provide a place to work the material ready for other uses.

The next part of Article 12 goes on to say '...a ditch, or arable outside the covert in arable land, on condition that it does not harm any neighbour'. The ditch reference is obviously also water engineering — if you live in bits of Britain where the land is either too boggy, or too dry, to successfully grow crops. It's often both at different times of the year, so you need a system of ditches and irrigation channels to drain the soil and direct water to where it's needed. The only thing you're not allowed to do is cut down the covert or cover in the Kings best hunting areas. But in any suitable clearing or on the edge of a woodland you can go ahead and prepare the ground for crops, and bring in as much water as you need by cutting channels, or drain the fertile peat land ready for sowing and harvesting.

Small scale industry

Small scale industries carried out within the bounds of the forests might include any of the modern day woodland crafts such as turning spindles with a pole lathe. You can use the small twigs or brash from underwood to make charcoal, for sale or to use in blacksmithing and forging iron. You were allowed to do all of these things to meet the needs of your own household, and make enough extra to have some small surplus for sale, provided that you could carry off the goods on your own back. What you were not allowed to do, or at least, not without paying a fee to the wardens, is bring a horse and cart into the woods, fell trees on a commercial sale, and then take it off to market as a wholesale business. Once you started using wheeled transport such as an ox cart, then you could be charged a toll for using the highway in and out of the forest.

Universal Basic Income and Why Your Electricity Bill is Illegal

The Charter of the Forest then, agreed in the thirteenth century and still Britain's longest lasting law, guaranteed you and your family rights including pannage, pasturing your pigs in the woodland in autumn; taking wood for making tools or as firewood, as estovers; cutting turf as fuel for your hearth by turbary; feeding your family on fish and rabbits as piscary; and pasturing your livestock on the common heaths known as agistment, providing meat, milk, and clothing from their fleeces, and mutton fat rushlights to brighten the winter evenings.

You had the means to furnish your everyday needs with pots and pans, build your own house, collect water, and run a small business with power from a mill, all rights which we have lost, forgotten about, or simply allowed to lapse through carelessness and the daily grind. In other words, the 1217 Charter of the Forest says that we can all feed our families, our dependents, our domestic and farm animals, and have our everyday needs of warmth, shelter, fuel, and water met without being charged or taxed for it, from the common wealth of our nation. And you can work and run a small business without losing these benefits. It's a mediaeval Universal Basic Income, an idea whose time has come again.

According to Maslow's 'Hierarchy of Needs', before a person's psychological needs can be met to pursue a fulfilling life, some vital physiological needs must be met first. This is the bottom level of his hierarchical pyramid — clean air and oxygen; health, food and water; rest and sleep; clothes, warmth, and shelter — and it is these needs which I would argue that the King Henry III's Charter of the Forest recognised and agreed for everyone. Not as a benevolent monarch, but because everyone needs these basic necessities, and that by throwing people out of the royal hunting forests he had deprived them of the stuff of life itself.

In 2015 I started off trying to write a book about renewable energy and the need to limit climate change (and our population), and realised that the way electricity is priced is grossly unfair and nonsensical if we agree that everyone needs access to the basic necessities of life. I was looking into the legality behind standing charges for electricity, water, sewage and other non-optional services, which for a small farmer or rural business now includes broadband internet access. These connection or service charges are taxes by any other name. I defy anyone to live in the middle of a town or city and manage, as we almost can on our small farm, to be unconnected to any of the major utility services.

The final inescapable implication from the Charter of the Forest, which says that you cannot stop people having access to (or tax them for using) life's necessities, is that for all the utilities, including water, electricity, gas if you have it, sewerage, phone and broadband (since the government requires some reporting online, such as tax or farm returns), there should not be any standing charges at all and instead the overheads included in the unit costs. That's what probably makes your electricity bill illegal today, because these charges are hidden taxes.

The remaining woodlands and forest of Britain cannot possibly support the entire population of the country for the sustainable future if everyone invokes the Charter and starts helping themselves to whatever they need from our forests, as mediaeval peasants were expected to, so we should all be getting a Universal Basic Income in lieu instead. But how could our society afford such a cost?

By coincidence, just over a year after the *Evolving the Forest* conference, the House of Commons actually debated Universal Basic Income. The concept had resurfaced precisely because so many people fell through the cracks of the government's rescue packages during the 2020 coronavirus pandemic, especially the poor and self-employed, and were becoming destitute, just as they had when the estates were declared Crown property as Royal Hunting Forests under King John. Which led to the barons' second revolt, forcing King Henry III to fix his seal to the Charter of the Forest.

Back in 1217 the Crown could afford to allow displaced peasants to return to their work and earn a subsistence living from the resources found in our forests. Today there are too many of us to do the same, but our nation is richer than ever, so do we need a new 'Charter of the People' based on our oldest and best law, the 800 year old Charter of the Forest?

Dr Angela Summerfield is a contemporary British artist and author, whose colourful paintings celebrate trees and Nature. She divides her time between London, North Yorkshire and rural North Gloucestershire, where she now lives. Her art practice aims to create new contemporary landscape categories, such as tree-nature portraits, treescapes and landscapes of wonder, as well as visualising ideas of the rural. Angela's book and art catalogue publications include the lead essay 'Why do artists paint trees?' in 'The Arborealists: the art of the tree', Sansom & Co. 2016. Angela is also an experienced art curator and public speaker, and in 2019, she was a guest speaker, on the subject of art and trees, at The Times & The Sunday Times Cheltenham Literature Festival. Her art works are in private collections in the UK and abroad.

www.angelasummerfield.com

Green Truth – the forest as a unique creative space

Angela Summerfield

Angela Summerfield *Being with Trees – Summer* 2020

Green Truth — the forest as a unique creative space

Angela Summerfield

Introduction

The colour green's etymological origins can be found in mediaeval written and illustrated studies of plant and tree life and their inter-relationships with the health of the planet and human beings. In text such as *De Proprietatibus Rerum* (*On the Property of Things*) 1240, written by the influential theologian and scholar, Bartholomaeus Anglicus, greenness was associated with plant and tree physiology and the healthy balance of the world's phenomena, such as the Four Elements. Greenness was identified as a substance found within all these things and became associated with the concept of Green Truth (Viriditas). In Causae et Curae (Causes and Cures) 1150, Hildegard of Bingen, polymath and theologian, introduced a new correlation between the state of human health (the body and the human soul) with the natural world: thus greenness could exist within humans too. Her writings also invited humankind into a communion with the essence of things; a communion which drew on ideas of contemplation, a state of grace and beatitude. Collectively Hildegard's writings and music can also be interpreted as a celebration of the role of the human imagination, as a creative force in accord with nature. In our contemporary world, we would associate these experiences with current ideas surrounding the concept of wellbeing and humankind's engagement with natural environments, such as forests.

Emotionally-engaged experiences of Nature, such as forest bathing, draw on all our senses, but require the process of Slow Time; the freely available Forestry England publication 'Forests for Wellbeing', highlights the benefits of this activity[1]. In contemporary UK healthcare terminology, forests are also defined as one of the 'living systems' which offer a beneficial 'green space' to be both experienced and understood as a model for a 'more regenerative way of life[2].' Recent research, published by the leading neuroscientist, Professor Susan Greenfield, has shown that walking in natural environments, as opposed to urban settings, enhances our cognitive abilities to notice, remember and develop deep thoughts (Greenfield 2016). These experiences have become more pressing and poignant within the context of the 2020 Covid virus lockdowns, individual economic uncertainties and loss of life which faces our worldwide communities. This current situation gives an urgency and focus to contemporary visual art which accords with nature. I am a British artist for whom the contemporary visualisation of trees and landscapes, relating to Empathy Aesthetics, is central to my creative art practice (Summerfield 2018). This essay explores the experience of forests as a unique creative space, whose appeal for contemporary painters, such as myself, lies in its very separateness from urban temporal sensibilities, such as the rush from A to B, and physical structures, such as pavements, road signage and street lighting.

1 Forestryengland.uk/resource: internet access 4th September 2020. Forestry England is part of the Forestry Commission.

2 *Green Space and Health* Centre for Sustainable Healthcare https://sustainablehealthcare.org.uk/courses/green-space-and-health, accessed 4th September 2020.

Angela Summerfield: *Treescape — Empathetic Green*

English Forests

Most of the forests in England permit public access and are managed by the Forestry Commission. They vary in scale, but unlike a wood, forests are large areas of trees and undergrowth, occasionally including pasture, such as the New Forest and the Forest of Dean. In terms of tree species, English forests include both native deciduous trees and, with the establishment of the Forestry Commission, the post-1919 planting of coniferous trees from Scandinavia and the North-West coast of America. In an English managed forest, a single tree species usually appears collectively and en masse with tall elongated growth habits reaching for the light. Such trees include the deciduous larch, English (pendunculated) oak and beech; and the coniferous trees douglas fir, Norwegian spruce and sitka. The under-storey of a well-managed forest offers a second group of trees which include the deciduous silver birch, hazel, holly and elder, alongside mosses, ferns and fungi. Forests vary too in origin, being either originally royal hunting grounds, and therefore including large swathes of ancient and native trees, or new 20th century commercial plantings of fast-growing trees. Forests in England, therefore, exist in a liminal state of managed naturalness. Walking these forests, an artist has a creative awareness of this past and present. As a British contemporary landscape painter, I have explored many forests, but the ones I know best and have a familiarity with are those from my childhood, in North Yorkshire, and where I now live in Gloucestershire.

Forest Sensibilities

Entering a forest means passing from one world of sensibilities to another, where physical orientation and decision-making can be determined solely by an individual creative impetus. Hearing becomes accustomed to shifting silences and sudden sounds of rustling undergrowth and bird song over head. Footsteps become more measured and take on a different pace, releasing quite literally the smells of the forest: rich and peaty with the fresh astringency of pine needles and with this too comes the experience of spaces as coolness or warmth. A forest's floor becomes an earthy softness to one's tread, with tree roots and fallen branches as traversing pathways. Confronted by a densely grown rank of trees, in a coniferous forest, light becomes both diminutive and distant. The forest's canopy limits the fall of light to the ground and therefore the possibilities of plant life. It is a natural inclination shared by all of us to walk towards the light and, in creative terms, this balance is often visualised by passages of deep tone, shadow and illumination which traverse the picture plane. So as to communicate the authentic experience of moving within the forest, traces of coloured light become forms of painted visual passageways and the use of conventional Western perspective is dispensed with in my paintings. Compared with a coniferous forest, in the company of deciduous trees in full leaf, the fall of light is more open and scattered in its variations of shadow and pattern. So that light once more becomes observed as falling shafts on branches and tree trunks, or as intricate patterns upon the ground. Light allows you both to trace and glimpse things: the smoothness of beech trunks or the deep weave of fissures to many conifers. Disconnected from obvious visible signs of the sky's sun or moon, light becomes its own natural force in the forest.

In an English forest there are often official way-marked tracks and pathways, but there is always the possibility of losing your way, or, as in life, perhaps finding it again. In our visual wanderings of the forest we can create the sense of paths or trails through and around trees, over up-rooted ones, tree stumps, unexpected tree roots, uneven ground, habitation holes, bushes, brambles, bracken and all manner of clinging undergrowth determining nature's pace and not our own. Forests as a form of space can in terms of spatial reading be disorientating: to walk the forest is to experience vastness, deepness and the impenetrable. Looking ahead only ever gives a partial sense of trees, whereas to look-up involves the receptors in our feet rooting us firmly to a spot, so as to avoid a sense of toppling. Our sense of space too moves from close compression to sudden openings, experiences which present a compositional challenge to artists. Alongside these personal experiences, artists such as myself explore forests with an awareness of how artists of the past have responded. The early 20th-century Canadian artist, Emily Carr, for example, captured the vertiginous experience of towering redwoods and larches in her paintings. While the mid-twentieth century British landscape painter, Ivon Hitchens, created what he termed visual 'compartments' of semi-figurative imagery and large dragged brushwork over double and triple-square canvas formats.

A Green World

To enter a forest is also to enter a green world of moss-covered trees, spring and summer leaves and undergrowth: a world which presents its own hidden order of living things — 'the ways of the forest' are still referred to as such by those who inhabit it. Artists have also been forest dwellers and there have been famous artists' colonies associated with forests, such as the Barbizon in France and the Abramtsevo in Russia. The 19th-century Russian artist, Ivan Shishkin, created a new type of landscape painting which encouraged other Russian artists to explore a wilderness of native silver birch and oak. Some of these artists responded to the geography of the forest as places of work, ownership and property, while others sought to exemplify forests as sacred and spiritual places associated with ideas of the 'natural church', The Old Believers and Pantheism. In 19th-century France the influential Barbizon colony of artists (named after a village of the district), developed around the Forest of Fontainebleau, noted for its ancient oak trees. These artists developed a new type of painting composition, known as the sous-bois, in response to the Forest's scale and depth, which evoked the experience of being immersed within a forest or woodland interior. The Dutch artist, Vincent Van Gogh, carried forward this visual legacy, with a group of paintings created 1887-90, which sought to capture the immediacy of the experience of an artist peering out from his surrounding undergrowth towards the light. The modern and contemporary artists' experience of a green environment of trees, however, does not necessarily mean an artist's palette of greens, or a pictorial representation. For the influential 20th-century art theorist and artist, Paul Klee, both trees and the forest environment held a life-time fascination. His colourful works, which exist between the abstract and the figurative, evoked a sense of being somewhere, rather than a formal depiction of a forest. His interest in Theosophy, a form of spiritual philosophy, informed his art theory which situated the development and expression of human artistic creativity within the context of a natural world. In his famous lecture, entitled 'On Modern Art', delivered at the Jena Kunstverein, in 1924, Klee explored the development of an artist as analogous to the growth of a tree, through his own drawings. Many contemporary artists, such as The Arborealists (www.arborealists.com), continue to celebrate trees and their green environments in multiple ways: such as living works of art; sources of personal creative inspiration; signifiers of eco-social impact; and as collective symbols or visual metaphors of humanity and survival.

The green world of the forest also evokes memories of a cultural past full of folk tales, folklore and classical mythology inhabited by woodland spirits, dryads and gods: the forest a place subject to magic, mystery and divine powers. In our contemporary world to walk the forest is also to be aware of multiple narratives: cultural, the autobiographical and eco-social. As a contemporary artist, the strong anthropomorphic qualities of trees in a forest always suggest both a presence and a sense of expectancy, even when all other living creatures are seemingly absent the forest, in terms of etymology, also offers a deeper human resonance still, for we can speak of entering the forest to reach its heart. To wander through a forest is, therefore, to become, by degrees, a part of something: a gradual fusion between human nature and Nature, the resultant art works being a visualisation of this accord between a living environment and an artist. From the 1880s, in mainland Europe, a new response to the forest in art developed in contemporary landscape painting. This was termed the psychology of the forest and featured in several international exhibition forums, such as the Vienna Secession exhibitions, notably in 1902. The psychology of the forest in painting was associated with a particular type of interior, dimly-lit forest scene of young, fast-growing and seemingly crowded trees, often silver birch or beech: Nordic artists such as Victor Westerholm (Finnish) and Prince Eugen (Swedish) alongside the Austrian artist, Gustav Klimt, created works of art as part of this development. The brooding presence of conifer trees in the paintings of the Norwegian artist, Edvard Munch, can be seen as a further development of this creative response. To be within a forest is to experience an atmosphere which can reach the core of the human soul and mind. In his essay entitled *Morality* that inveterate traveller and walker, Robert Louis Stevenson, observed:

> *'But indeed, it is not so much for its beauty that the forest makes a claim upon men's hearts,*
>
> *as for that subtle something, that quality of air, that emanation from the old trees, that so wonderfully changes and renews a weary spirit.'*
>
> *(Stevenson 1905: 169)*

This experience of 'that subtle something' may become so intense that one may simply not wish to leave the forest. Our sense of time, born of an urban world and its commerce, gradually receding so that we no longer recall how long ago it was that we entered such a place as this. We slow down with ease to see and study detail, rather than glance or look without regard. In pausing we discover the virtue of delight and wonderment. We sit, nestle-down even, on a fallen trunk or stump, with a sketchbook or notebook to hand: and so our creativity fuses with the calming green tissues of natural life. In the green world of the forest we have the possibility to notice, remember and develop deep thoughts - each of us finding answers to our own silent questions.

Artists can encourage a collective moral responsibility for the future of our forests. Through their artwork they can celebrate, investigate and explore with the aim to captivate both the intellect and the imagination of others. Above all they can share a passionate awareness of the human need for greenness in the world: greenness which is both an environment and a sensibility deep within us all. The creative possibilities, within such a unique natural space, are like the forests' own natural paths, simply endless. The mediaeval concept, Green Truth, informed pre-modern medicine and introduced the belief in casual relationships between nature and human nature: a belief grounded in observation (see Sweet 2006). In this essay, I have explored this affinity within a particular context, the contemporary artist and the forest: an exploration which reveals the contemporary significance of Green Truth, which in turn defines the forest as a unique creative space. This meaning of course resonates with us all, whether we are artists or not. By caring for forests, we can also care for ourselves and others creatively, emotionally, spiritually and physically — all of which adds up to the health of a human being and a green environment. The contemporary value of Green Truth is to be found in the future of our forests.

Kate Prendergast (D. Phil. Archaeology, Oxon 1998) has published extensively on ancient astronomy and climate change in prehistory. Her most recent book is Houses of the Gods. *Neolithic monuments and astronomy at the Brú na Bóinne in Ireland and beyond (LAP 2017). You can find out more about Kate's work on her blog: https://kateprendergast.typepad.com/*

Forests as Commons: a manifesto for future opportunity

Kate Prendergast

Forests as Commons: a manifesto for future opportunity

Kate Prendergast

photo: Kate Prendergast

This manifesto asks us to face the future and in particular, the role that forests may come to play in that future.

It places forests squarely within the concept of the commons, and suggests how there are manifold possibilities for regarding 'the forest commons' as containing and revealing opportunity.

Our day to day management of forests could be integrated with a new vision of the commons and their potential, enabling us to replace 'tragedy' with optimism and hope.

photo: Kate Prendergast

The Tragedy of the Commons

First coined by Garret Hardin in 1968, the 'tragedy of the commons' has been discussed extensively since.

The tragedy of the commons is a situation in a shared-resource system where individual users acting independently according to their own self-interest behave contrary to the common good of all users by depleting or spoiling that resource through their collective action .[1]

In modern economies the commons include a wide range of entities:

- Immense natural resources such as the atmosphere, forests or oceans
- Man-made objects such as highways.

The primary characteristic of the commons is:

Any resource, access to which is not exclusive except through further action such as the assertion of private ownership rights or regulation. Also known as common-pool resources, the assumption is that the resource in question is scarce and there is not enough of it to go around.

According to this view, forests are regarded as a crop to be harvested or sold, or an obstacle to development to be removed, with depletion in resource availability and negative effects for others as a result….

Tragedy as Comedy — of Errors

Among many assumptions embedded in the concept of the tragedy of the commons, two are of interest here:

- A focus on depletion of resources implies that they are scarce and even finite.
- A focus on individual users acting according to their own self-interest implies that human consumption is the central driving force of this tragedy.

So, what if we challenged these assumptions and argued that:

- There are examples of common resources that are infinite?
- Human consumption is not at the centre of the destruction and renewal of life?

What happens to the way we regard forests — and the tragedy of the commons?

1 Tragedy of the commons, Wikipedia: https://en.wikipedia.org/wiki/Tragedy_of_the_commons

Case Study: Carbon

Carbon is a building block of life.

- Carbon is the first heavier element to be formed when helium nuclei fuse in hotter cosmic conditions.
- It is an integral part of the formation of vegetation — carbon dioxide is an essential element in photosynthesis, carbon and sunlight create sugars, the carbon chain that is formed is the basis for the food chain.
- Trees comprise between 20-50% carbon.
- Carbon is relentlessly recycled through the food chain.
- DNA is also made out of carbon — through the patterns it helps to create, we can trace all life back to a Last Universal Common Ancestor (LUCA), around 3.5bn years ago. [2]

Radiata pine forest burnt during the 2003 Bogong Bushfires, Australia (image: flagstaffotos@gmail.com via Wikimedia Commons)

2 *What are living things made of?* Forces of Nature with Brian Cox, Episode 3, BBC: https://youtu.be/23A3C55XVLc

From Carbon to Forests

This view of forests — or their more fundamental building blocks — shows us that the commons are neither given or taken away by humans. They are intrinsically part of the cycle of life that occurs on this planet, with or without us….

It is comparable to the claim made in relation to global warming: We will 'destroy' or 'save' the planet! It reveals the anthropocentric nature of our views. In fact, the tragedy is that we will make planet Earth inhospitable or even uninhabitable for many species, including our own. What we really mean is, we will destroy or save ourselves!

photo: Kate Prendergast

From Tragedy to Opportunity

Carbon is a valuable case study because it demonstrates so clearly the opportunities that intrinsically inhere in the commons. With a focus on forests as the subject of this manifesto, these include the following.

Carbon is a 'greenhouse gas', so forests have a key role in climate change mitigation and adaptation. Some estimates say forests could sequester as much as 30% of emissions.

Reforestation is a key tool in our mitigation 'toolkit'. It is a primary variable in 'feedback cycles' and 'tipping point' models of the likely effects of global warming on sea levels, increased rainfall and desertification.

The resources forests supply are renewable: food, timber for fuel and building, shade in hot climates. They nurture and protect soils and improve water management and flood resilience.

They enable the protection of bio-diversity as many creatures live in and help to maintain and spread forests. This has further positive effects on resource availability for human consumption.

According to the European Commission, birds form an essential part of the ecosystems we depend on for survival. They are seed dispersers for plants and assist with germination. Birds also keep pest populations under control — for Jamaican coffee growers or Californian wine makers, a lack of birds might render growing coffee or vines unviable.

Because forest-dwelling species such as birds are high up in the food chain, they also provide good data about the health of wider environmental habitats.[3]

3 The Birds Directive, The European Commission: https://ec.europa.eu/environment/nature/legislation/birdsdirective/index_en.htm

The Commons as Yggdrasil the Tree of Life

This manifesto asserts that the concept of the tragedy of the commons ceases to be meaningful as soon as we separate natural resources from human-made resources.

The ways in which resources get made, consumed and recycled by and in natural environments such as the oceans or forests is not comparable to the way humans make, consume and recycle resources. Both the order and scale of production are completely different.

We utilise different languages and methodologies for each. To put it very simply, any discussion of natural resources has to engage with natural science methodologies, while any discussion of human created resources has to engage with the methodologies of the social sciences.

Studies of the natural world reveal that it has unlimited potential to create, recycle and regenerate the resources all living beings depend on, and indeed those living beings themselves. This puts it in a conceptual framework that lies beyond any concept of the tragic.

This view of forests is more akin to ancient belief systems that had a special place for trees, as coined in the traditional Celtic/Nordic concept of Yggdrasil, the tree of life.

Yggdrasil is an enabler for beings, human and animal, facilitating journeys along its roots, trunk and branches to other worlds.[4] This vision of trees as opening doors to new realms is in stark contrast to our vision of trees as human products in waiting, and waiting to be destroyed.

4 Yggdrasil: the sacred ash tree of Norse mythology, The Public Domain Review: https://publicdomainreview.org/collection/yggdrasil-the-sacred-ash-tree-of-norse-mythology

Flora Wiegmann is a Los Angeles-based dancer and choreographer. After a year at the Laban Centre in London, she earned her MFA from UCLA in 2007. She works in both live performance and film, often making research-based work that is specific to its particular site. Her projects have been presented at the ICA, Philadelphia; The Kitchen, New York; the California Biennial, Newport Beach; The Hammer Museum and the Music Center, Los Angeles; The David Roberts Foundation and The Camden Arts Centre, London; The Banff Center for Creativity in Canada, and Université Rennes in France.

photo: Richard Povall

Re-enchantment

Flora Wiegmann

Humbolt Redwoods (photo: Flora Wiegmann 2019)

RE-ENCHANTMENT

Amongst the old growth, it is strangely quiet; the deeply furrowed red bodies seem to absorb the sonics of activity between the forest floor and their distant crowns. The cushion underfoot is created by centuries of life posited back into the ground. Fallen trunks sprout new growth, continuing the lineage of these wise organisms. To call it awe-inspiring is inadequate. Miniaturized, I am humbled by the enormity of these trees, and by the knowledge that some have 2000+ years of tree-top perspective. Bodily presence, here, defies the act of description, overwhelms the mind, and opens the heart in an attempt to absorb what the brain can't fathom. It is sublime.

While sheltering-in-place during the global pandemic, I began to have a particular yearning to be immersed in a forest of Coast Redwoods (*Sequoia sempervirens*), the tallest trees on earth. I craved to be overwhelmed, to escape definition, to access the feelings of wonder, reverence, and awe. As my own physical position was limited, I traveled vicariously through the accounts of various explorers, both historical and modern day, and applied the lens of a feminist definition of the sublime in the face of nature—one that emphasies embodied understanding in lieu of human dominance over nature. To learn, not to conquer. In a vast array of locations, from 234,000 miles above the earth to a half-mile down underneath the sea, these explorers engaged their bodies (in often perilous positions) with curiosity. Each individual was powered by a true sense of reverence, recognizing that discovery involves the brain as well as the heart. In turn, imagination and emotion are integral to the process of studying, understanding, appreciating, and therefore, conserving nature. '[N]ature as a living whole...not a dead aggregate', in the words of Alexander von Humbolt, is experienced as the complexity of interdependent systems are felt.

Harnessing this impact is crucial as the extreme wilderness is shrinking and the mark of civilization is everywhere. In the midst of anthropogenic climate change, humans have become detached from nature, losing emotional connection with it. Without a personal connection, very few are moved to action of any kind. Here, I hope to encourage a re-enchantment with the earth, if even momentary, because the health of humans is directly connected to the health of our environment. We need to be moved.

Flora Wiegmann, dancer, artist and environmentalist, 2020

I understood what the Earth would look like, but seeing it with your own eyes was just unbelievable. I was actually looking at the pitch black space one day, and I wondered, 'How far does it go?' I was trying to find the 'bottom' of that darkness, and all of a sudden you kind of feel this fear, in a way, a sensation of getting sucked into that never ending, bottomless darkness....When I had that sensation, it made me think about the Earth as an even more unique and precious planet, supporting humankind, even on orbit. I still believe humanity must go on, but also felt that we cannot go on without the Earth. +254 MILES

Akihiko Hoshide, astronaut and space walker, 2013

I went to the forest-hills early in the morning when the forest awakes. Standing there I breathed in the wind, the unruffled voices of the birds and the silence which I love. And then I was concentrating on a picture, I stopped hearing the silence around me. It was as if I was somewhere else, like in a film. The forest started to move and, as I looked through the camera, I experienced fear. Maybe it was just the framing and the stillness of the evening. As if the birds and the crickets had stopped their singing, as if the wind had come to stop in the valley. Nothing but nothing to hear. No birds, no wind, no people, no crickets. The darkness of the light and this other silence made my hair stand on end ... I could not exactly place the fear, but it was coming from the inside. It was the first time I felt this so intensely, but not the last. I escaped! +1135 FEET

Jitka Hanzlova, artist, 2014

At the end of July 1800, they stepped out of the rainforest and into the open space of the Llanos. After weeks in a dense jungle where the stars appeared as if viewed from the bottom of a well, it was a revelation. Humbolt felt a sense of freedom that made him want to gallop across the wide plains. The sensation of 'seeing' everything around him felt completely new. 'Infinity of space, as poets have said in every language is reflected in ourself.' +141 FEET

Andrea Wulf on Alexander von Humbolt, naturalist, geographer and explorer, 1800

We have just splashed below the surf. SEA LEVEL
We are at our deepest helmet dive. -60 FEET
The Lusitania is resting at this level. -285 FEET
This is the greatest depth reached in a regulation suit by Navy divers. -306 FEET
We are passing the deepest submarine record. -525 FEET
A diver in an armored suit descended this far...the deepest point which a live human has ever reached. -600 FEET
Only dead men have sunk below this. -1426 FEET
We are still alive one-quarter of a mile down.

William Beebe, marine biologist and explorer, 1930

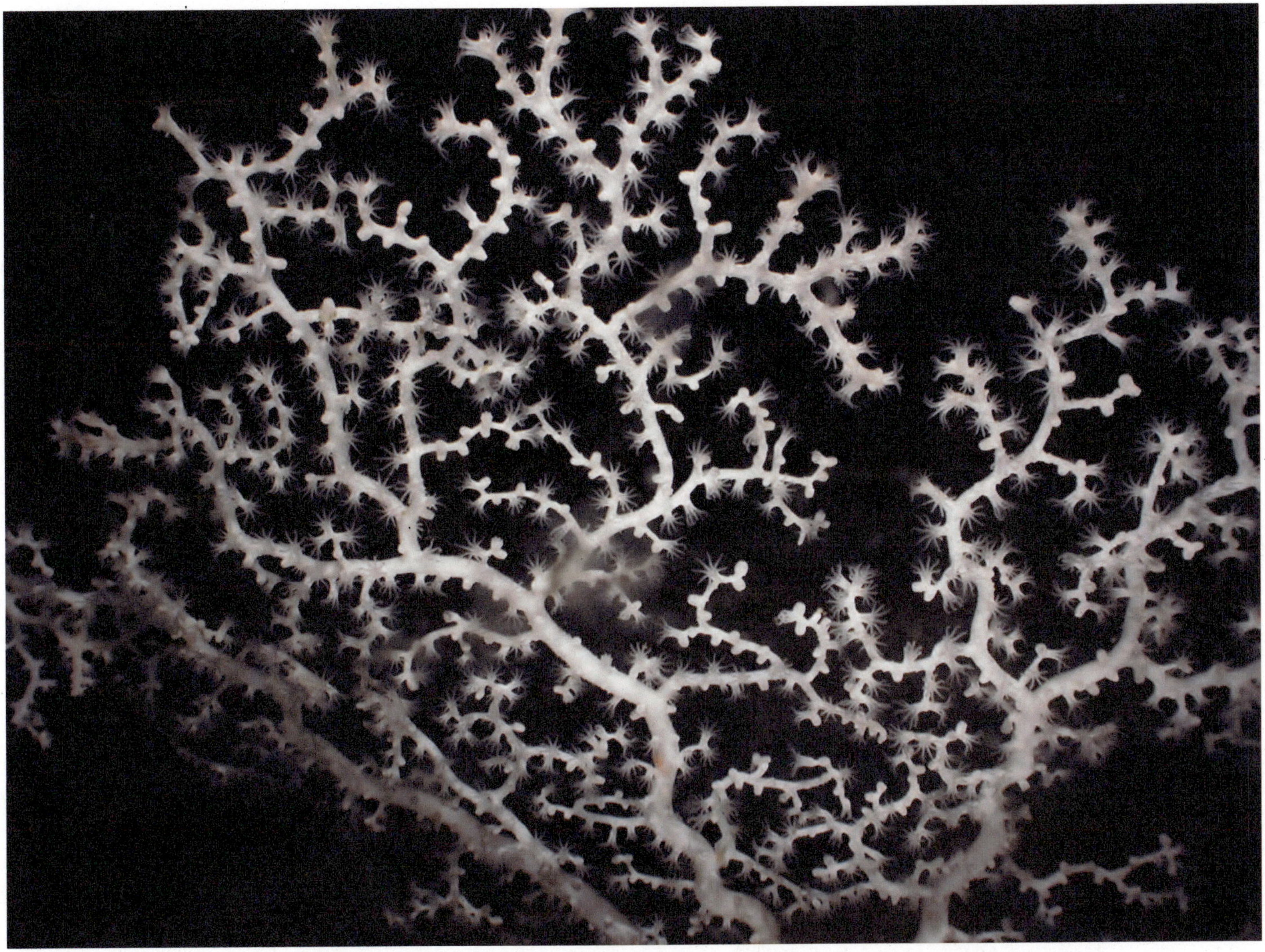

National Oceanic and Atmospheric Administration - Expedition to the Deep Slope 2007, NOAA-OE, 2007

I have heard other space travelers express a perception that I have had; the feeling of euphoria beginning and continuing several days after launch. I think it springs from the mind's realization that the reality without gravity is in effect a new dimension of form. It is a feeling that new possibilities must be present where physical orientation and visual perception are under control but always variable. +280 MILES

The old limits fade, to reveal new, different ones— it is not enough to be hundreds of miles above the Earth in free-fall. You want to be outside the confines of the cabin, outside the confines of the pressure suit. Perhaps you even, without consciously realizing it, feel closer to being outside your body. For each person, it is different, but it must also be the same.

Charles Walker, engineer, environmentalist and first non-governmental person to fly in space , 1986

There is a difference between intellectual knowledge and experience-based knowledge...all of us understand what gravity is, but I would argue strongly that you have no idea what gravity is until you have left it, come back, and experienced that horrible force trying to push you into the ground. It is a completely different kind of knowledge. +254 MILES

Sandra H. Magnus, astronaut and aquanaut, 2013

This embodied experience of being high up in the Arctic circle matters deeply. Questions like 'How can this place be, and how can I fathom being emplaced here?' ran like a current through the ship. 'How does my body fit?,' we asked. Subjectivity balked at the other-worldliness: The immense time of the earth, the epoch-long wildness of it, tugged at us. No theory can, or should, erase that. SEA LEVEL

And yet, while were pulled apart by a 'sense of belonging to a geohumanity,' the specter of the human—climate change—hovered around us: we knew the Arctic was disappearing, we found plastic on the beaches, saw glaciers retreating, heard dying ice streaming into the ocean. But even that knowledge—the knowledge of the Anthropocene—couldn't stop enchantment. We wove a fourth wall around ourselves, and willed that wilderness to be. Because it was wild. And stunning. And remote. And otherworldly. All of that was true, even as we heard 'it's melting, it's melting, it's melting because of us' drumming in our ears.

Alexis Rider, historian of science, 2018

The moment one is submerged — reality of absolute apartness of this place is apparent. In the air one weighs 160 pounds, here one can leap twelve feet, or lift oneself with the crook of a finger. A fall from a coral cliff is only a gentle drifting downward and one's whole activity is of a piece with the exquisite grace of a slow motion picture. In this kingdom, most of the plants are animals, the fish are friends, colors are unearthly in their shift and delicacy; here miracles become marvels, and marvels recurring wonders. -60 FEET

William Beebe, marine biologist, explorer and diver 1934

Inside the crystal cave at the Naica Mine (photo © Carsten Peter Photography & Film for National Geographic)

[I]t is virtually impossible to describe the beauty of the Earth. I don't have the vocabulary, and I have felt very frustrated in trying to describe it. ....you can scan the whole horizon, experiencing the 45 minutes of darkness, but then you couple that with the mobility of weightlessness while you are doing this, and the feeling is absolutely euphoric. My feeling was that I'd seen and done it all, and I didn't care whether I came back or not; it really didn't make any difference...just utter peace and contentment and fulfillment. +328 MILES

Edwin 'Jake' Garn, astronaut and first sitting Senator to fly in space, 1986

It's a terrible and magical environment all at the same time... The first time I entered Los Cristales, tears came to my eyes and I put my arms around some of the giant crystals and felt that I was actually a part of the cave system. That day, when I got out I wrote a poem about it: -980 FEET

The Deteriorated Climate of Fairyland

Gleaming spires longer than five humans put end-to-end,
Sparkling red ceilings and glowing crystal flowers
the size of my first compact car.
The Fairyland of my childhood was like this
but the climate has deteriorated significantly.
I now see that Real Life has the crystals of Fairyland
and the air temperature of Hell.
What a smug irony.

Penelope Boston, speleologist and astrobiologist, 2008

-1/4 MILE

[N]ever before had anyone had the chance to venture solo into that nearly dark, nearly light realm. [D]uring my momentous dive with JIM [an atmospheric diving suit] I was given license to let my curiosity take me where it would—to prowl around like a cat in a new house, whiskers twitching, alert to the slightest movement, sensitive to subtle nuances of shape, light, and sound. I was free to do what explorers elsewhere on Earth take for granted they can do—to walk around, touch strange objects, look for familiar patterns and be sensitive to new arrangements, and sometimes, simply to be quiet and reflect on the significance of that special environment and the nature of the creatures that live there.

Sylvia Earle, marine biologist, aquanaut and human depth record setter, 1996

-1/4 MILE

Here I was privileged to peer out and actually see the creatures which had evolved in the blackness of a blue midnight which, since the ocean was born, had known no following day; here I was privileged to sit and try to crystallize what I observed through inadequate eyes and interpret with a mind wholly unequal to the task. To the ever-recurring question, 'How did it feel?', I can only quote the words of Herbert Spencer. I felt like 'an infinitesimal atom floating in illimitable space.' No wonder my sole written contribution to science and literature at the time was 'Am writing at a depth of a quarter of a mile. A luminous fish is outside the window.'

William Beebe, marine biologist and explorer, 1934

BEAUTY

It was the third day on orbit before I had a chance to take 10 minutes out of the flight plan and, just as a tourist, look down at the Earth. When I did, it was a moving enough experience that it brought tears to my eyes. It was on two different planes. One was pure aesthetic beauty. I paint and I was estimating how many colors of blue there are just in the transition through the Earth's atmosphere from the horizon to the incredible blackness of space. I can remember 20 very intense shades of blue. Then you look down at an archipelago with hundreds of shades of green and blue-green and yellow in the shoals and the atolls. That also brought tears to my eyes. +155 MILES

Don Lind, astronaut and scientist, 1985

When the sun finally gets above the horizon and swings his daily circle, the color effects grow less and less, but then the sky and cloud-effects improve and the shadows in the mountains and clefts of the ice show forth their beauty, cold blues and grays; the bare patches of the land, rich browns; and the whiteness of the snow is dazzling...Above us the sky is blue and bright, bluer than the sky of the Mediterranean, and the clouds from the silky cirrus mare's-tails to the fantastic and heavy cumulus are always objects of beauty. This is the description of fine weather. +482 FEET

Matthew Alexander Henson, Arctic explorer, first to reach the North Pole, 1911

Our planet has changed color. Today, from space, the top of the world in the northern summer looks blue instead of white. We have created an ocean where there was once an ice sheet. It is Man's first major achievement in reshaping the face of his planet,' SEA LEVEL

Peter Wadhams, sea ice scientist, 2016

Seventy feet below the surface, the sub separated from the recovery platform and began falling through prism-blue water that seemed to glow with internal light. Shafts of gold from the midday sun penetrated the upper few feet, but gradually the colors mellowed into blue infinity, deep indigo shading to blue black, the blue-edged drones of deepest twilight or earliest dawn. And there were stars, or so it seemed; small bioluminescent creatures sparkled with brilliant silver-blue flashes as they brushed against the pane through which I viewed Earths 'inner' space. These mysterious, living constellations are as unknown and nearly as remote from human experience as distant galaxies. -1250 FEET

Sylvia Earle, marine biologist, aquanaut and human depth record setter, 1996

Dr. Mike Goebel, National Oceanic and Atmospheric Administration NMFS SWFSC, Antarctic Marine Living Resources (AMLR) Program, 1999

Looking out into space was the goal, but looking back has been the most dramatic part of it. I think we have been as surprised about how much it has meant to look back at the Earth, as it has to look out into space. I have flown in space, I have ridden a bike across the country, I have backpacked across much of the West, I have lived underwater for 10 days, and I have seen the Earth from many perspectives. Space is perhaps the macro-view, being on the surface is perhaps the mini-view, and underwater is the micro-view, where you see some of the world's tiniest creatures.

+254 MILES
to
-62 FEET

John B. Harrington, astronaut, aquanaut and member of the Chickasaw Nation, 2013

The days he had spent traveling from Quito and then climbing up Chimborazo, had been like a botanical journey that moved from the Equator towards the poles— with the whole plant world seemingly layered on top of each other as the vegetation zones ascended the mountain. The plant groups ranged from the tropical species down in the valleys to the lichens that he had encountered near the snow line. Towards the end of his life, Humboldt often talked about understanding nature from 'a higher point of view' from which those connections could be seen; the moment when he had realized this was here, on Chimborazo. With 'a single glance', he saw the whole of nature laid out before him.

+ 3 1/2 MILES
to
SEA LEVEL

Andrea Wulf on Alexander von Humbolt, naturalist, geographer and explorer, 1802

SEA LEVEL

Our own mini solar system underneath our feet is acting as practice as we try to...take our knowledge, take our science, take our melding of the discipline of science with the magic of exploration and the beauties of what we see and what we experience and combine those together in order to advance our knowledge of our universe.

Penelope Boston, speleologist and astrobiologist, 2008

My impressions of what we saw in the greater depths and of how I felt have kaleidoscoped. Darkness and flashing lights have become inextricably mixed, and parts of the descent might be compared to a journey through the heavens on some yet-to-be-invented machine at unheard of speeds — a constellation suddenly appearing and disappearing, a quick flash as some larger celestial body came into view—all of them disappearing with the rapidity of meteors arriving in our atmosphere.

-1/2 MILE

John Tee-Van, ichthyologist, zoologist and illustrator, 1934

Earthrise (photo: Bill Anders, 1968, courtesy of NASA)

I really believe that if the political leaders of the world could see their planet from a distance of...100,000 miles, their outlook would be fundamentally changed. That all-important border would be invisible, that noisy argument suddenly silenced. The tiny globe would continue to turn, serenely ignoring its subdivisions, presenting a united facade that would cry out for unified treatment.

+234,474 MILES

Michael Collins, astronaut and first person to orbit the moon alone, 1986

I found the experience of seeing the world as one distinct entity an enlightening one, realizing with my own senses the interrelatedness of the environment on the globe and the magnitude of the universe in which the globe sits. It extended my desire to have a first-hand feel for the world around us, and it sensitized me to learn as much as I could about the interconnectedness of the environment.

+280 MILES

Charles Walker, engineer, environmentalist, and first non-governmental person to fly in space , 1986

I'd studied environment at this formal level, but there was this informal level [traversing the planet by foot for 22 years]— I learned about people, and what we do and how we are. And environment changed from just being about trees and birds and endangered species to being about how we treated each other. Because if we are the environment, then all we need to do is look around us and see how we treat ourselves and how we treat each other.

SEA LEVEL

John Francis, environmental activist and the Planetwalker, 2008

The beasts of the forest retire to the thickets; the birds themselves beneath the foliage of the trees, or in the crevices of the rocks. Yet amid this apparent silence, when we lend an attentive ear to the most feeble sounds transmitted by the air, we hear a dull vibration, a continual murmur, a hum of insects that fill, if we may use the expression, all the lower strata of the air. Nothing is better fitted to make man feel the extent and power of organic life. Myriads of insects creep upon the soil, and flutter round the plants parched by the ardour of the sun. A confused noise issues from every bush, from the decayed trunks of trees, from the clefts of the rock and from the ground undermined by the lizards, millepedes, and cecilias. There are so many voices proclaiming to us, that all nature breathes; and that, under a thousand different forms, life is diffused throughout the cracked and dusty soil, as well as in the bosom of the waters, and in the air that circulates around us.

SEA LEVEL

Alexander von Humbolt, naturalist, geographer and explorer, 1807

People are under the impression that the planet is fully explored, that we've been to all the forests and climbed all the mountains. But in fact many of the forests have yet to be seen for the first time. They just happen to be underwater. We're still explorers. Perhaps the greatest era is just beginning.

SEA LEVEL

Sylvia Earle, marine biologist, aquanaut and human depth record holder, 1991

Adrian is an ecological researcher, with a particular interest in understanding human impacts on forest ecosystems. He has led projects throughout Latin America, as well as parts of Asia and Africa, in addition to the UK. His most recent research has focused on analysing how ecosystems collapse, or abruptly change, as a result of human activities. Many of his projects have also explored how forests can recover from such impacts, through approaches including ecological restoration and rewilding. Adrian is also a practising sound artist; he uses sound to provide a different perspective on the relationships between forests and people.

photo: Oliver Raymond-Barker

Increasing awareness of forest collapse through science and art

Adrian Newton

Should we paint trees blue? An ecological perspective on environmental art

Adrian Newton

Centre for Ecology, Environment and Sustainability, Bournemouth University, Poole, Dorset, UK

Email: anewton@bournemouth.ac.uk

Introduction

The title of this chapter was inspired by The Blued Trees Symphony, a site-specific artwork focusing on conserving threatened forests developed by the American artist Aviva Rahmani. The piece involved painting hundreds of sine waves on trees using blue paint, in locations across the USA where forests were threatened by the installation of fuel pipelines. The artwork aimed to address the role of fossil fuel corporations in the climate change crisis, with the painted score for a musical performance aiming to 'replace systems of extractive, ecocidal economies with one that acknowledges our interdependence with other forms of life' (Rahmani 2019). Using the score, the artist 'imagined the trees as silent operatic singers voicing their critical role in protecting the soil, air and water that all life depends upon' (*ibid.*). This project has many innovative features, including an attempt to protect the blued trees by copyrighting them as an artwork, an idea that appears to be untested in American case law. It has also been successful in helping to draw attention to the environmental costs of pipework construction, which has latterly become a major focus of protest in both the USA and Canada.

My aim here is not to critically evaluate this artwork; Aviva Rahmani is a highly experienced artist with an established international reputation and a long track record of linking her artistic activity with environmental activism. Using art to protect forests is surely a laudable goal. Rather, The Blued Trees Symphony provides a useful entry point to consider the broader role of both art and science in forest conservation. Specifically, it raises a number of interesting questions, such as: can art save forests from destruction? And if so, what kind of art is needed to achieve this? Furthermore, how can we ensure that art with environmentalist goals is itself ecologically benign?

Answers to these questions lie at the intersection between art, science, environmentalism and conservation practice. I approach these questions as an ecological scientist with research interests in the conservation of both tree species and forest ecosystems. For a number of years I have also been a practicing sound artist, and latterly I have begun to integrate these different interests and to explore their interface. Given that our focus here is specifically on trees and forests, the forestry perspective is also relevant. Given our societal needs, I accept the fact that many forests need to be actively managed to provide a wide range of different benefits, including carbon storage, recreation and regulation of water flow, as well as production of timber. However, it is also the case that environmentally sustainable approaches to forest management depend upon a scientific understanding of how forests function as ecological systems (Newton 2007). I suggest in this article that the same is true just as much for artistic practice as it is for forestry. After all, forest management is itself as much an art as it is a science.

Environmental context

It is widely appreciated that the world's forests are currently facing a global crisis. It has been estimated that more than 15 billion trees are cut down each year, and as a result of deforestation, the global number of trees has declined by almost half since the start of human civilization (Crowther et al. 2015). It is worth remembering that most of this decline has occurred within the lifetime of the world's oldest living individual trees. Tropical forests, which are home to most of the world's plant and animal species, are being cleared at an annual rate of over 10 million hectares per year. The main direct causes of deforestation are conversion to agriculture, wood extraction, and development of infrastructure such as roads and urban areas. Even in regions where forest areas have largely stabilised, such as Europe, the condition of forest ecosystems is being adversely affected by factors such as air pollution, fire, pest and disease outbreaks, habitat fragmentation and inappropriate management. In addition, climate change threatens all forest ecosystems throughout the world (Newton 2021).

While many people are aware of the problem of deforestation, there is much less appreciation of just how rapidly many forest ecosystems are now changing. Although climate change is a key driver of these trends, its effects are amplified by interactions with many of the other stressors currently affecting forests. As a result, forest ecosystems can decline very abruptly in a process referred to as ecosystem collapse (*ibid.*). The most striking illustration of such collapse is provided by the large-scale dieback of forest stands. Allen et al. (2010) identify 88 recent examples of large-scale tree mortality in different parts of the world as a result of drought and heat stress, while noting the occurrence of interactions with other climate-mediated processes such as insect outbreaks and wildfire. Many of the best-documented examples are from North America, including the recent death of >1 million hectares of multiple spruce species in Alaska, >10 million ha of *Pinus contorta* in British Columbia, and >1 million ha of *Pinus edulis* in the southwestern U.S.A (*ibid.*) Let us also not forget the 2019-20 Australian bushfire season, in which more than a fifth of the country's forest burned and three billion animals were killed.

The degradation of forest ecosystems can be seen as part of a wider ecological crisis, which has been referred to as the Earth's 'sixth mass extinction' (Barnosky et al. 2011). This reflects the fact that species are currently going extinct at a much higher rate than would be expected from palaeontological evidence. Unlike the previous five mass extinctions observed in the fossil record, which were typically associated with volcanism or asteroid strikes, the current one is entirely caused by human activity. While recent declines in groups such as mammals and birds are well documented, many people are not aware that many thousands of tree species are also threatened with extinction, including notable species such as the giant redwoods of California (*Sequoiadendron giganteum*), the monkey puzzle of southern South America (*Araucaria araucana*), and valuable timber trees such as mahogany (*Swietenia macrophylla*) (*ibid.*and Newton 2015).

Some insights from ecological research

How are these global trends relevant to the UK, which after all, has relatively little forest cover? Research that I have undertaken with colleagues has shown that profound changes are taking place in our woodlands, even if these are perhaps subtler than the extensive forest loss currently being observed in some other countries. For example in the county of Dorset, we have been able to identify how native woodlands have changed in recent decades by resurveying sample plots originally established in the 1930s. In the 86 woodland patches that we resurveyed, a total of 117 plant species were found to have been lost during the past 70 years. In addition, 47 new species were recorded, many of which had escaped from gardens. Composition of the woodland flora was found to have changed significantly, with different woodlands becoming floristically much more similar to each other over time, primarily as a result of increased nutrient enrichment (Keith et al. 2011 and 2009). This supports other research showing that increased deposition of nitrogen, principally originating from increased agricultural fertilizer use, has radically changed many ecological communities in the UK.

We recently extended these resurveys to other habitats in Dorset, and found a consistent pattern; the effects of nutrient enrichment are very widespread. In addition to this, many habitats have massively declined in area; for example, more than 97% of neutral grasslands and 70% of calcareous grasslands have been lost since the 1930s (Newton 2019). These trends are again attributable to the expansion and intensification of agriculture, which has had a devastating effect on our native wildlife. Although changes in woodland area have been less dramatic, this masks other important trends that have taken place: many native woodlands have been felled and replaced with plantations, often of non-native tree species. This again has had negative impacts on wildlife. Over the same period, the area of conifer forests expanded massively, as many lowland heathlands were converted into timber plantation (*ibid.*). The high ecological value of heathlands is now more widely appreciated than in the past, and latterly some of these plantations have been removed to allow the heathlands to recover. However, these observations remind us that since the Forestry Commission was founded a century ago, forestry has also been an important cause of ecological damage, which has occurred throughout the UK.

Some of our native woodlands are also suffering dieback. We examined this process in the New Forest National Park, which is one of the richest areas for native species in the country. For example, more than two thirds of the British species of reptiles and amphibians, butterflies and moths, fish, bats, dragonflies, and damselflies are found in the New Forest, together with at least one sixth of species in other groups (Newton 2010). The New Forest is home to some truly outstanding ancient beechwoods, which have been continuously forested since the end of the last Ice Age. They therefore provide a direct ecological connection with the wildwood that once covered much of this country, which is why the number of species associated with them is so high. Yet over the past 60 years, many of the beech trees in these woodlands have died. We studied this process in Denny Wood, a beechwood reserve that was designated in the 1950s, when two large survey plots were established within which all of the trees were measured and mapped. Resurveys of these plots have demonstrated how the stand has progressively died since then; some areas are now open grassland without a beech tree in sight. The cause appears to be increased summer drought and winter waterlogging associated with climate change, to which beech appears to be particularly susceptible (Martin 2015 and 2017). We also examined the impact of beech mortality on the other species associated with these trees in twelve different New Forest woodlands currently undergoing dieback. The results showed that the process is not linear (Figure 1); as the beech trees progressively die, there may be key thresholds or tipping points beyond

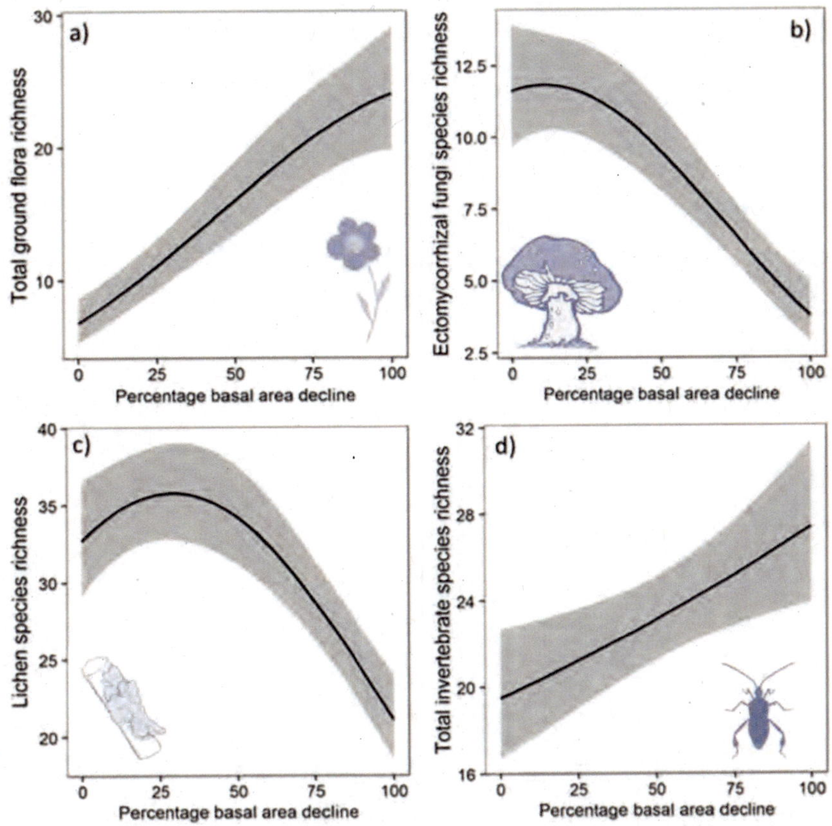

Figure 1. Impact of forest collapse on species richness in different groups of organisms. (a) vascular plants, (b) ectomycorrhizal fungi, (c) lichens, (d) invertebrates. From Evans et al. (2017).

which the rate at which other forest-dependent species are lost increases markedly (Evans et 2017 and Cantarello et al. 2017). This demonstrates that human activities can cause sudden and profound changes in our native woodland ecosystems, even if the environment itself is changing only gradually.

Some artistic responses

Can art help address the challenges of forest loss and degradation? My interest in this question is borne from a sense of frustration, arising from a growing awareness that these environmental problems cannot be solved by science alone. As a scientific researcher, I see my role as providing evidence of how human activities are affecting ecosystems, so that appropriate policy and management responses can be identified. Yet however much scientific evidence is accumulated, and however well it is communicated to decision-makers, there is no guarantee that any relevant action will be taken. This is a point well recognised by the environmental activist Greta Thunberg, who made the following comments to world leaders at the UN Climate Action Summit in 2019:

> *'For more than 30 years, the science has been crystal clear. How dare you continue to look away and come here saying that you're doing enough when the politics and solutions needed are still nowhere in sight.' (Thunberg 2019)*

Part of the problem, as appreciated by Thunberg, is that not all people are aware of environmental crises such as climate change, and the actions needed to address them. So for me, part of the reason for engaging in environmental art is to raise awareness of what is happening to our trees and forests. However, as readers of this book will surely be aware, art can potentially achieve much more than that. Most significantly, by providing an aesthetic experience, art can deliver an emotional impact (although quite how it achieves this is still the subject of debate (Silvia 2005)). This offers the possibility that art could help overcome the widespread indifference about what is happening to our environment. In 2019, it was reported that public concern about the environment had 'soared to record levels' in the UK (Carrington 2019). In other words, 27% of people surveyed ranked the environment among the three most important issues facing the country. This hardly represents a compelling majority, though. Since then, in the wake of the Covid-19 pandemic, the environment has slid further down the list of the nation's priorities[1].

With these goals in mind, during the past six years I have developed a series of artistic interventions that relate to the environmental crises affecting our trees and forests (Box 1). These provided me with a profound learning experience. It has been a privilege to work with skilled artistic practitioners and to learn how they express themselves creatively. I found how different it is to see a forest through an artist's eyes than to view them scientifically. To an ecologist, a fallen beech tree might represent evidence of dieback, or a valuable form of habitat for organisms such as fungi and beetles. To a photographer, though, they can be objects of plaintive beauty; the complex patterns of cracks and fissures in their bark provide a layered document of the processes of death and decay. Listening to musicians respond to the recordings of woodland sounds that I'd collected was a revelation; what I might perceive as sonic evidence of species interacting became for them a kind of symphony of sound, complete with musical structures and meaning. While developing my own artistic practice during these projects, I started to appreciate forests in a very different way, for example when discovering the delicate marimba-like sounds created when raindrops collide with ash keys. Or when finding that each individual tree has its own distinctive pattern of resonant frequencies, which both amplify sounds and conduct them through the branches and trunk. In fact after recording the internal sounds of trees, I came to understand that they can act as antennas, capturing sound in the branches and transmitting it throughout the tree. Trees might even be seen as living sonic sculptures, which can generate, transmit and amplify sounds.

Did these artworks make a difference, though? To an extent, perhaps. In our multi-media exhibition All trees

1. YouGov (2020). Regarding the overall impact on humanity, are you more concerned about the impact of coronavirus or climate change? April 22nd, 2020.

are clocks (Box 1), there is no doubt that photographs and video of ancient beech trees killed by climate change created an emotional impact, which exceeded anything that could be achieved by research data or graphs. Questionnaires completed by attendees of this exhibition indicated that a majority (>70%) were more concerned about climate change after having visited it. Hopefully the exhibition helped people understand that climate change is happening now, and is already having a tangible impact on woodlands that they know. The most striking impacts were perhaps achieved by *Heartwood* (Box 1), where many visitors were visibly entranced by listening to the sound-world hidden inside trees, of which they had hitherto been unaware. The most vocal responses were certainly elicited by *The Forest of Mendacity*, an installation featuring a grove of plastic Christmas trees rescued from landfill. Exhibiting these in a public shopping mall at the height of summer clearly infuriated a number of passers-by, judging by the amount of verbal abuse hurled in our direction. It is interesting to parse the reasons for this: did these people think that we had somehow made Christmas less special? This piece taught us that there is no better metaphor for our society's current relationship with trees than the artificial Christmas tree. This is the only time of year when families traditionally engage in a bit of tree worship, by bringing them into their homes to be decorated and celebrated. Yet latterly, real trees (typically *Abies nordmanniana*) have often been replaced by plastic substitutes; around 2 million artificial trees are now purchased each year in the UK, most of which are made from PVC. The carbon footprint of plastic trees is up to ten times higher than that of a real tree, and people just throw them away, creating a massive waste disposal problem. Think about that: once we venerated real trees, now we have replaced them with plastic substitutes that we consider to be disposable, while harming the environment in the process.

✦ ✦ ✦

Box 1: Selected recent artworks focusing on trees and forests

Heartwood

Heartwood is a sound art composition, featuring the internal sounds of ash trees (*Fraxinus excelsior*). The piece was developed to celebrate ash trees as living, dynamic organisms, of high cultural and ecological value, and also to increase awareness of what we are in the process of losing because of ash dieback disease. The piece has been presented as a site-specific installation, with a complementary suite of choral compositions by Karen Wimhurst celebrating the historical and cultural meaning of ash.

All trees are clocks

A multi-media exhibition featuring the results of recent ecological research, presented together with photography, video, sound art and music. The research examined the impact of recent climate change on the ancient woodland ecosystems of the New Forest National Park. A soundscape composition and accompanying video documented how the woodlands change throughout the year, with the sound of a ticking clock created by breaking the twigs of trees killed by climate change.

Figure 2. Illustration to promote the exhibition All trees are clocks, showing the recent death of a veteran beech tree. Based on photography by Paul Allen

Tipping Points

An interactive sound installation exploring the impact of environmental change on ecosystems, developed in collaboration with the sound artist Ambrose Seddon. Field recordings of different ecosystems were transformed electronically using chaotic feedback processes similar to those associated with ecological systems. Audible tipping points in the system were triggered by movement of the listener near to the installation. In this way, the installation provided a metaphor for human impacts on ecosystems.

By the Way: sounds in a common wood

Contribution of sound art elements to a site-specific production by Wimborne Community Theatre in Leigh Common, Wimborne in 2018, which featured broadcast of soundscape compositions via radio headphones during the theatrical performance. Recordings of woodland sounds were combined with poems about woods and spoken performances by cast members.

Multi-media installations of sacred groves

In many cultures, sacred forests or groves of trees are places of transformation. As Albertina Nugteren (2005) described it: 'In many sacred geographies, the botanical continues to connect the present with the past, the material with the symbolic, and the contemporary ecological with the traditionally sacred'. These installations represent an attempt to create sacred groves for the 21st century, and each involved creating tree-like sculptures from the rejectamenta of modern society. Each of these was a collaborative project with maker, Lynn Davy.

The Forest of Austerity. Installation of kinetic sculptures of found objects with a culinary theme, situated in a kitchen garden, celebrating a century of DADA.

The Forest of Plasticity. Installation of a grove of tree sculptures created from broken beach umbrellas and plastic objects found on the shore, raising awareness of the environmental issue of ocean plastic.

The Forest of Mendacity. Installation composed of a renegade grove of plastic Christmas trees, using abandoned baubles to display lies sourced from politicians, corporate advertising, the international media, anti-science conspiracies, etc.

Further details at http://nemeton.org.uk.

✦ ✦ ✦

Collectively these artworks were viewed by several thousand people, many of whom clearly enjoyed the experience. However, after talking to some of them, I began to feel that many visitors to art events simply view them as a form of entertainment. While the pieces definitely helped to increase awareness and understanding of environmental issues, and maybe changed some opinions, did they encourage any shifts in behaviour? If art is going to help address environmental crises, then it surely needs to help overcome the indifference about these issues that is currently widespread.

The '*Evolving the Forest*' event in 2019 provided a valuable opportunity to explore this topic with both creative and forestry practitioners. In the discussion following my presentation, I asked how art might encourage people to care more about trees and forests. The discussion was

Figure 3. Illustration for the Forest of Mendacity installation, showing what a forest of lies might look like. Use of terrain generation software offers the possibility of an environmentally benign form of landscape art, where no trees need to be felled. Image by Arthur Newton.

instructive and wide-ranging, but for me the most valuable contribution was made by Christine Fentz (of the Secret Hotel, Denmark), who emphasized the importance of creating empathy for a subject. One way to achieve this is to begin to see things from an organism's point of view. This idea was explored further in a workshop on 'biocentric participation' that Christine and her colleagues offered, which for me, was the absolute highlight of the event. During the workshop, we were taught how to move across the landscape like a swarm of ants, using the same rules that many animals follow to form flocks, shoals or herds. We spent time behaving as a meadow of grass stems, standing with our eyes closed, moving in response to subtle shifts of wind and sunlight. Finally we each chose a woodland creature that instinctively appealed to us, then explored the environment by moving as if we were that creature. While these actions were simple to follow, they induced a remarkably profound shift in understanding, increasing our awareness of how different organisms perceive the environments in which they live. So perhaps performative process art, such as this example, can help build empathy for trees and forests, and thereby contribute to their conservation. It also has the advantage of causing very little environmental impact.

Ecological impacts of environmental art

Although '*Evolving the Forest*' provided a unique opportunity to experience a wide diversity of creative responses to trees, I was struck by how few artists viewed trees from an ecological or environmentalist perspective. Furthermore, the environmental impacts of the artwork itself rarely seemed to be considered. For me, the tone was set by a centrepiece of the art exhibition that accompanied the event, which included suspension of a large number of banners from 'special trees' in the Dartington Estate. Was no thought given to the diverse communities of epiphytes that cover these trees, which will surely have been damaged by all of the ropes tied to tree branches, from which the banners were suspended? Also, does this kind of artwork imply that trees are nothing more than an easel, or a canvas, on which we might display our artistic ideas? Weren't the trees special enough already?

This issue is not limited to the art profiled at this particular event. In the past three years of attending other environmental arts events, I have encountered:

- a theatre piece exploring the environmental impact of plastics that constructed an extensive stage set entirely out of newly purchased plastic items,
- an installation examining aerial pollution that introduced chambers of polluting gases to a nature reserve,
- an installation that attempted to raise awareness of our use of petroleum by installing a large tank of oil near to a beach,
- a gallery exhibition focusing on river environments, which featured boulders extracted from a river,
- proposals to develop a mobile creative space for environmental art by converting a 4WD vehicle, which would then be driven around a threatened habitat.

Environmentalist critiques of environmental art are nothing new, of course. The development of land art, landscape art, 'earthworks' and associated approaches in the 1960s soon attracted criticism from environmentalists, for example when Robert Smithson used a bulldozer to reshape the land in construction of his *Spiral Jetty* (1969), or when Christo surrounded eleven islands with half a million square metres of pink plastic (*Surrounded Islands*, 1983). Such interventions have been branded as unethical and an affront to nature (Carlson 1986). While 'ecological art' (or 'eco-art') has since developed, with a stronger focus on environmental ethics, there is still widespread scepticism about the aims and results of much recent art focusing on the environment; even art exhibitions dedicated to environmental sustainability may themselves be unsustainable. There have been few previous attempts to examine the role of art specifically in relation to forests and forestry; a leading example is the *Seeing the Forest* exhibition that toured Oregon in 2000 (Demos 2009). Here, one of the main conclusions was that artists are part of the 'general public', who generally live in urban locations and often have little first-hand knowledge of forests.

Interestingly, artists' awareness and impressions of forests were often found to reflect commonly held public beliefs. This can be a strength, in terms of engaging the public, but also a liability, if those beliefs need to be challenged. For example, this exhibition generated little interest among either artists or members of the public in the condition or health of forest ecosystems.

Partly this issue can be understood in terms of how people value trees differently. To an artist, for example, the principal value of a tree might lie in its aesthetic qualities or its cultural resonance, such as its role in myth or metaphor. In contrast, a forester might be more interested its economic value as a potential source of timber. Conversely, an environmentalist would emphasize its ecological value. Many of the conflicts that occur between different uses of forests, as illustrated by the environmentalist campaigns to protect ancient woodlands, veteran trees and tropical forests, can be understood in terms of the contrasting values held by different groups of people. Those individuals who value a forest for recreation, for example, are likely to campaign bitterly against plans to clearfell it, which to a forester might seem to be the most sensible silvicultural option in terms of optimising timber production.

So what is meant by ecological value? There are two main elements. The first relates to the role of trees as habitat for other organisms. Many groups of species live either within or on the surface of trees, or in close association with them. Examples include the lichens, mosses and algae that live on tree bark; the beetles and other insects that live in wood; and the mycorrhizal fungi that live in association with the roots of virtually all trees. Secondly, trees and their associated organisms play a key role in a range of ecological processes such as the flows of carbon, water, energy and nutrients within ecosystems. Many of these processes underpin provision of benefits to people, such as regulation of water flow and reduction of flood risk, mitigation of climate change through carbon storage, and reduction of aerial pollution through capture of particulates.

Another way of thinking about the value of trees is from an ethical standpoint, which considers the intrinsic value of life. This is perhaps best understood from the standpoint of 'deep ecology', an environmental philosophy that recognises the inherent worth of all living things, regardless of their utility to people. The concept of deep ecology originated in the early 1970s with the work of Norwegian philosopher Arne Naess; since then, his ideas have developed into an influential social movement (Nugteren 2005). A core principle is the belief that all living things should be respected, and regarded as possessing moral and legal rights to live and flourish. Except to satisfy vital human needs, humankind does not have a right to reduce the diversity and richness of life (Drengson 2011). It is this kind of ethical standpoint that has led to the Whanganui River in New Zealand recently being given the same legal rights and protections as a person, in a landmark case. Suggestions have been made that trees or forests might be granted similar protection, and a recent court case brought by schoolchildren has established this legal principle for the Colombian Amazon.

What are the implications of these ecological and ethical values for artistic practice? There are perhaps two key points worth highlighting:

Not all trees are the same. Viewed from an aesthetic standpoint, there is perhaps a tendency to view one tree as largely equivalent to another. However, trees differ markedly in their ecological value depending on the species involved and where they are growing. For example, native tree species consistently have a much higher value than exotic species as habitat for other organisms. Trees growing in semi-natural woodland have higher ecological value than those growing in plantations. Trees that have established through natural regeneration have higher value than those that have been planted. Older, more structurally complex individuals, such as ancient or 'veteran' trees, are more valuable than trees with a straight trunk and few branches (Newton 2007). From this, it follows that not all forests are the same; 'old growth forests and ancient woodland typically have much higher ecological value than plantation forests.

Trees are not just plants. As noted above, trees provide habitat for many other organisms. The number of species associated with trees is remarkably high; for example, in the UK more than 2,300 species are associated with oak (Mitchell et al. 2019) and more than 1000 with ash (Mitchell et al. 2014). Any individual tree could therefore have hundreds of species associated with it. Like lichens, trees can be considered as dual organisms, with two partners in a symbiotic association: the plant itself, and the mycorrhizal fungi associated with its roots. Trees should therefore be viewed as diverse ecological communities or systems, rather than as simply plants made of wood.

These perspectives should ideally inform any artistic intervention undertaken with trees. Tree bark, for example, should not be viewed as something dead and disposable, but as a vital part of the organism. Bark provides an important source of protection against fungi and other pathogens, and the living part of the tree lies just below its surface; any damage to bark integrity could therefore threaten the life of a tree. Trees essentially breathe through their bark; covering them with paint threatens this important process of gas exchange. Furthermore, tree bark is often covered with diverse communities of lichens, bryophytes, algae, fungi and invertebrates, which can vary markedly within a single tree. Lichen communities, for example, may differ from one side of the tree to another, and at different heights above ground. Patterns of stemflow of nutrients and water play a major role in structuring these communities, so if any substance (such as paint) is applied to the surface of a tree, it is likely to have a negative impact on the species living there by influencing these processes. So anything tied to, suspended from, applied to or hammered into a tree is likely to cause ecological damage of one kind or another. Even developing an artwork near to a tree without touching it could disturb species that are roosting or nesting there, such as cavity-nesting birds or bats. Removing plant materials, such as wood, leaves or seeds, from a forest to a gallery setting will also inevitably destroy habitat for some species.

True 'eco-art' should seek to minimise such negative environmental impacts, and ideally avoid them altogether. Consideration of these potential impacts should form part of the planning of any art project, perhaps as part of an environmental risk assessment. It's important to do your ecological homework: don't claim, as one group of artists did, that an area with some of the country's largest and most ecologically important native woodlands has few trees. Furthermore, following the principles of deep ecology, artists should respect trees as the marvellous living systems that they are, rather than viewing them as simply an artistic canvas, easel, or source of materials. Similarly, foresters should view trees as more than a source of timber. If we as artists or foresters do not view trees as a community of living creatures, each of which has a right to life, then we will fail to communicate the kind of ethical values that people need to adopt if global environmental crises are to be averted.

Box 2: Initiating ecological change through sound art

Although contemporary eco-art focuses primarily on the visual arts, progress has recently been made in developing ecological approaches to sound art. Potentially, sound art may have particular value in helping people to connect with environmental issues through creation of metaphors, articulating the relationship between people and the Earth's ecosystems, and increasing awareness and respect for invisible areas of the environment (Gilmurray 2017). A number of artists have begun to explore whether sound art approaches such as soundscape composition might also help initiate ecological change. Recent developments in this area are reviewed by Jo Kennedy, who presents a simple model of how sound art might encourage a shift towards pro-environment behaviour (Figure 4) (Kennedy 2019). This model incorporates three key elements: connectedness, knowledge and structural support. She proposes that all three elements need to be in place for a piece of sound art to have the best chance of nudging people towards more environmentally sustainable behaviour. With regard to 'connectedness to nature' she considers how best to generate this affective experience in audiences, and believes that ultimately this might best be achieved through work which invites the audience to take part in the creative process — to be the creators themselves. The work must also, at a fundamental level, be informed by an understanding of ecological processes and environmental issues, and not shy away from sharing some of this knowledge with audiences, including small ways in which they could change their behaviour having experienced the work. Thirdly she notes the need to support and embed such artworks in frameworks that serve to aid their creation, public performance and dissemination. These ideas might potentially be relevant to other areas of artistic practice.

✦ ✦ ✦

Acknowledgements

Heartfelt thanks to everyone who contributed to the art projects, especially Lynn Davy, David Rogers, Paul Allen, Emily Burridge, Karen Wimhurst and Arthur Newton, and the participants of Campfr workshops, especially Jo Kennedy.

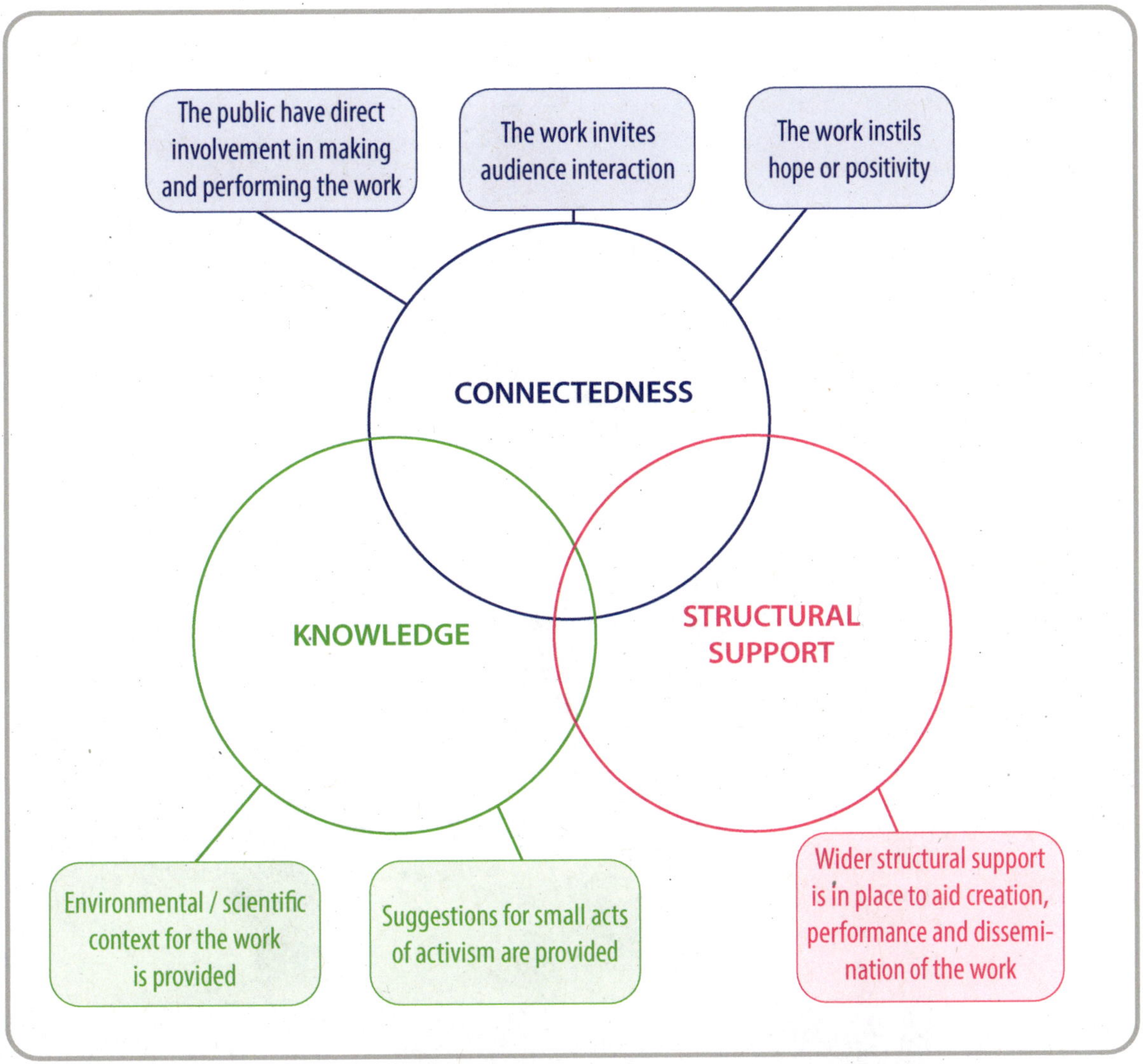

Figure 4. A proposed model for ecological sound art, suggesting elements needed if pro-environmental behaviour is to be initiated in audiences. From Kennedy 2019:30.

Jason Griffiths is co-director of Reading the Forest, the research and public engagement project uncovering the literary heritage of the Forest of Dean. In 2019 he received a PhD from the University of Gloucestershire for his thesis on the history of Forest of Dean literature. Jason has worked on a number of community projects in the Forest including Forest of Dean Radio, and the Voices in the Forest Festival, and was instrumental in the setting up of the Dennis Potter Archive. Jason has been a Senior Lecturer at the University of Gloucestershire School of Media; at the same time qualified as a Freeminer after completing his 'year and a day' working underground.

photo: John F French

Reading the Forest

Jason Griffiths

PEOPLE and TREES
NOT PROFIT + GREED

Reading the Forest: Insights into people — forest relationships through the study of a local literature

Jason Griffiths

As the snow fell on 3rd January 2011 in Speech House field in the Forest of Dean, three thousand people gathered to protest against the UK Government's plan to privatise the public forest estate. A march, speeches, and music, were rounded off by the burning of a wooden effigy of Big Ben, symbol of the UK Parliament. This was the first major demonstration of the HOOF (Hands Off Our Forest) campaign.

The Forest of Dean is situated in the West of England between the River Severn to its East, and River Wye to its West bordering Wales. Though its administrative boundaries and extent have shifted down the centuries, today as a local government district it covers around 200 square miles, whilst 35 square miles of this is statutory forest[1]. The Government's proposals would have seen large areas of the nation's state-owned woodland sold to commercial interests; some offered for sale to community groups; whilst 'heritage woods' such as the Forest of Dean and New Forest were to be run by a newly set up charity or offered to the Woodland Trust or similar (Vidal 2011). Retaining state ownership of the Forest of Dean's woodlands was seen by many there as the best way to protect them, and of guaranteeing the continuation of existing freedoms of access and traditional rights and privileges (such as Freemining[2] and the common grazing of sheep).

As other protests sprang up around the country HOOF became part of a highly organised and successful nationwide protest movement that eventually saw the Government back down. For those familiar with the history of the Forest of Dean the HOOF campaign and its wider support in the local community would have come as no surprise. This was in fact just the latest in a long line of similar battles fought repeatedly over hundreds of years (including as recently as the 1980s and 1990s) by people in the Forest of Dean against attempts to privatise access to the Forest's[3] woodlands and its resources. So strong is the identification for many in the Forest with long standing freedoms and traditions in relation to its woodlands that the Government's plans were seen as nothing less than a threat to the community's very own sense of identity. This is a region with a strong sense of a distinctive identity tied up with its unfettered access to and a love of its

1 Beyond the more general understanding of forests as wooded landscapes, in England forests as set aside spaces for the exclusive enjoyment and exploitation by the monarch were first established under William I (though may have existed earlier in some form under Cnut). For a more detailed exploration of the topic see for example Havins, 1976. For a succinct summary of the history and definitive qualities of the statutory forest within the Forest of Dean region, see HOOF, 2011, 8-11.

2 Freeminers: Miners exercising their rights to get iron ore or coal in the Hundred of St Briavels (in the Forest of Dean) under Royal Charter since the thirteenth century. These rights were more formally codified in law through Parliamentary Act in 1838. Freeminers continue to operate in the Forest of Dean to this day. See https://www.forestfreeminers.org/

3 The term Forest (as opposed to forest) is used throughout here to refer to the Forest of Dean region rather than just the forested area within it. Similarly, Foresters here refers to the inhabitants of the Forest of Dean.

photo: John F French

woodlands, an independent and anti-establishment[4] spirit, suspicion of outside influence, and, perhaps most important in regard to the HOOF campaign, a willingness to robustly defend its traditional rights and privileges.

These ideas about Forest of Dean identity are long-standing and have informed portrayals of the Forest and its inhabitants in works of history, poetry and many of the novels set in or about the Forest of Dean, and this writing has in its turn served to further reinforce these ideas. Stuart Laing's writing on the powerful role played by images in rural popular culture is instructive here. Laing writes that the 'construction of meaning', takes place 'through language and symbol, through the available stories and images circulating within their culture' (Laing 1992:133). Many of the 'available stories', about the Forest of Dean depict a community with a deep love of its woodlands, and one that, when its woodlands are felt to be threatened, is willing to defend them. These stories have circulated through its literary culture and have thus fed back into Forest identity. These same stories of a community that robustly defends its Forest, often through riot and disorder, could arguably be seen to have been reverberating amongst the crowd at a public meeting held in the Forest of Dean by MP Mark Harper (on 4th February 2011) to explain the Government's sell-off plans. Such was the strength of opposition feeling in evidence at the meeting that the MP left under police escort (The Forester, 2011).

What then are some of the ideas about Forest identity that have been transmitted through its literary culture and what are their origins? In choosing to narrowly explore only Forest of Dean literature, what insights might be gained and shared that could inform a wider understanding of people-forest relationships? As our trees and woodlands take on an ever more important role in regard to climate-change, species diversity, and human wellbeing, what value might these insights have in helping to value and protect them?

A Sort of Robustic Wild People

One of the earliest literary descriptions of the Forest of Dean appears in William Camden's (1551-1623) Britannia, first published in Latin in 1586, and later in various English translations (Camden 1701). Amongst his brief description of the Forest at that time he writes that the Foresters had once been fierce and dangerous, and that they had been shaped so by their woodland environment:

> *This Wood was formerly so thick with Trees, so very dark and terrible in its Shades, and various Cross-ways, that it render'd the Inhabitants barbarous, and embolden'd them to commit many Outrages [...] they so infested the Banks of the Severn with their Robberies, that an Act of Parliament was made on purpose to curb and restrain them.*
>
> (Camden 1710:280)

For Camden the Foresters had been shaped to be brutish by their dark woodland environment. The 'outrages' were raids on shipping travelling up and down the River Severn by small bands seeking to capture cargo such as grain. Such were their frequency that a specific law was passed in 1504 to counter these attacks carried out by 'divers

4 Historically this has rarely included the monarchy. The Crown as landowner, identified with the ruling monarch, was often seen as guarantor of Forest rights and privileges in the face of Government expediency or outside interests. See for example 'The Foresters' Song' by Richard Morse (1811-1875) (Morse 1840 cited in Morse et al. 2012:30).

misruled persons inhabiting the Forest of Dean' (Davies 1871:408). In his short section on the Forest Camden also notes that there are furnaces making iron from its ore, but in regard to its people his only comments are those above. Just a few years after Camden a more mythical, poetical history and topography of Britain, Poly Olbion (1612), by Michael Drayton (1563-1621) was published, and again the lawlessness of the Foresters is noted amidst a recognition of the region's significant woodlands:

> *Here (Queene of Forrests all, that West of Severne lie)*
> *Her broad and bushie top Deane holdeth up so hie,*
> *The lesser are not seene, shee is so tall and large.*
> *And standing in such state upon the winding marge,*
> *Within her hollow woods the Satyres that did wonne*
> *In gloomie secret shades, not pierc't with Sommers sunne,*
> *Under a false pretence the Nymphs to entertaine,*
> *Oft ravished the choice of Sabrins watry traine;*
> *And from their Mistris banks them taking as a prey,*
> *Unto their wooddie Caves have carried them away:*
>
> (Drayton 1612:102)

The Forest's inhabitants are portrayed here as 'Satyres,' a half-man half-beast figure drawn from classical mythology. Again, much as in Camden's earlier formulation, Drayton's Foresters are shaped by their woodland environment, and again are noted for their raids on Severn traffic ('watry traine'), the river here taking on her mythical guise of 'Sabrin' (or Sabrina).

Drayton and Camden's literary characterisations of the Forest of Dean and the people who lived there drew on long-standing literary motifs regarding forest woodlands that saw them as wilderness or wastelands, and the people who dwelt there as persons living beyond the norms of courtly life, civilisation and conventional morality: forests were places that harboured rebels and misfits (Harrison 1993). The Forest of Dean was thus noted as part of Britain's landscape in these generic terms, a place occupied by a wild and lawless people, shaped by their lives lived in a dark woodland wilderness. As much though as these ideas were based on long-standing literary convention, they also did have some basis in reality. As Peter Havins has pointed out, there was a long history in England of real woodland outlaws, such as 'Eadric the Wild, or 'Eadric of the Woodland'', who until his capture in 1070 had fought against the Norman invasion and took refuge in the woodlands of Shropshire; Malcom Musard and his gang in the early 1300's operating out of Feckenham Forest; Piers Veneables of Derbyshire active in the 1430s and described in one contemporary account as behaving like, "Robyn Hode and his maynee" (Havins 1976:73-79). Though in the Forest of Dean there was no single notable outlaw figure from such an early period, there were many incidents, besides the raids on Severn river traffic, to inspire the literary depiction of Foresters as lawless and ferocious, and some of these incidents were contemporary to Camden and Drayton.

In 1612, for example, the very same year that Poly Olbion was published, there were riots in the Forest of Dean provoked by the Earl of Pembroke's grant to exert monopoly control over the Forest's timber, (a resource the local inhabitants were used to having access to, not least as pit props in support of their mining activities) and its iron ore. The exclusive nature of the grant to Pembroke contravened the longstanding privileges and customs of the Forest, and in particular those of the Forest of Dean's Freeminers, and action was taken by them that included the setting fire of timber felled by Pembroke's men. The rioters were described at the time as "those Robin Hoods[5]", driven to their actions of riot and vandalism by their 'wild humours' (Earl of Northampton First Lord of the Treasury cited in Hart 1966:91). Though in this case those involved were relatively small in number, the authorities lamented that there was widespread support for them in the area, and thus they could be seen as representative of the wider Forest community.

There were similar revolts in the decades that followed the 1612 disturbances as the Crown enclosed parts of the Forest of Dean's woodlands in order to exploit it more efficiently, in particular to provide fuel for the region's expanding iron industry. As Buchanan Sharp (2010) has made clear though, just as such enclosures were not peculiar to the Forest of Dean at the time, neither was its inhabitants' resistance to them. Disorder was in fact so widespread during 1626-1632 in response to enclosures across England they became known as the 'Western Rising' (Sharp 2010:55-80). John Williams also known as 'Skimmington', one of the leaders at this time in the Forest of Dean, may, according to Sharp, also have been actively involved in protests in other regions as well. What is significant though in regard to the Forest of Dean is the role that such revolts have played in shaping Forest (of Dean) identity, something reinforced through its literature. With repeated incidents of open revolt[6] in the Forest of Dean throughout the seventeenth century against the various attempts at the curtailing of customary rights and freedoms, and such was the Foresters' reputation that by the end of the period the Chancellor of Gloucester Richard Parsons felt justified in describing Foresters as 'A sort of robustic wild people, that must be civilised by good discipline and government' (cited in Nicholls 1858:56). It would be characterisations of Foresters such as this, and those of Camden and Drayton, repeated in the early county histories, and in H. G. Nicholls' three histories specifically on the Forest of Dean, that informed many of the subsequent portrayals of the Forest and the Forest characters that peopled them.

We Foresters'll deal wi' him

One such inheritor of these descriptions of Foresters was the character Rob Wilde, in Thomas Mayne Reid's (1818-1883) novel No Quarter! (circa 1885). Its story is set in and around the Forest of Dean during the English Civil War of the 1640s and follows the fortunes of popular (fictional) local landowner Ambrose Powell, his daughters Sabrina (see above) and Vaga (the Latin name for the Wye), and a host of other characters. Wilde's first appearance in the book sees him emerging from concealment in woodland undergrowth at the edge of a track, strongly suggesting he is a man of the woods, a product of nature. Reid describes him as a "true free-born Forester", 'majestic in his mein', and possessing a 'savage grandeur' (Reid c.1885:82-88), and, as his name Wild(e) suggests, he might be seen as a literary descendant of those same Foresters described by Camden and Drayton.

Wilde joins the local Parliamentary forces, is rapidly promoted, and is involved in the fight against local

5 The legendary outlaw figure appearing in literature from the late-Medieval period onwards, he 'offered a dangerous but, at the same time, carefree life of which the sweating ploughman and the overworked apprentice could at least dream' (Anderson,1990:29).

6 As well as riot, Foresters were equally capable of making a successful defence of their longstanding woodland rights and privileges in court, as they did the following year in regard to Pembroke's grant. This willingness to resort to law (as well as direct action) were qualities later noted by the Forest historian Rev. H. G. Nicholls writing in 1863 as he described Foresters as being a people 'very impatient of control' (Nicholls,1863:176) but also in possession of a 'litigious spirt' (180).

Royalist Sir John Wintour. At one-point Wilde states with conviction, "Sir John Winter won't hae it all his own way much longer. We Foresters'll deal wi' him" (Reid c.1885:85). Wintour[7] was a real historical figure, a local landowner who helped in the suppression of the riots in the Forest in 1628 for which service he was made a country deputy lieutenant (Anstis 1996:27). It was Wintour to whom Charles I sold rights to exploit all the minerals and timber of the Forest of Dean in 1640, something the historian Cyril Hart described as 'the virtual sale to Wintour of most of Dean' (Hart 1966:124), and a transaction described by another modern author as 'the biggest land and property deal in a generation' (Anstis 1996:27). Such was Wintour's impact on the Forest's tree cover, over successive grants, that one contemporary assessment suggested that he was responsible for the destruction of nearly 30,000 trees (Anstis 1996: 67). In Reid's novel it is Wilde, the ordinary Forester, a man of the woods, who is pitted against Wintour, the destructive businessman who sought to exert monopoly control of the Forest of Dean's natural woodland resources for his own private gain.

In another more recent example of Forest of Dean literature dealing with the same period Wintour is once again assigned the role of villain. In Forest Heart: A Civil War Tale of a Forest of Dean Family (Tye 1998) it is again 'ordinary' Foresters, (here two young brothers, sons of a local innkeeper) who are instrumental in his defeat. And, just a few years after Tye's book, in 2000, when a local community arts project, The People's Opera, wrote and performed its drama set in the same period (the plot inspired by Reid's novel), Wintour was again the wicked industrialist seeking to have the Forest for himself. The People's Opera performed several times in venues across the Forest of Dean and were seen by hundreds of local people. In an opening scene Wintour's bid to buy the Forest was depicted, its woods symbolically represented by a model handed to him on a plate: it was a highly evocative image, coming as it did only a few years after the most recent threat, a proposal for privatisation of the nation's forests in the early 1990s.

Whilst some academic assessments of Wintour have been kinder to him[8] in regard to his impact on the Forest's woodland, to this day, his portrayal in Forest of Dean literature means that for many he is the Forest's bogeyman, a symbol of what might happen if private commercial exploitation of the Forest is given free rein. If Wintour is a villain for the Forest, there is another later local historical figure who is seen by many as a hero for the Forest.

Warren James: Freedom Fighter

When Thomas Mayne Reid was writing *No Quarter!*, he was living on the edge of the Forest of Dean[9], and in his frequent visits into the Forest he would no doubt have heard about a more recent example of Foresters defending their woodland rights and privileges. The Dean Forest riots of 1831 was a revolt involving up to 3,000 people prompted by an extension of the period, and extent, of recent woodland enclosures. The enclosures took the land

7 Spelled variously Winter / Wintour, including by Reid within *No Quarter!*, and also Wyntour.

8 Antis (1996:72) cites assessments by Cyril Hart, George Hammersley, and Richard Newman all of whom suggest Wintour has been unjustly maligned in regard to his impact upon the Forest of Dean's woodland cover.

9 This Irish-born adventurer turned author lived in the region from 1875 to 1883.

out of use for grazing and curtailed the getting of timber for use in coal mining or other uses. The resulting riots were led by a Freeminer, Warren James, and his status to this day in the Forest of Dean as a local hero is exemplified in the dialect poem by Keith Morgan (1945-), 'Warren James: Freedom Fighter' published in 1985. The poem begins with an assessment of his character:

Warren James wer' sart o' mon
As allus zin as right wus done.
All 'is life 'im'd zin vair ploy,
An' feared not any mon nar bwoy[10].

(Morgan 1985)

Morgan emphasises James' innate sense of justice, but also importantly his fearlessness. The remainder of the poem recounts James exercising that fearlessness in leading the 1831 revolt against enclosure, and lest this be left as simply a story of the early nineteenth century, Morgan leaves the reader in no doubt of James' contemporary significance with his final line of the poem: 'The 'Freedom' mon as zhowed the woy[11]'.

The story of James and the riots have also featured in a number of works of Forest history over the years, for example Nicholls (1858), Hart (1966), Fisher (1981), and has been the subject of monographs by Ralph Anstis (1986), and Ian Wright (2008). The riots were the backdrop to a short story too in Dickens' periodical Household Words, in 1851, written by popular Forest-born novelist of the period Rev. William Wickenden (1796-1854). The leader of the revolt in Wickenden's 'A Tale of the Forest of Dean', is a regular Wickenden character, Jack Prosser, 'a wild Orson of a fellow', later described in the story, somewhat sarcastically due to his ineffectual role in the riot, as 'that Robin Hood' (Wickenden 1851:462-463). It is a comical tale, but yet again, at the heart of a story set in the Forest of Dean is riot and resistance. As leader of the real riots, Warren James was found guilty and transported to Van Diemen's Land (present day Tasmania). Although he never returned to England he was later given a free pardon at the behest of the Forest of Dean authorities, partly in recognition of the Foresters' claims and partly as an attempt to mollify them (Anstis 1986:240). Though not in support of the means, such was the respect in some quarters for the Foresters' robust defence of their legitimate rights, that even one of James' prosecutors, local Justice of the Peace P. J. Ducarel (1778-1855), described Foresters with some admiration only five years later in his epic poem De Wyrhale: A Tale of Dean Forest, in five Cantos (1836). As we meet them for the first time, Ducarel, the man who had issued the warrant for James' arrest (Anstis 1986:110) describes Foresters as in possession of 'stout hearts of brass', and with 'Spirits untamed like wildfires[12]' (Ducarel 1836:123). What suggested to Parsons that Foresters 'must be civilised by good discipline and government', were by the pens of Ducarel, Reid, and later Morgan turned into qualities

10 Warren James was the sort of man,
Who always saw that right was done,
All his life he had seen fair play,
And feared not any man nor boy.

11 The 'Freedom' man that showed the way.

12 Ducarel also draws on Camden's and Drayton's story of raids on the Severn: 'They say we are Pirates too' (Ducarel, 1836, 123).

of character that instead might be respected and even admired.

Whether 'barbarous', 'Satyres', or persons of 'savage grandeur', these literary images of the people of the Forest of Dean and their willingness to stand up for their rights have become woven into the Forest's very sense of itself and have arguably been a source of inspiration for campaigns such as HOOF. Warren James in particular is today considered so iconic by many within the Forest of Dean that the 1831 riots were the focus of one-day festival in 2010[13] featuring talks, music and a community play, whilst James is celebrated as hero in his home village of Parkend with a mural inside The Fountain Inn.

For the Love of Trees

The motivation for protests such as the 1831 riots, and earlier ones, should not of course be misunderstood. These were not organised by proto-environmentalists. They were primarily led by Freeminers, keen to protect their economic interests vested in their right to mine for iron or coal, quarry stone and get timber. They were though supported by the wider Forest community because, as Simon Sandal (2013) has argued, there were a series of ancillary benefits such as common grazing and the gathering of firewood (let alone work, such as transport, in direct support of mining) that were also threatened when private interests sought to take ownership of, or the Crown to enclose, the Forest of Dean's woodland. This gave all Foresters — actively involved in mining or not — common cause to guard jealously access to these woodland resources. To what extent at this time the community also valued the Forest's native flora and fauna for its own sake or had any aesthetic appreciation for the woodland landscape, is unclear. However, as the first Forest of Dean authors began to write their own native descriptions of the Forest in the early nineteenth century, and from then onwards, the value to them of the woods as part of nature, and a place of beauty, becomes evident.

The 'Forest Poetess' Catherine Drew (1784-1867), for example, in her poem 'The Forest of Dean In Times Past Contrasted With The Present', published in her collection of 1841, details the story of the Forest's development, including its recent rapid industrialisation and the independent character of the Foresters, but she also notes her own appreciation of the natural world around her:

> *In yonder grove I've many sweet hours spent,*
> *And listened to the wild notes with content,*
> *That issued forth from every bramble bush,*
> *The blackbird, white-throat, and the tuneful*
> *thrush.*

(Drew 1841:18)

Whilst in part reflective of the period's turn towards nature in Romantic poetry and literature, this section of the poem also suggests a genuine appreciation by Drew of nature in her native woodlands. This same appreciation of woodland nature can be found in other work of the period, for example that by Morse, Wickenden, and Ducarel. In a later section of Drew's poem, she mourns the felling of an individual oak tree: 'Oh! I regret, for thee to be cut down, But so it is, 'tis ordered by the crown' (Drew 1841:20). This is not the response of someone who only sees the woods as

13 In a 2017 a similar type of event marked the 800th anniversary of the Forest Charter.

a source of personal economic gain or domestic resources, but rather an expression of disinterested appreciation of her woodland environment, and even suggestive of an emotional connection to trees (the tree after all is addressed with the singular pronoun 'thee').

Just over a century after Drew's poem was published a similar, if more expansive response to the felling of Forest of Dean trees was expressed by poet, author and literary editor from the Forest, Leonard Clark (1905-1981). Having left the Forest to continue his teacher training, Leonard Clark regularly returned, eager when he did to catch sight of Chestnuts Wood which was just a short walk from his family home. Trees and woodlands in general remained important to Clark throughout his life and they feature in many of his poems. In his memoir A Fool in the Forest, he describes the source and depth of his feelings about trees:

> *I was brought up in a forest, which means, if you like forests, that trees become part of you, your brothers and sisters, as it were. The trees of my forest became part of me [...] I pale when I hear that one is to be cut down. I become a different creature when I move among trees; their woody spirit seems to enter into me. I inherit their silence.*
>
> (Clark 1965:7)

Clark was horrified to discover on one visit home in 1945 that his beloved Chestnuts Wood had been entirely felled, (partly due to disease and partly as a contribution of timber to the War effort). Though it was soon replanted he mourned the loss of the particular trees (as individuals) that he grew up amongst and was especially sorry for the elderly residents 'who grieved most of all' as they had amassed an even longer period of cohabitation with the same trees. For Clark and his neighbours, the woods were not merely scenic backdrop, or a pleasant environment to live amongst, they were a repository of memories and part of their very identity. As the trees were felled so they felt part of themselves was being lost (in Clark's case the felling was a metaphor too for the passing of his youth). This identification with and strength of feeling for trees and the wider Forest as a place can be found in other examples of twentieth-century Forest of Dean literature.

Dennis Potter (1935-1994), for example, remembered as a child the first time he left the Forest of Dean for any length of time: 'I cried with the kind of sick passion of those who love a place almost as they love a person'[14] (Potter 1960:41). A young Winifred Foley (1914-2009) shared similar feelings when, as a fourteen-year-old, she travelled to London to take up her first job in service. '[W]hat a bloody 'ole to come to', was her first thought on arrival, as recalled in her memoir A Child in the Forest (1974:161). In an interview she gave in 2002, talking about that first night away from the Forest, she revealed that it was a tree that afforded her some solace:

> *My bedroom was a little junk room, and through the window I could see the top of a tree. And that first night I made friends with that tree. And I cried with the tree, being stuck in London, and me being stuck in London, I felt a real affinity with that poor old tree.*
>
> (Foley 2002)

14 Cultural geographer Yi-Fu Tuan used strikingly similar terminology some years later when he wrote that 'To know a place fully means both to understand it in an abstract way and to know it as one person knows another' (Tuan 1975:151).

It is from within the branches of a tree, 'securely lodged in the saddle-like cleft of the upper branches of the tall old oak', that Dennis Potter's young 'Singing Detective' Phillip Marlow delivers his memorable lines, 'When I grow up, I be going to be — a detective' (Potter 1986). The tree for Phillip is his safe heaven, a place for daydreaming, and his god-like viewing platform on the world.

Trees can be imbued then with significant symbolic resonance. As part of nature they can also facilitate opportunities for spiritual renewal too. For the Gloucestershire poet who came to live in the Forest of Dean, F.W. Harvey (1888-1957), writing after World War One, being amongst woodland nature afforded 'pardon', for 'memory of evil done' in his poem 'Absolution', and in another of his poems, 'Lydney to Coleford (By Rail)', the natural woodland surroundings of the journey allow one to 'Discard Life's fret and fear', and to 'Forget — forget — forget' (Harvey 2017:12). For popular Forest poet and author Joyce Latham (1932-2007), writing in the 1980s, the Forest of Dean's woods were too a place to access 'nature's cure, away from crowds, the traffic's angry roar' (Foley et al. 1984). Whilst none of these motifs of trees and woodlands are particular to Forest of Dean literature, they do demonstrate the importance of these Forest writers' deep connection to the woodland surroundings.

A Woodland Sense of Place

As important as the Forest's woodland environment was for these and other Forest poets and authors, the network of people, places, and stories of the Forest of Dean also widely populate their work. As Winifred Foley eloquently put it, as a child at least, she 'took it for granted that hundreds of massive oak trees bordered our village, that the woods were full of ferns' (Foley 1974:14). The Forest's trees and woodlands are in reality only one part of a broader sense of place in which its towns and villages, open wastes, rivers Severn and Wye, streams and valleys, its industrial history, its dialect, free-roaming sheep, and perhaps most significant of all its people, all come together to create a distinctive sense of identity and belonging. In writing about the Forest of Dean in his memoirs, Leonard Clark for example does indeed describe the importance of nature and trees but he is also concerned with his human neighbours and extended family. So too with Foley, her writing focusing on people, their stories and their relationships. The Forest's woodlands are integral to and indivisible from this wider sense of place, but only one part of it. Understanding this, that the Forest of Dean's woodlands are part of a place rather than simply an element of landscape or natural environment, gives an insight into the true strength of feeling evident in the HOOF campaign. As cultural geographers Oakes and Price put it (2005:254), place consists of 'space infused with meaning', and according to Benyon and Hudson (1993 cited in Muir 1999:281) for people attached to particular places they 'come to have socially endowed and shared meanings that touch on all aspects of their lives, helping to shape who they are by virtue of where they are.' In just this way the Forest's woodlands are part of what is 'Forester identity'. As suggested above, Forest of Dean literature both expresses this and is a part of it; part of the complex web of people, place, culture, nature, landscapes and environment that come together to inform this sense of place-specific identity. This being so, what more widely applicable insights — beyond this particular small corner of England — might this highly localised literature offer regarding our complex relationship with trees and woodlands?

The HOOF campaign encompassed people from a wide range of political positons (there was support from both local Conservative and Labour councillors for example) and though there were environmentalists amongst its supporters, one of the leaders of HOOF was a Freeminer, Richard Daniels who, though motivated by the wider concerns, also recognised that a change of regime might threaten the Freeminers' right to mine in the Forest. What united such a variety of people in the campaign was that they shared such a strong sense of identification with the Forest of Dean as a distinctive place, with unfettered access to its woodlands as part of the public forest estate at the heart of it. When that was felt to be threatened it was seen as an assault on the Forest of Dean's sense of itself as a place, and for many in the area their own personal sense of self as Foresters. This, and the image in literature of Foresters throughout history resisting such assaults, offered a deep cultural well from which to draw energy and inspiration for the campaign.

The Forest of Dean, and other 'heritage' forests, are then places that have accrued intense cultural meaning for people. They are cultural landscapes in that they are not only physically shaped by human activity but shaped in terms of their meanings and value to people by their histories, and the telling and retelling of their stories. In recognising their cultural value, we are not discounting their importance too as ecological habitats, or their value as vital natural capital in our response to climate change. However, understanding the distinctive cultural identities tied up with each individual forest means that we understand their true irreplaceable value to the people who live amongst them or come to appreciate them. It is this that helps ensure they will be safeguarded, cared for and enjoyed, and, should they ever come under threat, that they will be robustly defended. As the UK begins to create new forests, and enlists them to help tackle the climate emergency, what the Forest of Dean experience shows us is that the creation of new stories and histories for these new forests as they grow, will allow people to develop a deep feeling of identification with them, and if necessary, should they be threatened, that they will want to robustly defend them.

photo: John F French ▶

NOT FOR SALE
FOR SALE

Space for Imagining installation, Troutbeck Alder, Cumbria (somewhere-nowhere 2017)

III. Artistic responses

Uphold (from below): from One Life to Another

Cherie Sampson

Cherie Sampson has worked for thirty years as an interdisciplinary artist in environmental performance, sculpture and video art. She has exhibited and presented live performances in art-in-nature symposia, art installations and conferences in the U.S., Chile, Cuba, France, Finland, Germany, India, the Netherlands, Norway, Spain, South Korea, UK and other countries. In 2018, the Pori Museum of Art in Finland acquired photographic and video documentation by Sampson of site-based installations and performances for their permanent collection. Sampson is the recipient of many grants including two Fulbright Fellowships, a Finnish Cultural Foundation Grant and university research grants. She is a Professor in the School of Visual Studies at the University of Missouri, USA, dividing her time between teaching and her husband's organic farm near the Mississippi River, where she creates many of her works. Sampson received her MFA degree in Intermedia & Video Art from the University of Iowa, 1997.

ash & soil (Photographic series, 2017. Cherie Sampson, w/ Lisa Wigoda, photographer)

Cherie Sampson: still image from *Uphold*

Uphold (from below): From One Life to Another

Cherie Sampson

> *'I am no longer afraid of*
> *mirrors where I see the*
> *sign of the Amazon…*
> *There is a fine red line*
> *across my chest where*
> *a knife has entered,*
> *but now a branch*
> *winds across the scar*
> *and travels from arm*
> *to heart. Green leaves*
> *cover the branch,*
> *grapes hang there, and*
> *a bird appears. What*
> *grows in me now is vital*
> *and does not cause me*
> *harm…I have designed*
> *my chest with care*
> *given to an illuminated*
> *manuscript…On the*
> *book of my body, I have*
> *permanently inscribed*
> *a tree.'*
>
> —Deena Metzger

Deeply moved by a photograph of Deena Metzger's torso — arms open wide against the sky, surgical scar overlaid with a sinuous leafy tattoo over the site where her right breast had been, I drew an undulating line in pencil around the quote accompanying the image. In the decade of my twenties, I had been reading various books on the subject of goddess revisionism and feminist art, including *The Once & Future Goddess* by Elinor Gadon in which Metzger's image, 'Tree' (1979) appeared. (Gadon 1989)

It was the first time I had ever seen an image of the oncosurgical results of breast cancer. It provoked a visceral response — impressed by Metzger's courage to transform trauma into healing by identifying with the body and spirit of the legendary Amazon warrior and the figure of a tree as archetypal symbol of vitality and new life. I could never have imagined then that my inscription in the book thirty years ago I might one day think of as prescient. I found my marks when the book was recently re-opened in preparation for a talk in which I discussed the influences of early feminist art on my work.

The most impactful of those second-wave feminist artists was Cuban-born, Ana Mendieta, who was the primary reason I pursued my MFA in Intermedia at the University of Iowa, the same program in which Mendieta did her graduate study two decades earlier. An equally iconic image as Metzger's *Tree*, is Mendieta's *Tree of Life*, (1976) in which the artist's body, plastered with a mud and grass mixture, stands against the trunk of a very large deciduous tree at Old Man's Creek just outside of Iowa City. Mendieta's arms are also outstretched, bent at the elbows with palms facing forward in a posture akin to goddess iconography found in many world cultures, from the Afro-Cuban diasporic religion of Santeria, its rituals profoundly informing her work, to the ancient Minoan snake goddesses and many others. Curator, Olga Viso, and other scholars have written about the traumatic experience of Mendieta's childhood exile from the Castro regime on the development of her artistic work and an autobiographical nucleus in much of the body of work Mendieta referred to as 'earth-body sculptures.' (Viso 2004)

> *'I have been carrying on a dialogue between the landscape and the female body (based on my silhouette). I believe this to be a direct result of my having been torn away from my homeland during my adolescence. I am overwhelmed by the feeling of having been cast from the womb (nature). My art is the way I re-establish the bonds that tie me to the universe.'*

Ana Mendieta eventually traveled to Mexico and returned to Cuba to create many her most well-known works. Her work gave me permission to explore my body as an artistic medium, the natural environment as my studio and the performative process as a form of ritual. My childhood experience could not have been more different. My passage 'backwards into [my] mother,' led me to Finland, the home of my maternal ancestors. (Jung 1980) My Finnish great-grandparents homesteaded and made their livelihoods in the boreal landscapes of northern Minnesota, very similar to the forested environments that they left behind in the motherland. I traveled to Finland for the first time on a Fulbright grant in 1998 and a number of subsequent trips over a twenty year period since. Many of my site-based installation, video and performance projects were informed by and created within the cultural and geographical landscapes of Finland. I have never considered these works autobiographical, in the sense of negotiating the circumstances of life experience and identity, but rather emerging from a more primal and ancestral, genetic memory of 'place', 'home', 'origin' and 'self'. (Heddon 2008)

For over 25 years, I have been making video-performances with my naked body embedded in what Finnish environmental aesthetics scholar, Yrjö Sepänmaa, once described as 'found landscapes,' a practice initiated during my graduate studies when I worked in the mixed deciduous woodlands around Iowa City. The works, then and now, are characterized by slow improvisational, site-responsive movement, often mimicking the 'architecture' of the treed spaces in which they take place. The process initially involved minimalist, one-take videos in analog format, but with the advance of digital technologies, the work gradually became more layered and mosaiced. Now, the pacing of my movement in real time is maintained in post-production, however the imagery is often manipulated to represent multiple gestures and selves within the frame. The interplay of the quiet performances with simple visual effects in the completed video invokes a sense of time alternately stilling and stirring, alluding to the temporal in nature. The video-performances have been created throughout the forests and tundra of Finland and Lapland, a sugar cane grove in Cuba and in my own 'backyard.'

✦ ✦ ✦

On a late spring day in 2017, I walked along the paths of our property on a Mississippi river bluff in northeast Missouri in the American Midwest. The paths, tractor-mowed by my husband who is an organic farmer, meander at the edges between woodland and prairie, prairie and orchard, orchard and our pond. Though on this route many times, this particular morning an old cottonwood caught my attention in a way it had never done previously. It appeared figurative, like a majestic forest goddess with massive arms widespread, beckoning me into her embrace. The tree was half-alive, having been struck by lightning at some point — the scars of charring still visible at its base. Later, I took a ladder and climbed up to look inside. Its interior was hollow. But it had weathered the storm and was full of foliage and thriving. When I saw the monumental form of the cottonwood that day, I knew I had to create a video-performance work at the site.

At that time, I was in between treatments for hereditary breast cancer that had been diagnosed in February of that year. In an act of foresight and/or absurdity, I began documenting the cancer experience from the moment the biopsy radiologist informed me of the results, through the subsequent months of treatment and recovery. I turned the camera on myself, compiling a collection of video, audio and photographs, in addition to filing hundreds of medical scan images. The documentation process itself was therapeutic, permitting me to step back and at times, observe the difficulties as if a witness. In a disquieting prescience, my somatic work as a performance artist for nearly three decades inquiring into 'liveness' had set the stage for probing this unknown, scary territory — my body, life, environment and art impacted by cancer.

In her 2008 book, *Autobiography and Performance*, performance theorist, Dierdre Heddon, wrote in the introduction, 'Creative practices are always informed by who we are, as subjects embodied in time and space, with our own cultures and histories (although it is nevertheless to be noted that some endeavors are unproblematically taken to be more universal — less personal — than others).' (Heddon 2008) I have understood that to be true in my art, though thought of my work as leaning more toward the universal than the personal. Autobiographical storytelling, at any point in the narrative spectrum from linear to decentered, always seemed to me to be most poignant when told by artists with compelling stories to share. In collecting all of that documentation, I was cognizant that the material would be the foundation for some kind of artistic work, even a live performance, someday. This was the time to explore autobiographical work and I could attend to a creative endeavor that would be completed in *my future*. In the words of feminist poet, Audre Lorde, translating my cancer experience into artistic work provides an opportunity to 'examine it, put it into perspective, share it and make use of it.' (Lorde 2006)

In addition to documenting the cancer itself, two performance works for the camera were created in the spring and summer of 2017, before my body as I had known it as a woman and worked with it as an artistic medium most of my life, would be forever altered by surgery. These endeavors impelled my 'self as subject, embodied in time and space' much closer to the 'personal' than my work had ever been. The effects of chemo were visible on my hairless body. The first work was created in the cultivated landscape of our apple orchard, the trees in full spring bloom. It was an impromptu series of performance-photographs, sited at the bottom of the orchard where my husband had just conducted a maintenance burn of the orchard floor a couple days prior to the shoot to recycle nutrients, return carbon to the soil and stimulate dormant seed species.

ash & soil (Photographic series, 2017. Cherie Sampson, w/ Lisa Wigoda, photographer)

Dan also dug over sixty holes, awaiting the planting of new apple trees. On a beautiful April afternoon (between the first and second rounds of chemo), a series of interactions with trees and charred land — punctured every few steps with gaping holes — was shot. Naked, I laid on the blackened remains of grasses and clover and lowered my bald head into a dark crater. Cognizant that the process was at once an intimate ritual as well as the making of a work of art, I contemplated the ash as representative of renewal and the deep hole as the void of the unknown and a promise of new life.

The second performance was created in the woodland west of the orchard with the cottonwood tree, that would later be completed and edited as the 'Uphold (from below)' video-performance work. Over a several-day period, just ten days prior to my impending surgery, a series of improvisational performances were shot with and around the gracious tree. I had just completed the last round of chemotherapy and was to undergo a bilateral mastectomy to remove the cancer and as a measure to prevent future malignancies. Without prophylactic surgery, my lifetime risk for additional breast (and other cancers) would remain exceptionally high as a carrier of the BRCA genetic mutation.

A simple platform was constructed of wood found on site at the base of the tree to elevate my body slightly from ground level. As characteristic of my work, I set up a tripod, also on an elevated platform, to remain stationary for the shoots and to capture a single vantage point, with the cottonwood's limbs spanning one edge of the frame to the other. I pressed my body and breasts up against her course bark, feeling the textures of the forest like I had done in countless environmental performances for the last opportunity before surgery would render my chest with

◀ *ash & soil* (Photographic series, 2017. Cherie Sampson, w/ Lisa Wigoda, photographer)

little to no sensation. I stretched and torqued my body in multiple movements and postures while standing on the platform, mimicking the limbs and embodying the physical, cellular and energetic manifestations of her life force. Barefoot on the woodland floor, I slowly paced toward and away from the tree and around her circumference, reaching to touch the trunk, to look up into the canopy full of verdant green. With the assistance of a ladder (and an extra set of hands), I climbed into the tree to be cradled high in the crook of each limb.

During production, I anticipated that these various performance shots would be edited later into an image consonant with magic realism in which the multiple appearances of my body represent the liminality of the self between states of wholeness and illness, being bound to and transcending the earth, at the juxtaposition of life and death. Just as the hollowed, but living tree, the woodlands and nature itself are in a perpetual dance of evolution and dissolution, so was (and still is) my body and our collective human body. Cells are renewed approximately every seven years, yet once 'cast from the womb' we are ultimately breathing evanescence. In the completed '*Uphold (from below)*' video, the figurative apparitions co-exist and progress intermittently through presence and absence, absence and presence. Each state of being is a witness to the other/s. The 'witness that speaks of having been there' appears a little over half-way through the video when a glimpse of the post-surgical body is revealed for a few moments. (Frank 2013) A few months after surgery in the fall, leaves drifting to the ground, I returned to the site to perform again, body changed, but cancer-free.

✦ ✦ ✦

There is a growing field of integrative oncology in which combined modes of healing, including mind-body, movement, music and art therapies, yoga, visualization, ritual and spiritual practice, herbal, botanical and naturopathic supplementation, CBD and many others, are used in combination with conventional oncology to create personalized programs of 'anticancer' treatment. (Society for Integrative Oncology). These interdisciplinary evidence-based approaches address multiple dimensions of a patient's experience from the management of drug side effects to wellbeing and quality of life. A visit to a park, natural environment or simply exposure to fresh air, however one may be able to access these spaces, has regenerative and healing potency for any patient struggling with illness. The conventional medical field broadly recognizes the value of such activities, but they usually aren't part of a cancer patient's comprehensive anti-cancer treatment plan, as they often are when a patient is being treated by an oncologist whose practice involves integrative methods.

In a segment on National Public Radio's *Morning Edition* program in July 2017, correspondent Allison Aubrey reported on her participation in a 'forest bathing' adventure led by Forest Therapy guide, Melanie Choukas-Bradley, that took place along the banks of the Potomac River in Washington D.C. 'Forest bathing' is an approximate translation of the Japanese, Shinrin-yoku, a practice named by the Japanese Ministry of Agriculture, Forestry and Fisheries in the early 1990's to define a practice in which one visits a forest, or other natural space, with the intention of absorbing its environment holistically through all senses. Aubrey described,

'As we passed through a stand of pawpaw trees, we touched the bark. We smelled the black walnuts, which give off a lovely citrus fragrance. We got a little shower of ripe mulberries, too...

It took me a few minutes to clear out the clutter in my brain, and tune in to the natural world...

After I opened my eyes, the green looked a lot greener. And I began to see things I hadn't

noticed before: the flutter of birds, the ripple of the water, the swaying of trees.'

Aubrey continues with a discussion of research on the health benefits of forest bathing that found stress and blood pressure reduction, positive increases in parasympathetic nerve activity, and immune system improvement. She cited a Japanese study that discovered that the inhalation of phytoncides (tree-derived compounds) reduced stress hormones in the participants and enhanced the activity of NK, or 'natural killer' cells. NK cells are a form of cytotoxic lymphocytes (one type of white blood cell in our immune system) that respond quickly to virus-infected cells as well as play a vital role in tumor immunosurveillance by actuating the death of malignant tumor cells. Simply stated, deep breaths taken in a forest abundant with phytoncide compounds may have cancer-fighting, cancer-prevention benefits.

I partook in many integrative modalities myself during treatment, digging up echinacea root from the prairie at the orchard's edge to make tinctures, hiking through our deciduous forests to hunt morels in the spring, chanterelles in the summer and medicinal turkey tail whenever available. I will never know what combined therapies and/or singular modalities, alongside the three-drug cocktail of chemotherapy, may have contributed (or not) to the 'pCR' (pathological Complete Response), indicating the eradication of disease in my left breast. Of all the complimentary methods that I used, continuing to do my artistic work, engaging my body physically through yoga, dance, improvisational movement and time spent in and among the trees in my 'forest bathing' (whether on a walk or in an purposeful performative process), are those that I believe had the most rehabilitative and healing impact. These practices were, and still are, at the center of my personal integrative medicine.

Not one to participate much in the ubiquitous 'performance of the self' via social media, it took me many months after the diagnosis to go public with the cancer. When I finally posted a couple images of the orchard and cottonwood tree shoots on Facebook, a friend and ovarian cancer survivor, commented: 'Every. Single. One. Of us who has been with this disease is validated, loved and to a certain extent, freed by this image.' If my images have any capacity to be freeing to a viewer, it is because I was freed from my own limitations in the act of being fully present in nature while performing improvisationally, a 'discipline of spontaneity and awareness' that involves 'a process by which the evolving nature of the world around and within the artist is revealed by their actions.' (Steinman 1995) The environment of the deciduous woodland encompassing the presence of the cottonwood was the evolving world that informed the revelation of my actions. In addition to the dance with the cottonwood, I did a series of improvisational movement sessions for the camera in my barn studio in which I 're-performed' various events and activities that I had endured in the cancer experience. Those movement phrases have become some of the elements, along with the video and audio documentation

aforementioned, of 'every.single.one', an autobiographical theatrical solo performance (in-progress) depicting my experience with hereditary breast cancer.

In his extensive tome, *Performance Studies: A Critical Introduction*, renowned performance studies scholar and pioneer, Richard Schechner, writes about the interrelationship of ritual and performance: 'Performances — whether in the performing arts, sports, popular music, or everyday life — consist of ritualized gestures and sounds' and rituals, when transforming the life of an individual (or collective) permanently, can be referred to as 'rites of passage — from one life role or status to another.' (Schechner 2006) Artists invariably understand that many aspects of our practice, whatever expressions they may take, involve ritualized gestures that actualize the works of art. Unless an artist is creating a work from within and according to the canons of a specific religious or sacred tradition, Schechner would likely define the artist's work (particularly in the west in the present time) as associated with everyday life and activity, therefore secular. The countless video performances I have made with my body for many years in a myriad of forest and woodland landscapes are certainly characterized, aesthetically and materially, by the rituals and repetitive actions that I employ, from in-situ production to post-production. While I experience the creative process as reverent — new perspectives always opening and limitations transcended, I have not considered the deliberate actions of art-making as life-changing transpersonal rites of passage, that is, until preparing to do the cottonwood performance that would become the '*Uphold (from below)*' video.

The moment I saw the cottonwood tree in the spring of 2017 as a site to create the final work with my body as I had lived in and with it for the entirety of my life, I was cognizant that the performance was to be a significant rite of passage. The performance action would mark one stage of life to another, though at that time, I had no idea what new phase of life (or death? with a type of breast cancer consistently described as 'most aggressive' and 'deadly') might be awaiting me. Schechner describes the essential phase in the rite of passage as the 'liminal — a period of time when a person is 'betwixt' and 'between'' where the work of transformation occurs and out of which new realities and identities may emerge. The limen is an architectural feature — a threshold, rim or physical delineation of some form connecting one space and another,

> *'a passageway between places rather than a place in itself. In ritual and aesthetic performances,*
>
> *the thin space of the limen is expanded into a wide space both actually and conceptually.*
>
> *What usually is just a 'go-between' becomes the site of the action...It is enlarged in*
>
> *time and space yet retains its peculiar quality of passageway or temporariness.'*

In most of my video-performance work with a stationary camera and frontal vantage-point, the environment in which I am situated is the stage and the totality of the image, including the four edges of the rectangular frame, the proscenium. In '*Uphold (from below)*', the limen in its physical manifestation, was the tree — the wide horizontal span of her two largest limbs akin to the lintel, elevated above and extending outward from the trunk. (Architecturally, lintels have been traditionally comprised

Performance photograph: Cherie Sampson, w/Lisa Wigoda, photographer of either wood or stone.) The main axis of the tree was purposefully composed to be centered in the image. While my multiple bodies in shifting translucence walk along the ground, crouch and lie in the branches, most of the performance action takes place at the trunk, the interior of which is completely hollow, empty. Standing parallel and against the axis, I extend outward and upward, alternately recoiling. Just prior to the revealing of the mastectomy scar, that only occupies a few moments in the complete sixteen minute video, I turn around to face the camera, arms crossed over chest, then slowly curl in on myself. Like the universal axis mundi, the cottonwood trunk was the site of opening and passing between — from one state of being into another, from the terrestrial realm of the living to the underworld of malignancy…

And back again.

Schechner depicts two stages of the ritual liminal experience: First, the individual engaged in the ritual enters into a state of vulnerability, where they become 'nothing,' open to change. They enter a realm that is neither here nor there, at the center of a passage from one self to another, and for a time, without identity. In the second phase, 'persons are inscribed with their new identities and initiated into their new powers. There are many ways to accomplish the transformation. Persons may take oaths, learn lore, dress in new clothes, perform special actions, be scarred, circumcised, or tattooed.' (Schechner 2006)

When returning to the woodland site in September, three months post-surgery to do another series of performances with the tree, I was 'dressed' in a new body, cancerous tissue carved out of the breast 'pockets,' replaced by silicone. Nipples were removed, each breast bearing a vertical scar from the incisions made to open them up. I covered my body in a green-gray clay harvested nearby from an opening in the earth that the deer like to graze. Around the base of the tree, I found chunks of charred wood, not from the lightning strike that occurred at an unidentifiable time, but from a controlled burn in the woods that my husband had carried out a couple years previous. Lightly wetting the black carbon on a small bit of bark, I drew a line over each suture, following the dimensions, temporary tattoos inscribed over permanent marks of change.

Unlike Deena Metzger, I did not make a permanent inscription of a tree branch on my chest. I now have four scars — two on each breast, from additional reconstructive surgeries, as well as several small sutures from a prophylactic bilateral salpingo-oophorectomy to remove the high risk of ovarian cancer BRCA genetic mutation carriers also have. These are the signatures of my vulnerability and transformation, ultimately symbolizing the impermanence of the body and the transience of life. Instead, I inscribed my body on the tree, and in the environment in which it exists, within the fleeting moments of an ephemeral performance. (Rosenberg 2012) What remains of that performance-ritual is the simulacra of a digitized moving image, transfigured into a video artwork, a description of its process chronicled in the pages of this book.

Metzger, now a recognized poet, storyteller, healer and teacher is still alive and 84 years old at the time of this writing. I may live into my eighties as well; I may not. Perhaps the wounded, hollowed cottonwood, a fast-growing species having a similar lifespan to humans, 70–100 years, will outlive me. I still walk by, visit the tree and forage mushrooms on the ground where she stands regally, where the chanterelle mycelia have been spreading abundantly since the spring of 2017. The platform I built at the base of the tree to raise my body is still solid and situated, but I am unlikely to ever do a performance there again. For a short time, I was held within and passed through the threshold of her embrace; one state of being when I was immersed within her, another state when the time came to be released. We continue, the cottonwood and I, each on our own evolutionary pathways, aware — one possibly a little more self-referentially than the other — that whatever we endure, rough bark and soft flesh are coequally momentary.

Direction, performance and post-production by Cherie Sampson; Musical composition and arrangement by Charles Gran

still from *Uphold (from below)*

Ash Tree

Chris Poundwhite

Chris Poundwhite is a poet concerned with ecology, climate, and the human relationship to land and the non-human. His poems have appeared in a number of journals and magazines, including the Reliquiae supplement, Longshore Drift, and Otata. He teaches ecopoetry courses & workshops through Go to the Pine, and works on poetry commissions that fall within his spheres of interest. Chris also co-curates SALT, an annual festival of place & environment based in Folkestone, Kent.

Ash Tree

In so few strides I circumambulate the tree, its centuries
centred in rings of heartwood, sapwood — the circularity
of years, charted seasons, bud & leaf-fall, bloom & icicle

Myth in its fibres, wood made word; the fissured bark
of Yggdrasil, world-tree, tree of Ask — the first man, tree
of manna, foe feller, child healer, known by eye & fingertip

Here, see the fine and delicate strata of its leaves, how they gift
sun's light one to another, on and on down through themselves,
filter & diffuse it, release of form & structure, release as gesture

✦

Chalara, the trees' killer, gets to work in summer:
spore to leaf, hypha to stoma, appressorium splits
the epidermis, fungus threads the pith, xylem & phloem

In months leaves wither, stems drop, branches purple, suffer
lesions. Crown slides low, turns winter-brittle off season.
Disease strips whole hills of trees, makes place memory

I cannot know the tragedy of moths & lichens, their soft
dusty bodies, their searching mouths, their ecosystem
syphoned out of other, larger, ecosystems, last generations

of their species. I only know how names on maps — Askrigg,
Askham, ashford — will slip their meaning, trip the tongue,
the way word follows world, & how forest light will alter

Tracing paper
£9.50

Naomi Hart is an artist whose work looks at human interaction with the environment, especially themes around elements, journey and memory. Her work ranges from intricate drawings and paintings to large-scale installations. Naomi was Leverhulme artist in residence with glaciologists from Sheffield University and the University of Norway in Svalbard and exhibited the work at the Royal Geographical Society in London. She has been artist in residence with scientists and researchers in Terra Nova National Park Canada, outback Australia (Kimberley and Tasmania), on a wooden boat sailing to Greenland, and with ExeterMarine and The Galapagos Conservation Trust. She was commissioned to create an outdoor aerial sculpture for The Crown Estate and has work in the permanent collections of National Museums Scotland and Exeter Cathedral.

Jenny Pickerill is Professor of Environmental Geography and Head of Department of Geography at Sheffield University, England. Her research focuses on inspiring grassroots solutions to environmental problems and in hopeful and positive ways in which we can change social practices. She has published 3 books (Cyberprotest; Anti-war Activism; Eco-Homes) and over 30 articles on themes around eco-housing, eco-communities, social justice and environmentalism. She is currently completing a book on Eco-communities: Living Together Differently.

◀ workshop at Evolving the Forest (photo: Oliver Raymond-Barker)

Old growth Forests of Takayna/ Tarkine in north-west Tasmania

Naomi Hart & Jenny Pickerill

Stopwatch (Naomi Hart, 2017)

Forest Time

Images and sound[1]: Naomi Hart; text: Jenny Pickerill and Naomi Hart

Temporality, our relationship to time, is shaped by culture, nature, economics and history. Time is a form of social change. Time is non-linear, it is unstable, and continuously being made. Time has multiple rhythms, continuity and moments of discontinuity. This non-linearity can lead to chaotic outcomes. A small change in, for example river flow speed, can become amplified to trigger a response out of proportion, a 'jump'. Therefore nature has multiple temporalities; plants, seasons, light and climate all create and shape time. Nature does not have a stable equilibrium state or a moment where it is perfectly balanced, rather it has multiple stable states which nature alternates, or oscillates, between.

We have been exploring time in the forest in the Tarkine, an old growth forest in NW Tasmania, Australia. We have explored these multiple temporalities: the tensions of time between the slowly evolving trees, organisms and ecosystems, the carbon cycling through the system, charcoal and ashes nourishing the new growth, and the rapid human incursions as destructive and protective forces. The art was made in place and in timed moments, deep in the forest. It evolved through a process of sitting uncomfortably, becoming part of the landscape, being absorbed into the drawing and the forest, yet utterly alien to it, not belonging. We explore these temporalities through a series of timed, blind drawings drawn through graphite paper onto eco paper, and sound recordings of the ancient forest.

We are not in Britain, we are in Australia. Not mainland Australia, but an island off the southern shores: Tasmania. Not mainland Tasmania, but an island to the south: Bruny Island.

I am making myself do timed drawing - not setting a time to complete it, but letting the clock run until I think it's finished.

My phone counts the seconds, minutes, hours that I take to study the tree, the light, the forest.

I make marks, sometimes drawing through graphite paper onto ecopaper: carbon on carbon on tree. Blind drawings, not knowing where it will go, where I am in the picture.

Bruny Island, Adventure Bay. The first European to sight the bay was explorer Abel Tasman in 1642, though it was already inhabited, and Captain James Cook anchored the HMS Resolution here during his second voyage to the Pacific.

Apparently you can still see the stump of the tree where he tied the boats.

The anchorage was excellent for resupplying vessels with fresh water, plenty of fish and

1 Listen at https://artdotearth.org/media/Forest-Time_Naomi-Hart-2017.mp3

31.12.16, 7.54.22, *Adventure Bay*, blind drawing through carbon on ecopaper

'a great many gum trees and of a vast thickness and height, one of which measured in circumference 26 feet'.

In 1798, Adventure Bay became the site of whaling and timber stations.

Recording the sound of the brook, feeling the warmth, concentrating happily on the trees, the noises, the joy of being here; only after several minutes do I notice and recognise the land leeches charging up my boots and towards my ankles. Frantic stamping and flicking, my heart races, I remember I'm in Australia, where nothing seems benign.

✦ ✦ ✦

We are in woods further into Bruny Island, dry eucalypts, a strong wind.

Hidden in the trees, a wedge-tailed eagle sitting unperturbed on a high branch.

The sound makes me think of bushfires, the crackling of flames, fanned by the wind.

Bushfires reducing in a matter of hours what has taken hundreds/thousands of years to grow.

We burn coal to speed up work -
using something which has taken millennia to create and burning it in minutes to make our lives go faster.

Edge (Naomi Hart, 2017)

The burning is destruction, but in Australia it is also rebirth. Natural events, mimicked and controlled by the local inhabitants for more than 40,000 years to provide food for the animals they hunt.

Birth, growth, death, decay, rebirth (Naomi Hart, 2017)

✦ ✦ ✦

North West Tasmania, Takayna / Tarkine, old growth forest and partially protected area.

07.01.17, 15.45.89, Tarkine, Whyte River Track graphite on ecopaper
(Naomi Hart, 2017)

In many parts logging trucks operate 24 hours a day. There are walking tracks through thick forest to the totemic trees where protestors fought the logging concerns to protect the giant forest. Thick moss now grows on fallen trunks that are as thick as I am tall.

Eucalyptus regnans, known also as mountain ash, swamp gum, stringy gum, Tasmanian oak, is the tallest flowering plant and one of the tallest trees in the world, second only to the redwoods of North America. Many of them have been logged, including those higher than trees of any species alive today. One tree of 132 metres was recorded.

07.01.17 (b), 49.03.57, Tarkine Telegraph, graphite on ecopaper, (Naomi Hart, 2017)

They regenerate by seed, which are released by heat. They also need light, so a mature tree canopy will prevent this. A large bushfire can kill all the trees in a forest, but prompt a massive release of seed, which takes advantage of the nutrients in the ash.

Mature *Eucalyptus regnans* forests have been found to store more carbon than any other forest known.

A burned remnant on mainland Australia as a living tree had a DBH, or diameter at breast height, of nearly 11 metres or 35 feet.

The current title is 77 metres high (253 feet) and nearly 7 metres, or 23 feet in girth.

I draw, concentrating on the light, the shade, the layers, the interwoven and criss-crossing lines. The more I look, the more species I see, the more detail. Drawing makes me see things properly, I am lost in the moment, slowing down time, not noticing it pass.

06.01.17, 23.41.85, Tarkine, Pieman-Arthur, graphite on ecopaper (Naomi Hart, 2017)

Beside me my collaborator and long-suffering friend paces up and down, thumping the ground with her feet to ward off the deadly tiger snakes, which we have already had two close encounters with that morning.

'Ten minutes' I say; she knows it will be twenty-five.

Time sitting in the space, hearing growth around me.

The time the tree has taken to grow.

The time, immeasurable to us, which this forest has taken to form.

Time, cut down, washed away, washed ashore like matchsticks, the size of trees.

The word 'Time' probably comes from Old English, 'tima', from 'dimen', related to 'Tide' and meaning to divide up.

The word 'Timber' comes from Old English 'Zimmer', a room, or Old High German 'Zimbar', a wooden structure and the Indo-European base 'dem' or 'dema', meaning to join together, to build.

Seconds, minutes, days, years, millennia.

Birth, growth, death, decay, rebirth.

Life offers many opportunities, they often piggyback each other.

Relocating to Scotland in 2003, I learnt to walk in the Cairngorms and explore further afield by foot, discovering the joys of solo travel. Edinburgh, intended as a three year stay, extended another ten years in Oxford. Here I embarked on an MA in Social Sculpture at Oxford Brookes University Studies underpinned by the question 'what's hidden, ignored, denied?' a line of enquiry that led to projects in Italy and Iran examining historic and contemporary waterscapes. In Oxford I also acquired my first bicycle. A latecomer to the art of cycling, I fell off and broke my elbow almost immediately (the first of many falls). Despite the injuries, a passion for cycle touring was ignited.

Raised in the tradition of Penelope the weaver, Penelope Pitstop was always whispering in the margins, beckoning. So, embracing an itinerant lifestyle, with fellow adventurer, Roberto, I began cycling towards Australia. Writing has become an instrument for examining and sharing these experiences.

Evolving the Forest: Encountering Trees (and what they tell us)

Marita Davidson

Evolving the Forest: Encountering Trees (and what they tell us)

Marita Davidson MA (Social Sculpture) Oxford, UK

Introduction

The desert may seem a strange place to begin thinking about Evolving the Forest but the absence of trees, of shade, of water, and a lack of respite from the relentless sun focuses the realisation of our dependence upon trees. In June 2019, just as 'Evolving the Forest' is convening in Dartington, I arrive in Darwin: three years and 30,000km after cycling out of Oxford with my partner, Roberto. The next stage of our journey: 4,000 km traverse from Darwin to Melbourne, includes one of the longest stretches of desert that we cycle. We reach the Central Desert of Australia, having cycled through Iran's *Dasht-e-Kavir* (Great Salt Desert), the Steppes of Kazakhstan and Tajikistan's Pamir Plateau.

Fig. 1. Map of the route cycled in Australia

I Darwin to Alice Springs

Approaching Alice Springs, in central Australia, Tjoritja (the MacDonnell Range) stretches east-west across the land. It rises from the seemingly endless, flat expanse of red ochre, typical of the desert here. In August when overnight temperatures can drop to below zero, the western light inflects the landforms with violet and blue shades. Cool tones that suggest eucalyptus trees, shade, and water holes. We approach the landscapes depicted by Arrente man, Albert Namatjira, whose watercolour paintings capture the distinct clarity of light and colour that are characteristic of this part of the world. It seems ironic that watercolour is an apt medium to describe a thirsty land.

Gum tree (Photo: Lazydaz | Dreamstime.com (reproduced under license))

Fig 2. Australia Post First Day Cover, 2002, commemorating the centenary of the birth of Albert Namatjira. © Australia Post (by permission)

'By the 1950s, reproductions of Namatjira's work adorned the walls of many Australian middle-class living rooms'[1] (this was at a time when the white Australia policy was yet to be dismantled)[2]. The distribution of those images meant that early tourist itineraries to the Red Centre were likely to include a stop, 16 km west of Alice Springs, at the site where Namatjira made several paintings of twin ghost gums (*Corymbia aparrerinja*). The National Gallery of Australia describes his landscapes as 'iconic images synonymous with the Australian outback.'[3] His watercolours 'challenged misconceptions of a lifeless inland by presenting the flora and ancient geography in an ever-changing palette of tone and light'[4]. Such acknowledgement was not always forthcoming, with some Directors of state galleries refusing to display his work.

Divergent ideologies within the art establishment saw conservative landscape artists such as Han Heysen appraise his work. In 1937 Heysen wrote to his daughter Nora about:

> *...a brilliantly clever Black at Hermannsburg who has taken to watercolours and within two weeks of watching him (Battarbee) paint, he turned out some remarkable watercolours, with good colour and a fine feeling for light. (Hans Heyson quoted in Mendelssohn 2014)*

The modernists, however, disregarded him. Either ignoring him (dubious of his popularity and antagonistic towards those who championed him) or dismissing his works as inauthentic: 'Namatjira's art has nothing of the original outlook — it is purely Europeanised.' (Charles Lloyd Jones quoted *ibid.*). (Similar criticism of inauthenticity was levelled against the Papunya Tula artists' use of acrylic paint in the 1970's.) Depending on one's perspective, his gum trees were considered clichéd or iconic, his colours garish or vibrant.

---

1 https://www.nma.gov.au/explore/features/indigenous-rights/civil-rights/albert-namatjira-citizenship/expansion-folder/from-ward-of-the-state-to-australian-citizen retrieved 22/08/2020

2 The Immigration Restriction Bill, 1901, which enacted the white Australia policy was one of the first acts of parliament after federation. It was not completely eliminated until the introduction of policies like the Racial Discrimination Act 1975 by the Whitlam government. https://www.aph.gov.au/about_parliament/parliamentary_departments/parliamentary_library/pubs/bn/1011/indigenousaffairs1 retrieved 22/08/2020

3 https://nga.gov.au/namatjira/ retrieved 22/08/2020

4 *ibid*

In 1984, when the Araluen Arts Centre opened in Alice Springs, its inaugural exhibition presented a retrospective of Namitjira's work. Highlighting the exhibition's role in reassessing attitudes towards his art, *When the Wind Changed* traces the conflicting attitudes towards his work. Of particular importance to this reassessment is the experience of viewing the work in context:

> *...seeing Namatjira in his own landscape makes you realise how good he is. He got two essential aspects of the landscape absolutely right: the cleanness of the air and the clarity of the light. Unlike most white artists painting the landscape of Central Australia, he didn't melodramatise it. (Patrick McCaughey quoted ibid.)*

Our departure from Alice Springs takes us past the site of the twin ghost gums. It is disheartening to learn that they no longer stand, having been 'felled by fire' in 2013. Media reports cite arson as the cause of the fire[5]. 'An appallingly tragic act of cultural vandalism,'[6] the trees were found burned just as they had been approved for inclusion on the state heritage register.

II Alice Springs to Watarrka

Namatjira Drive runs parallel to the Larapinta Trail, a 223 km walking track in Tjoritja/ West MacDonnell National Park. The

Fig 4. Ghost Gums, Watarrka National Park

Fig 5. Ghost Gums (detail)

landscapes depicted by Albert Namatjira lie all around here. A series of commemorative stamps, issued in 2002[7] to mark the centenary of his birth, show works that he painted at Simpson's Gap (where we camp the first night and hear the haunting chorus of dingoes moving along the dried river bed), Mt Hermannsburg (close to his birthplace at the Hermannsburg

7 In 1968 Namatjira's image had appeared on the 'Famous Australians' series of Australian postage stamps. He is said to be the first named Aboriginal person to be portrayed on an Australian stamp. A 1952 stamp of Gwoya Tjungurrayi (known by his nickname One Pound Jimmy) had been released with the title Aborigine.

Lutheran Mission), Glen Helen Country, and Mt Sonder (the highest point on the Larapinta trail). Just after Redbank Gorge, the last access point to the trail, also the last place to buy provisions, the road turns 90° south and after 52 km runs out of asphalt. Here begins the Meerenie Loop, 125 km of unsealed road plus a bit further (35km) before the next supply stop. Wild camels and horses, buffle grass and cattle are all evidence of introduced species that degrade this pristine desert environment. On day three an over-confident driver passes us, towing a caravan. No doubt he'll be surprised to arrive and discover that it no longer has a door!

Most tourists come to Watarrka (Kings Canyon) for the spectacular Rim Walk that winds its ways around the canyon. Signage in the car park reminds people:

> *Watarrka, as with all National Parks is a protected area. Disturbance of plants, animals and natural features is an offence. It is prohibited to: break branches for fly swats; write or etch names on rocks; remove or displace the natural landscape i.e. rocks or flora.*[8]

The online information pack for schools specifically cautions that 'unfortunately school groups are among the worst offenders when it comes to damage to the Park's environment. Graffiti on the rocks, building stone cairns, littering, vandalising trees and breaking rocks are all offences under the Territory Parks and Wildlife Act.'[9]

On my first foray into the canyon, arriving too late in the day to tackle the exposed rim walk, I take the gentler route along Kings Creek instead. Towards the end of this walk, where the sandstone face of the canyon towers abruptly ahead, I pass a ghost gum wrapped in hessian bandages to protect and heal the wounds gouged into its bark. Nearby signage documents the initials that have been incised into the living dermis of the tree. For the Anangu people (the traditional owners who jointly manage the park) the ghost gums are sacred. The incisions disrespect the Anangu people and the natural environment for which they are guardians.

In a chapter entitled Anima Mundi, James Hillman describes how 'spontaneously, the human hand makes its mark, insisting on personalized messages, as human nature everywhere immediately chalks its initials on monuments' (Hillman 1990). He writes that such 'defacing of monuments actually put(s) a face on an impersonal wall or oversized statue. The human hands seem so want to touch and leaves its touch…'(*ibid.*)

Although writing about alienation in the city, his use of the words 'chalk' and 'touch' conjure images of aboriginal ochre hand prints found on rock surfaces, more than the aerosol spray-cans used for 'tagging' in urban environments.

Aboriginal rock paintings are often busy surfaces, active with images of ancestral spirits from the dreamtime, non-human animals and representations of human figures sharing space, sometimes overlapping with stenciled hands. Located in concealed places, these sites protect the fragile materiality of the paintings whose thin layers of iron oxide impregnate the rock. Sacred sites, visited for ceremonial purposes indicate an ongoing connection to place. The gesture inherent in this mark making speaks

8 http://www.macdonnellranges.com/Watarrka-National-Park-visitors-information-guide.htm retrieved 15/07/2020

9 https://nt.gov.au/__data/assets/pdf_file/0010/359083/watarrka-np-info-for-school-groups.pdf retrieved 15/07/2020

of connection the graffiti signals 'owning': naming being an unmistakable act of claiming possession as is evident throughout the entire colonial history of Australia, beginning with the fallacious declaration of terra nullius.

The act of tagging or carving initials into trees seems to arise from an urge for existential assertion, not only I AM but also I AM HERE and I AM HERE NOW. They are marks that express the transience of a specific individual passing through rather than an act embedded in a cultural context that signals an ongoing connection to place.

These trees are protected.

If the graffiti detailed above is viewed as an act of vandalism, this raises an awkward question regarding Aboriginal dendroglyphs (the complex geometrical patterns, incised and painted onto trees). In both instances markings are carved into the living tree. From the perspective of the tree perhaps there is no difference.

For both Indigenous peoples and white colonials, trees represented a resource: settlers saw the forest as timber to be extracted and land to be cleared for agriculture and grazing. For them 'trees were mere impedimenta to agriculture.'[10] Long cites early settler publications that 'detail the most efficient ways to clear a forest, including the practice of ringbarking. The aim was to kill the tree with a minimum of effort, thus increasing the carrying capacity of the land for pasture grasses (Long 2003). The practice of ringbarking involved 'cutting of a concentric groove or the removal of a concentric strip around the base of a tree trunk, which generally kills the central bole and any higher limbs;…It invariably kills the tree.' (*ibid.*) Long notes that 'in general, the historical European use of bark was highly destructive to the environment, whereas deliberate care appears to have been taken by Aboriginal people to manage and preserve the resource for future use'. (*ibid.*)

Aboriginal scarred trees indicate where bark has been harvested for functional use. Dendroglyphs, differing from these, 'are a form of visual expression that reflects affiliation with the land and special cultural association with the landscape and its resources.' (Buhrich 2015) The intricate geometrical markings bear witness to cultural practices embedded in place. The trees themselves are considered sacred beings, and afforded respect. 'A prominent tree can represent an Ancestor as being still present in the landscape' (Hercus 2012).

Cultural pillaging saw dendroglyphs removed from the sites where they stood as markers for graves and bora grounds (ceremonial sites), also serving as cultural repositories for Indigenous knowledge. 'Only the carved sections of the trees were taken, both whole trunks and fragments.' (Purcell 2001). In her text for the exhibition: Carved Trees *Aboriginal Cultures of Western NSW*, Purcell includes correspondence between Lindsay Black (amature anthropologists who sought to document and collect Aboriginal material culture) and Dr Winterbotham (University of Queensland) regarding the procurement of two trees. Transactional in nature, the correspondence unsurprising lacks any acknowledgment of indigenous voices. The dendroglyphs are viewed as cultural artefacts to be preserved and possessed. The connection between place,

10 *ibid*

sacred object and the people that created them is entirely absent. In her poem Seeing the *Carved Trees Exhibition* (Kennedy 2011), Gayle Kennedy addresses this cultural theft:

Did giving them these cold, hard words
Calling them the tree carvings of a primitive people,
Make it easier for the scientist,
The anthropologist, the land coveter
To rip them from their belonging place?
To destroy the warriors' classrooms or
Desecrate the graves of our lost ancestors?

III Watarrka to Uluru

After three days of rest, showers and cold beers we are ready to move on. 166km on the paved Luritja Rd delivers us to the Lasseter Hwy intersection. We camp 5km before the turn off, footfall of wild camels passing in the night. Rounding a bend the next morning, Mt Connor looms unexpected, in the distance, mistaken by many for Uluru. We are still 138km from Yulara, the campsite outside Uluru-Kata Tjuta National Park. The ride allows for a slow approach over a couple of days with a

Fig 5. Watarrka National Park, NT

Fig. 6 Cycling the Meerenie Loop near Tnorala Conservation Reserve, NT

mounting sense of anticipation.

The last time I was here, the nation was focused on the disappearance of a baby, taken by a dingo from the family tent. This time we enter into the media affray surrounding the imminent closure of the climb that scales Uluru. In the 1960s a

300-metre-long stretch of chains, attached to 138 steel posts was installed to facilitate climbing. They are to be removed after the closure. For the Anangu people, the traditional owners, Uluru refers not only to the monolith but also encompasses the surrounding area. It is a sacred place containing several sacred sites. The planned closure has been announced two years earlier and in a fervor of 'last chance' opportunity to 'climb the rock' tourist numbers have soared over the recent school holidays. In the communal kitchen at Yulara campground, talk revolves around who has climbed and who is planning to. A group of French school students moan in unison at the prospect of a 5am wake up the following day. They are planning to see the sunrise before they climb. An Italian alpinist (one of the top two in the world: I know this because his autographed book lies on the table) has travelled here with his young son whose ascent earlier in the day he has timed and is proudly discussing. As a 16 year old I made the climb, ignorant of the cultural disrespect inherent in doing so. Forty years later I circle Uluru by foot, taking time to stop at waterholes and rock overhangs protecting ochre drawings. It is astonishing.

In the Uluru-Kata Tjuta Cultural Centre I read about sorry rocks: souvenirs of stone and sand that have been collected by tourists in the past and later returned with accompanying letters of regret. There is a database where these notes are documented. In response to these acts of remorse a statement reads:

Uluru is Aboriginal land

> *Anangu the traditional owners of Uluru, believe that rocks and sand belong at Uluru, not in the homes or pockets of visitors. Under Tjukurpa, the Anangu law governing life and land, there are consequences for disrespecting the law of the land. Anangu recognise no curse associated with removing rocks and sand but refer to the respect that should be shown to the land, especially as a visitor.*[11]

From the Mala car park, every person who now climbs Uluru passes an information board, translated into seven languages. It reads: 'please don't climb' and in wording similar to the above text, explains why. Known variously as Ayers Rock, The Rock and Uluru, names that signify possession, object and place.

IV Coober Pedy to Parachilna

From Coober Pedy, I set out alone. The road starts well with a tailwind galvanising my resolve to ride this stretch solo. I cross into the 'Forbidden Zone', where military exercises are scheduled in ten days time. The people I encounter on this stretch are helpful and encouraging, checking whether I need anything, those that stop mostly offer cool water, always welcome. By day four I am expected in Williams Creek. News and gossip are conveyed along the 'bush telegraph' by radio. Passing vehicles kitted out for the realities of isolated rural homesteads or 4WD adventurers heading to the outback, stay connected in this way. I must be a peculiar sight. I set up my last camp before reaching the township. A ute drives out to offer me a ride: 'heard you were out here…we can chuck your bike in the back'. I am grateful for their concern but explain that I will camp here the night and ride in the following day. In the morning, an emperor gum moth (or a close relation) has landed on

11 https://sacredland.org/wp-content/uploads/2017/10/Media-Fact-Sheet-Sorry-Rocks-2.pdf retrieved 25/08/2020

Fig 7. Wild camping outside William Creek, NT

Fig 8. Emperor Gum Moth

one of my panniers. It has such seemingly mournful eyes patterned onto its wings.

The boy who lived next door during my childhood was slightly older than me and taught me how to climb trees. I recall his look of bewilderment that I was unable to do so. Several established eucalypts stood in his backyard. His preparatory instructions to me were simple. He held out some gum leaves and pointed to a black and white patterned caterpillar, quite hairy with red and yellow markings: 'These are spitfires: don't touch them'. And then he found a juicy big green caterpillar exceeding the size of my largest finger. It was beautiful in its detail. This was the emperor gum moth before it's chrysalis. He identified different-shaped cocoons: the scattered ones camouflaged with sticks that we used to roll like cigars between our fingers until they became soft and squishy, now held a new reality. Advancing in front of me, he indicated where to place my feet as I climbed, cautious and fearful. My world of play had never extended beyond ground height. Settled in a secure branch, he pointed to nests higher up and I was amazed by this world that had been previously hidden.

Both the caterpillars and the moths are scarcer now than they once were. One reason could be habitat loss, especially the loss of eucalypts in suburbia where the moths and caterpillars are more readily seen.[12]

The danger posed by some gum trees is very real, hence their nickname 'widow makers' after their habit of unexpectedly dropping when under the stress of drought. And the well-known adage: never camp under a gum tree! The trees next door that I learned to climb as a child still stand, much to the ongoing chagrin of the neighbours. Their abundant detritus and bark shedding tendency constitutes an ongoing battle for the upkeep of swimming pools.

12 https://www.thecourier.com.au/story/3736506/gum-emperor-moths-scarcity-concerning/retrieved 20/09/2020

Suburban antipathy towards native tree species is long standing and given voice in the part autobiographical novel, My Brother Jack. From the roof of his new suburban home in 1960's Beverly Grove, David Meredith laments the lack of trees. Observing that 'the place was not really flat' he begins to notice 'fold, rises and declivities', imagining 'good sturdy blue-gums or stringy barks' and 'slopes brown with bracken'. Against the reality that 'now there was nothing but a great red scab grown over the wounds the bulldozers had made, and not a single tree remaining. (Johnston 1964) He protests by planting a sugar gum, 'one of them quick-growin' eucaltyps' (*ibid*.).

Suburbia echoes historical colonial narratives that reflect the desire to establish order and eradicate mess. The Golden Spruce related the sentiments of a faller in British Colombia:

'I love this job', he explained, gesturing toward the wild chaos of the old-growth forest he was in the process of levelling. 'It's a challenge to walk into a mess like this and get it looking civilized.' (Valliant 2005)

V Parachilna to Wilpena Pound

I reconnect with Roberto at Parachilna, 570km (12 days) after parting. From here we head east into the Flinders Ranges that rise from the ochre drenched plain into a landscape of monumental eucalyptus trees. Mature stringy bark and river red gums stretch their massive limbs in every direction. Dry riverbeds are scattered with rounded boulders testifying to waters that have coursed through here in the past. The soundscape is completely altered by vegetation: fallen bark, dried leaves and snapped branches amplify the movement of every unseen reptile, rodent, marsupial, bird and insect. The smell of eucalyptus is a welcome relief from the relentless stench of road kill. It takes time for our eyes to adjust to this verdant environment. Being unaccustomed to elevation and topographical features, the effect of filtered light and shadow is disorienting, confusing our spatial perception after months in the flat, constant desert. We enter the landscapes painted by Hans Heysen.

By the beginning the 1900's most inhabitants of Australia occupied the eastern seaboard and the bush was an object of nostalgia. Titles of Hans Heysen's paintings: Early Morning Pastoral, Twilight at the Billabong, Gums Under Mist, and Lord of the Bush reveal romantic tendencies towards portraying the landscape. Places that he painted such as Hahndorf and Ambleside reflect naming practices that speak of distant locations and other histories. (There is something uncanny about passing a turnoff to Todmorden along the Oodnadatta Track in outback Australia.)

Heysen was acclaimed as 'the first artist to use eucalypts as a persistent subject in his art, celebrating the nobility of certain species and presenting them as symbols of heroic endurance'[13]. The symbolic role of trees to represent heroism and nobility had already entered into the Australian psyche via WWI. On the Gallipoli Peninsular, a solitary pine tree remained where the Ottoman army had dug their trenches. It didn't survive the encounter with the landing forces. In the aftermath of the Battle for

13 https://nga.gov.au/exhibition/heysen/default.cfm?MnuID=3&GallD=4 retrieved 17/09/2020

Fig 9. Eucalypts in dried river-bed Ilkara - Finders Ranges National Park, SA

Figs 10 and 11. Cazneaux's Tree, Ilkara - Flinders Ranges National Park, SA

Lone Pine Ridge (6-10 August 1915) two pinecones were retrieved from the site and returned to Australia (acts that today would breach biosecurity). These were eventually propagated and the seedlings planted as ANZAC memorial trees[14].

The years that saw Heysen painting in the Flinders Ranges also attracted photographer Harold Cazneaux to the area. At the edge of Wilpena Pound in the Ilkara /Flinders Ranges National Park there still stands the river red gum that he photographed in 1937. The gelatin silver print is entitled *The Spirit of Endurance*.[15] A short walk from the interpretation board approaches the cavernous interior of the tree. It is littered with the skeletal remains and matted fleece of decayed sheep. I wonder whether this scene speaks more accurately of the reality of trench warfare than the heroic individual: carnage and death seeping into the ground.

✦ ✦ ✦

Between 1926 and 1933 Heysen made nine trips to the Flinders Ranges. In a letter home he complains:

> *...it is so difficult to paint clear space—by clear I mean there is no thickness of atmosphere between you and objects, and also the circumstance under which one has to paint—heat, wind & millions of flies—is most trying.*[16]

The geological forms and individual trees that he painted remain 'objects' to him. He is an observer, situated in the landscape, but separate from it. This detachment contrasts with the Australian poet, Judith Wright whose relationship to the landscape 'articulates ... an apparently inseparable bond of self and land' (Collett & Jones 2009). Her autobiography Half Life, recounts a train journey during WWII and looking out at the landscape: 'These hills and valleys were—not mine, but me.' (Wright, J. quoted *ibid*.)

✦ ✦ ✦

Like Heysen, Cazneaux sought to capture a landscape that he perceived as essentially Australian. He believed that 'Australia had not yet clearly seen the true Australian sunlight'. [17] His aim as a photographer was 'to show our own Australia in terms of sunlight rather than those of greyness and dismal shadows.' (*ibid*.) Other discourses might question whom 'our own Australia' signifies and whether the 'dismal shadows' include those shadows where as a child Judith Wright imagined 'seeing old men, dark-skinned and shadowy, standing with spears in their hands among the few trees left standing on our sheep-ridden land'. (*ibid*.)

VI Mt Gambier to Portland

14 https://www.nationalregisterofbigtrees.com.au/listing/762.pdf retrieved 17/09/2020

15 The tree is listed on National Trusts of Australia Register of Significant Trees as Cadzneaux's Tree https://trusttrees.org.au/tree/SA/Blinman/Off_The_Blinman_Hawker_Road_About_1Km_N_Of_Wilpena_Pound_Intersection_And_Then_500M_W_Along_Wilpena_Creek__Off_The_Blinman_Hawker_Road retrieved 17/09/2020

16 https://nga.gov.au/exhibition/heysen/default.cfm?MnuID=3&GalID=8 retrieved 17/09/2020

17 Harold Cazneaux, letter to Jack Cato, May 1952. NLA MS 5416 quoted in Harold Cazneaux Photographer-the Catalogue. (2004, April, 15). https://webarchive.nla.gov.au/awa/20040415123514/http://www.nla.gov.au/exhibitions/caz/cat.html retrieved 17/09/2020

We map a route through secondary roads but don't escape the articulated timber haulage trucks, stacked with trees felled from nearby pine plantations. They dominate the narrow winding roads, bound for the chip mill and Portland's wharf. Both bike and breath shudder each time they hurtle past. Knuckles white from handlebars gripped too tightly, awaiting the inevitable vortex that follows the displaced air. Feeling a short breath away from becoming road kill ourselves. Huge flocks of Black Cockatoos amass in the tops of cone-laden trees, shrieking in unison as we cycle by. Bloated and bloodied, the bodies of wombats and koalas are scattered along the margins of the road in bizarre poses set by rigor mortis.

I stop to photograph *Xanthorrhoea australis* (native grass trees that send up spectacular flowering spikes). They are widely distributed throughout this area. I discover that the stretch of native vegetation along the roadside is deceptive, extending only a few meters in depth. Then I recall Douglas Pavlicek, a character in *The Overstory*, driving through Idaho in North America, discovering 'the curtain of concealing trees…the illusion of the thinnest artery of pretend life' (Powers 2018). And his horror when told by a cashier at a gas station: 'They're called beauty strips. Vista corridors.' (*ibid.*)

My attention is drawn by the stark quality of the light beyond. Unlike sunlight filtered through a multi-layered forest, the light following a clearfell glares, harsh and unbroken. Ruth Cunningham describes: 'I drove through patches of clearfelled forest, past the shattered, dismembered corpses of trees lying in the mud… Whatever your view on logging, seeing clearfelling like this is to see a wounded landscape—and this particular wound was still bleeding.' (Cunningham 2019) In another part of Australia, Anna Krein revisits Tasmanian logging coupe SX10F soon after it had been felled. 'It is like a sharp intake of breath. What you were looking at a second ago is suddenly gone.' (Krien 2012)

Later in the day, we stop for a hasty lunch on the verge of a logging track that grants access to symmetrical rows of plantation pines: a deadening conformity of colour, height and spacing in an unnatural silence that dulls the senses.

At Portland an impressive pile of blue gum woodchips, 40-metres high, sits on the wharf, ready for export. Our campground lies a few blocks back from the main street. A resident koala and its joey are wedged into the forked branch of a gum tree that stands near the toilet block. The owner of the campsite tells of a koala (lost, displaced, homeless?) that spent days circling a nearby traffic roundabout, attracting many onlookers. There is something quite disturbing in this image of dislocation, like a tragic figure from Greek mythology, stuck in an endless pattern of futile circumambulation.

By the 1930's, the fur trade meant that koalas had been hunted to the point of extinction in South Australia. The species was later reintroduced to the mainland from island populations.

Koalas are solitary animals living within a network of overlapping home ranges…By 12 months of age, the young is weaned and takes up a home range, which overlaps with its mother, for much of the next year. Between the age of two and three years, these young disperse beyond their original home.[18]

18 https://environment.des.qld.gov.au/wildlife/animals/living-with/koalas/facts retrieved 21/09/2020

Unlike other native species, koalas do not regulate their breeding according to available habitat. The implications of habitat loss are obvious: their need to traverse greater stretches of ground makes them vulnerable to predators and road traffic. Terms such as edge collapse and functional extinction have become part of our lexicon, as more recently have zoonosis and social isolation. It seems that the eremocene, O E Wilson's *Age of Loneliness* is upon us.

VII The Otway Ranges to Melbourne via the Great Ocean Road

Our last stretch to Melbourne enters the Otways where we are again surrounded by a treed landscape. Bushfires last ripped through here in 2016, closing the Great Ocean Road and evacuating local communities. It was a Christmas when we sat transfixed to our screens in another hemisphere, seeking updates. The coolness of dense blackwood forest and fern tree gullies smells so familiar, a sense of home coming.

In the northwest of the state, the Djab Wurrung Heritage Protection Embassy has been set up to challenge and protect against the proposed removal of 3,000 eucalyptus trees, including Indigenous scarred trees and birthing trees. Their removal is part of a major roads extension project. 'Over 50 generations have been born on these sites & the birthing trees themselves are 800 years old.'[19] For the Djab Wurrung people:

> *'This is a place where we connect and heal and unite as a people.'*[20]

> *'They (the trees) are living beings that embody our stories throughout this significant landscape'*[21]

We arrive back in Melbourne after an absence of eighteen years. The lemon tree out the front of our house has been devoured by gall wasp and is beyond saving. In the backyard a pink peppercorn tree that I planted as a sapling, now provides shade all through the summer. On some days the air in Melbourne is dense with smoke, an uncanny end-of-world atmosphere, that creates spectacular sunsets while further north and east, bushfires rage.

✦ ✦ ✦

Acknowledgements

I would like to acknowledge the Wurundjeri people who are the Traditional Custodians of this Land where I work and live. I would also like to pay respect to the Elders past, present and emerging of the Kulin Nation and extend that respect to other Indigenous Australians in particular those whose lands are recounted in this piece of writing.

---

19 https://www.abc.net.au/news/2020-08-10/commonwealth-rejects-protection-for-western-highway-trees/12540782 retrieved 18/07/2020

20 Lidia Thorpe quoted in Martin, Lisa (2019) https://www.theguardian.com/australia-news/2019/aug/22/protesters-defend-sacred-800-year-old-djap-wurrung-trees-as-police-deadline-looms retrieved 18/07/2020

21 https://www.abc.net.au/news/2020-02-05/bushfires-and-history-of-australia-trees-carving-colonisation/11913214 retrieved 18/07/2020

Vincent van Gogh, Public domain, via Wikimedia Commons

It is the materials, site and history that shape the context of Stacey's practice, translated through the use of performance, sculpture, sound, drawing, film, and photography. It was during her MA (2002-2004) that Stacey's practice became more focused on environmental art. Stacey was involved with several artist led projects in Cornwall. The Poetics of Materials, Eden Project (2004), Research Art Nature Environment (2005-06), 'Wheal Art' at King Edward Mine (2006), 'Eek' in Redruth (2006), 'Transition: Curators Edition' at Newlyn Art Gallery and resident artist for 'Build' at Cornwall College (2008). In 2010 she performed with the Oxford Improvisers' Cohesion 4 Festival, and in 2014 she presented a pop-up museum of her Grandmother's collections, which received a wide social and geographical audience. In 2018 Stacey exhibited her mulberry related works in the Garden Space at Dartington Hall, and in 2019 presented some of this research at the Evolving the Forest *conference.*

Under the Mulberry

Stacey Righton

Morus nigra at Dartington Hall Gardens, 2019

Under the Mulberry

Stacey Righton

I ate the berries greedily, sucking the juice from my fingers, one berry after another, not being able to stop feeding because they were so enjoyable. Until at last I lay under the Mulberry tree exhausted from the gorge, my belly full and satisfied, my hands stained red with the blood like liquid that oozed from my mouth.

The mulberry has a fascinating history, there are many stories and legends associated with this tree, it provides inspiration for artists, writers and poets and represents faith, nature, growth and decay.

Still from video *Under the Mulberry Tree 1 Love and Death* 2018

I began my research into the mulberry tree when I stumbled across one at Dartington Hall gardens,[1] in the summer of 2018. The tree was in fruit, I picked and ate some of the mulberries and was struck by the blood-like colour that stained my hands, I wondered at the deep burgundy colour before me. What was this tree and what was its history?

The story of Pyramis and Thisbe as told to us by the Roman poet Ovid in his *Metamorphoses*, is one of tragedy, love, life and death and, like all legends, has been told and re-told many times. Pyramus and Thisbe were lovers whose neighbouring families were rivals; they could only communicate with one another through a crack in the wall.

They arrange to meet secretly under a white mulberry tree. Thisbe arrives first, veiled so as not to be recognised, and as she waits by the tree a lioness approaches, her jaws are fresh with blood from a recent kill. Thisbe flees to hide behind a nearby rock, and in so doing drops her veil by the tree. The lioness tears at the veil, and discards it as she leaves the scene. Shortly after this Pyramus arrives but sees only Thisbe's veil stained with blood and ripped to shreds beneath the tree. Believing his dear Thisbe has been killed by a lion and unable to bear the grief for his lover, Pyramus kills himself with his sword. Thisbe returns to the tree to see her bloody veil next to Pyramus' lifeless body; on realising he has ended his life for his love for her and in an attempt to unite with him, Thisbe takes her own life by plunging his sword into her breast, dying by his side.

The fruit is fabled to have thereby changed from white to deep red through absorbing the lovers' blood.

Genus Morus

The mulberry (gen. *Morus*) has according to Britannica about ten species of small to medium sized trees belonging to the family *Moraceae*. Mulberries are native to Asia and North America and several species are cultivated for their fruits and as ornamentals. The major species are the red mulberry (*Morus rubra*), white mulberry (*Morus alba*), and black mulberry (*Morus nigra*). The fruits of the black mulberry are apparently superior in flavour to the fruits of the red mulberry. There are several varieties of the white mulberry including the Russian mulberry (*Morus*

1 The gardens at Dartington Hall in South Devon are of great historical interest and a monument to the vision of the families who have owned and transformed them. The estate originated in the 1390s when John Holland created a manor house overlooking the river Dart. In 1925 Dorothy and Leonard Elmhirst purchased the neglected estate. The Elmhirsts were pioneering and inspirational thinkers and extremely well off so poured their resources into setting up farming, forestry and educational projects, resulting in the Dartington Hall Trust. During the Elmhirst years Dartington became a centre of creative activity and remains as such today.

alba, var. *tatarica*), introduced in Western North America for shelter belts and timber use, and fruitless sorts such as 'Stribling' and 'Mapleleaf' cultivars. There is also a weeping mulberry (Morus alba 'Pendula'), which is used as a lawn tree[2]

The mulberry trees I am mostly interested in are the common black mulberry and the white mulberry. *Morus nigra* has been cultivated in Europe for so long that its true origins are obscure, Morus alba is native to eastern and central China and was cultivated to feed silkworms. It has a longer growing season than Morus nigra, the leaves of the white mulberry being more palatable to silkworms than those of the black mulberry, and it provides the right nutrients for the worms to thrive, so their silk production is of finer quality.

These two mulberries are associated by incredible historical events. When researching and collecting together these historical stories, I found that some of them interlinked and I also observed the difference in gender of the characters involved and how this seemed to effect the content of the stories; the stories that embody war, wealth and power include men at the helm, and the stories that express creativity, insight and awareness have women as their central characters.

Silk

> *'Once upon a time a dainty little Chinese Empress, while idling in her garden, had her attention drawn to a caterpillar which was building for itself a beautiful little house with threads spun from its own body' (Yamaguchi 1950)*

The yellow empress Lei Zu, wife of Huangdi (born 2704BC and ruled from 2697BC) discovered silk, she may well have been dainty and little but this story suggests someone who is clever, intuitive and determined.

Lei Zu watched a caterpillar wind a fibre produced from its own body around itself until it became shrouded and cocooned in a soft casing, she marvelled at how delicate it was and how it shimmered in the light. As she sat under a mulberry tree drinking her tea and contemplating this phenomenon, a cocoon fell into her cup, she watched it begin to soften and unravel, and she gently pulled at the loose thread and wound it around her finger. She wondered if she could unravel the slender thread as one piece, so this she carefully did, and unravelled it to the length of her garden.[3] She asked the Emperor to give her a grove of choice mulberry trees, then worked hard at cultivating the worms. She took their cocoons and unravelled each one until one day succeeded in twisting together the strands from several of the cocoons into many long threads. From these threads she made a fabric so exquisite that the Chinese named it after the Empress 'si', the name given to silk in China, as she is also known as Si Ling-Chi. Lei Zu invented the silk loom and went on to introduce sericulture across China.

Silk was a symbol of wealth and higher social status so was highly desired. The making of silk was so secret in China that it was forbidden for silkworms or the eggs to leave the country and the penalty was death. In Italy and at the

2 www.britannica.com/plant/mulberry-plant 2020

3 A silkworm cocoon is about 2.5cm in length, when unwound this gives up to 0.5 miles of continuous thread.

time of the esteemed Roman poet Virgil (70-19 BC), silk was held to be a product of the mulberry leaves, the work of the silkworms not yet understood. It was the Roman Emperor, Justinian (who ruled from 527 to 565 AD) who brought silk to Europe, he persuaded two Persian priests, who had lived in China for many years to go and bring back some silk eggs. The priests returned with the precious eggs hidden in hollows in their pilgrim's staffs. This is what brought silk to the Western world and the West continued to be supplied with silk for twelve centuries. Through time, trade with China dropped off and Chinese silk became more and more rare. There must have been mulberry trees in Rome for the silkworms to feed on, (mulberry pips have been found in Roman excavations), unless the thieving priests took mulberry saplings too.[4]

By the 13th century Italy had a flourishing silk industry and from the 15th century France too. In England black mulberries had been planted during the medieval times in monasteries and abbeys and in their infirmary gardens for medicinal purposes. But in the 16th century Henry VIII's reformation of the church (for the purposes of divorcing Catherine of Aragon), meant few mulberries survived the devastating acts of the dissolution of the monasteries. Elizabeth I believed it was fashionable and impressive to provide exotic black mulberries to guests, so many mulberries were once again planted.

King James I of England desired a silk trade for Britain and wrote letters in 1607 and 1608 asking nobility to plant 10,000 mulberry saplings for silk worms to feed on. The wealthy

4 '... mulberry seeds found in excavations of Roman settlements near the Thames suggest that the Romans planted black mulberries for their fruit. The berries perish soon after being picked, so could not be imported. In this case, mulberries would have been growing in London before the 5th century CE.' https://www.moruslondinium.org/research/timeline 2020

were sold mulberry saplings and the less well-off endeavoured to establish mulberry plantations from seed. It is well known that James failed in his attempt to start a silk trade in Britain because the wrong trees were sent from France, James had black mulberry saplings imported instead of the white variety. Some suggest that the French deliberately tricked him, however the facts seem otherwise. James successfully planted thousands of white mulberries in Virginia in the American colonies, suggesting therefore that he did in fact have the 'right' mulberry. The climate was more suited in Virginia so the trees thrived, but he still did not succeed at sericulture. The climate of Britain at this time must have also contributed for his failure, particularly as during this time Britain experienced the coldest part of the 'Little Ice Age', so even if James had planted white mulberries in Britain, they would have been unlikely to survive. [5]

◀ *The wrong seed* 2018: seed packet — made from a map of China, from an Atlas of the World — containing Black Mulberry seeds from Dartington Hall Gardens

Metamorphosis

There are four stages of development in the life cycle of a silkworm, the egg, larvae, cocoon and moth.

In 1647 in Frankfurt Maria Sibylla Merian was born. At the age of 3 her father Matthaus Merian, died and her mother Johanna Catharina Sibylla, married the artist Jacob Marrel. Growing up in Marrel's studio, Merian collected insect specimens for Marrel's compositions and she also learnt the techniques of watercolour, preparing pigments and copper plates for printing. From a young age she started her own caterpillar collection and at 13 years Merian kept silkworms, in her journal she recorded her efforts to rear them and drew and painted her observations of their life-cycle. In 1665 she married, and in 1670 after the birth of her first daughter moved to Nuremberg where she opened a studio and worked as a flower painter and engraver and published three volumes of flower engravings between 1675 and 1680. She also taught embroidery to the wealthy daughters of merchants who not only provided an income to Merian but subject matter of exotic plants from their greenhouses. Her books became popular botanical guides for watercolour and embroidery. After her second daughter in 1678 she published her first book on the metamorphosis of European butterflies, this she called her 'caterpillar book'. Merian was familiar with the paintings of Jan Goedart (1617-1668), who also painted insect life cycles but used dried specimens, Merian's approach was meticulously detailed and depicted the plants that the insects thrived on, she made a revolutionary breakthrough with regard to entomology. Entomology was not recognised as a distinct field of science until the 19th century. During the 17th century 'spontaneous generation' was widely believed, a notion that creatures could arise from non-living matter, Merian was one of the first to challenge this by closely observing and recording insect transformation. Her depictions of metamorphosis and her studies of plants and creatures during her voyage to Suriname (1699) caught the attention of the Royal Academy 250 years prior

5 The 'Little Ice Age' occurred from the 13th century through to the mid-19th century. Today scientists use it to distinguish the period between 1500-1850 but it is more commonly applied to the period between 1300-1850. The 'Little Ice Age' followed the Medieval Warming period (roughly 900-1300 AD), and preceded the present period of warming that began in late 19th century to early 20th century. Frequent cold winters and wet summers throughout northern and central Europe led to crop failures and famines. https://www.britannica.com/science/Little-Ice-Age 2020

'Homage to Bombyx mori, Fukusa' 2020 Silk threads embroidered on French linen backed with red cloth. (see note below).

to the first woman permitted to join the academy. After catching a tropical disease and returning to Amsterdam where she had lived and worked from 1691, Merian never fully recovered and died in 1717.[6]

The eggs or 'seed' take 3-7 days to hatch the worm, at first the worm is black, 3mm in length, covered with long hair and has a shiny nose. The skin of the worm cannot keep pace with its growth so it has four moulting periods or 'sleeps' when it sheds its old skin for a new one. At each moult the hair gradually disappears and it lightens in colour, at its last moult it becomes cream or white. When the worm moults it ceases eating, fastens itself to a fixed object and remains in a listless state for nearly 2 days. After each moult the worm gains strength by resting, rejuvenates and is hungry again. The worm lives for about 40 days, and attains around 7-8 cm in length. Then it knowingly attaches itself to a twig and begins to spin itself a precious silk cocoon. The worms secrete the silk within a glutinous liquid from a small orifice below the mouth called a spinneret, the liquid sets into a long thread that is wound around and around their bodies, the worm achieves this by swinging its head from side to side. Working incessantly the worm creates a protective layer that thickens and can take up to 48 hours to complete. Inside the cocoon the silkworm has its final moult, then after 10-14 days of developing into a silk moth it hatches from the cocoon. At hatching stage, the moths aim is to find a mate so they dance wildly and frantically towards one another, and lock into an embrace. After mating the females immediately deposit their eggs usually from 600-800 of them. The farming of silkworms to produce silk is known as sericulture. When farmed the cocoons are collected and boiled before they have a chance to pupate, at the mating stage superfluous moths are cast aside and the female moths once they have laid their eggs are disposed of.

In the moth's natural state, she lives for two days, she does not eat or defecate, she just lays eggs.

Note: A *Fukusa* is a Japanese ceremonial cloth used for gift wrapping and is used in tea ceremonies for ritually cleaning the tea utensils. The Fukusa is square and can vary in size from 23cm to 91cm, is usually highly decorative, embroidered, dyed or woven. The design on a Fukusa has a symbolic image and the reverse is usually red or orange for those used by women and purple for those used by men.

Listening to the Mulberry

When the silk caterpillars eat the leaves of the mulberry, they eat so voraciously that it sounds like rain. When the tree buds it happens so quickly overnight and with such

6 https://www.nhm.ac.uk/.../maria-sibylla-merian-metamorphosis-art-and- science.html

force that their breaking forth may be heard. There are other sounds that can be heard from the mulberry.

The Old Testament tells us that King David, at battle with the Philistines, inquired of the Lord saying,

> *'Shall I go up to the Philistines?'...The Lord replies "Thou shalt not go up; but fetch a compass behind them, and come upon them over against the mulberry trees." And let it be, when thou hearest the sound of a going in the tops of the mulberry trees, that then thou shalt bestir thyself...to smite the host of the Philistines. (King James Bible, Samuel II, 5:23-4).*

The 'sound of a going' can be interpreted as the sound of marching and hooves of the enemy's horses. Not surprisingly it's the mulberry tree that features in the King James Bible, and in other editions, the poplar, the balsam, the pear or aspen trees are mentioned.[7]

At Dartington, I waited under the mulberry tree and recorded the sounds I heard; I hoped for a pure natural sound but of course the birdsong, the bumble bees, the leaves rustling in the wind and the rain falling on the canopy were all interrupted by road traffic in the distance, airplanes, a steam train, garden machinery and human chatter. Initially frustrated I soon realised that these sounds were all a part of nature, a modern-day industrial nature. Human beings will always have an effect on the Earth we belong, we are in the age of the Anthropocene, but perhaps during the lockdown of 2020 the sound, under the mulberry, returned to a pre-industrial one, or at least

Under the Mulberry Tree 2 - Waiting 2018: loudspeaker embedded into a Holy Bible, King James edition. Old Testament Samuel II, Chapter V, versus 19, 22-25. Sound recording made under the Mulberry Tree at Dartington Hall Gardens, looped.

we paused for a moment able to hear the natural sounds more clearly.

All these threads I link together in *Under the Mulberry Tree 2 Waiting 2018*.

Descendants

Depending on their care the common black mulberry can live for hundreds of years, the white mulberry for just over one hundred. The majority of black mulberries alive today are likely descendants of King James' planting, (there is still a royal collection of mulberries today, to the north of Buckingham Palace), there are very few instances of *Morus alba* in England.

However, in 1718 John Appletree had a go at planting both varieties, feeling undeterred by James' first attempt he decided to produce silk on land in Chelsea Park, that

7 The New International version mentions the Poplar, the English Standard, New American Standard and the Berean Study Bibles all mention balsam, the Douay-Rheims Bible mention the pear and *A Faithful Version* mentions the aspen. https://biblehub.com/2_samuel/5-23.htm

was once Thomas More's estate. He planted both black and white mulberries and the industry flourished but by 1724 Appletree was bankrupt. A new lease on the land was given to Sir Richard Manningham who sold and sadly took out most of the mulberry trees, Chelsea park was sold as lots and gradually developed over the next century.

William Shakespeare planted mulberries in his Stratford garden, and was clearly captivated by the mulberry as they feature in his plays. In 'A Midsummer Night's Dream' the story of Pyramis and Thisbe is well known, and in 'Corialanus' the war hero at a humbled moment likens himself to the tender and ripe fruit of the mulberry. In 1609 Shakespeare's famous mulberry of which there are descendants at Kew, is said to have been taken from the mulberry garden of James I and planted in his garden at New Place in Stratford-upon-Avon. The tree was highly celebrated but around 1752, Revd Francis Gastrell, the then new owner of New Place got so fed up of requests to see the tree that he abruptly chopped it down. The wood was sold and various makers including Thomas Sharpe, George Cooper and John Marshall made mementos like snuff boxes and weight scales, some of them being inscribed with the punning motto 'Memento Mori'. (Grieve 1976) The number of souvenirs and other items on the market couldn't have possibly come from the one tree so people became suspicious of the authenticity of the wood.

Memento Mori Paper knife made from the Stratford Mulberry Tree? Found object from my Grandmother's belongings 2020

Motherhood and wisdom

> *'Of all the cultivated trees, the mulberry is the last that buds, which it never does until the cold weather is past, and it is therefore called the wisest of trees' (ibid. p 58)*

The generic name for the mulberry being Morus derives from the Latin word mora meaning delay, the tree was dedicated by the ancient Romans to the Goddess Minerva. The display of this late budding by the mulberry also led to the ancient Greeks dedicating it to the Goddess Athena. Interestingly there are differences within the qualities of these particular Goddesses, this is due to the specific differences between the two cultures, stories and language. Athena is the Greek Goddess of wisdom and war, yet the Romans made less emphasis on war and added the influence of trade and the arts.

The English nursery rhyme *Here we go round the Mulberry Bush* [8] perhaps celebrates this wisdom with its repeating line 'on a cold and frosty morning'. The rhyme is said to have been inspired by a tree at Wakefield prison and devised by female prisoners in

8 The mulberry is a tree not a bush, however when farmed for silkworms the trees are kept short, often not more than 1-2 meters high. The branches are cut in the spring to make way for new branches to grow, they grow rapidly and produce tender young leaves for the silkworms. When pollarded these trees look more like shrubs.

the 1800s (still within the grip of the Little Ice Age), who exercised around the tree and sung the rhyme to entertain their children.

Listening for the 'sound of the goings' with ear trumpet 2019 at the Mulberry Tree at Torre Abbey, Torquay

At the end of the summer of 2020 I came across a black mulberry at Batsford Arboretum in Gloucestershire where with my children and nephews we spent some time looking for and savouring the last of the fruit that this wonderful tree has to offer. As we foraged, we sang and reflected on the famous rhyme, I thought how the eating of the berries, which are so rich in iron and vitamin C would certainly help boost our immunity in preparation for the colder seasons ahead. The repetitive rhythm of the famous nursery rhyme reflects the tree's continuous cycle, it's budding, being in leaf then in fruit then resting again for the winter; this pattern can echo our own existence with nature (if we allow it). A more simplistic way of life comes to mind, one of gathering, stocking our larders, making preserves and wine, keeping warm and resting as the days darken, then re-emerging with the new life of spring to repeat the cycle once more.

I graduated from the Art and Social Contexts course at Dartington College of Arts in 1980, subsequently working on my own art council funded film projects and as assistant film editor for Channel 4 productions before returning to education to study Architectural Glass and Photography at the State Academy of Fine Art in Stuttgart, Germany, where I graduated in 1991. I continued to live and work in Germany mainly on Architectural Glass projects until 1998, before returning to England to raise a family.

As the 90s progressed, I gradually returned to the rural and environmental themes and concerns I had as a student at Dartington, producing installations and sculptures, working freely in terms of materials. Since then, I have worked on many temporary site specific projects in rural and urban environments, alongside permanent public art projects and exhibitions - in the UK and mainland Europe.

Bob Budd: Felled redwoods in Dartington's North Wood

Three sculptures

Bob Budd

My photos show three works installed at Dartington during the *Evolving the Forest* summit; two in the North Wood behind Schumacher College, on the periphery of the estate, and one in the formal Dartington Hall Gardens near to the Great Hall.

These works are both a personal and emotional response to a physical location as well as to the wider social and environmental concerns implied by the project title, *Evolving the Forest*.

I had worked in the North Wood the previous year. My impression then was that the woods were a tranquil, majestic place, with its tall redwoods, at moments having an unearthly beauty. The wide tracks carved out by logging machines in the forest floor (reminding me of dried out river beds) were littered by layers of fallen branches, suggesting that forestry work here was a thing of the past. Given the great age that Redwoods might attain, one could project into a far future where these trees had continued to grow and thrive and any signs of human presence had long disappeared.

A subsequent visit showed some serious logging had taken place, with substantial lengths of healthy redwood arranged in piles. My dream of a far future had woken up, a pleasant fiction while it lasted. Further visits saw the piles disappear and the logging tracks freshened up by new rubber tread. This place was in flux and not even pretending to be forever.

I know these are managed woodlands but I didn't care to visualise these magnificent trees being felled. As it transpired, in all my visits and days working in the woods I never once saw a forester nor even the flash of a hi-vis jacket, although I would often hear the ominous sounds of chainsaws, heavy moving gear and crashing in other parts of the woods. If I looked away, and back again, would I find another part of the forest had been removed? The woods presented a picture of growth and beauty as well as loss (emotional as well as mechanical). This had an unsettling quality, which somehow matched our times.

I was happy, though, for a bit of friendly company, a chat with a passer-by, or when various birds would visit my work place, perhaps curious about what I was doing, I imagined, until I sussed out they were only waiting for me to disturb the leaves and soil on their behalf, to uncover or unearth a grub or juicy worm for their lunch. My pride hurt, I pondered on whether every time they saw a human stumbling through the trees they thought `Worm'. Working in nature is a great leveller.

Work 1 (North Wood)

A felled Redwood in parts, wrapped in bandages secured with safety pins, the parts held together with metal hinges and marked with black paint.

Work 2 (Dartington Hall Gardens)

Bandages wrapped around a fallen then chain sawed ancient tree, held by a very large safety pin.

Work 3 (North Wood)

An infant's swing chair hanging from a Redwood branch, which had snapped off the main trunk, suspended between two Redwoods with thin metal rope.

Data of the Heart
Duddon Valley

Monterey pine suspended from the Duddon Valley Oak, Cumbria, 2018

Harriet and Rob Fraser are environmental artist researchers collaborating as somewhere-nowhere. Their projects explore the nature and culture of rural spaces, using walking, research, conversations and the practice of pausing to bring together the knowing and feeling of place. Photography, poetry and landscape installations speak of environmental and cultural issues in rural spaces, and share knowledge from environmental sciences. The Frasers' projects, workshops, exhibitions and books consider value systems and complexity, without losing sight of the wonder of the natural world. They encourage debate and collaboration between disciplines, and promote active participation in caring for the planet, beginning with local solutions. They have exhibited and presented across the UK and in America; and are founders of the newly established PLACE Collective at the UK's Centre for National Parks and Protected Areas.

Website: somewhere-nowhere.com

Space for Imagining: an installation and an invitation

Harriet & Rob Fraser

Space for Imagining: an installation and an invitation

Harriet & Rob Fraser (somewhere-nowhere)

in the shade of the oak
I realise

the problem
                    of the page
                    is that it is too

                              two dimensional

here I sit
cradled by a triple-centuried tree
my summer-bare arms pressed against bark
light dappled, leaves loosely dancing

my two dimensional page
is an invitation for words

but my multi-dimensional sense
within the space of trees

is wind and song and coolness
the certain seat of a curved root
the smell of grass pollen
                                        drifting
                                        from the meadow

there is suspension
of the cultured-known

            just for a brief swaying moment

the floating of trees
the dance of a chestnut
no bigger than my hand

and a jackdaw hopping

            from branch to branch

its black eyes fixed on me

Horse Chestnut suspended from the Dartington field oak, 2019

A Space for imagining. Seven books of seven colours, each containing a sapling, hang suspended from the boughs of a vast oak. Light streams through leaves, the earth is redolent with the scent of recent rain, rotting wood and the presence of cattle. We pause, allow our minds to float with the slowly spinning books, and follow prompts to consider our place in relation to a single tree and to the wider world.

Connected to this old, established tree, the tiny trees that could be the beginning of future woodlands drift in mid-air, their young roots symbolically nurtured by the compost of knowledge held in books: but the suspension of this knowledge above thin air suggests the possibility of change and the necessity to rethink and re-contextualise what we know.

The experience of stepping into a dynamic art piece, and in so doing matching its rhythm both physically and mentally, has a way of cutting through the noise of the intellect. It can still the mind yet rejuvenate thought. This gentle art piece was shared during the *Evolving the Forest* symposium at Dartington Hall in 2019, and has been installed in three other locations between 2015 and 2019, one of which was an artful protest against the felling of irreplaceable ancient woodlands to clear ground for England's new high-speed rail link, HS2. It has become a portal for discussions and an invitation to imagine a future that is not about business as usual or repeating errors of practice and judgement, but is a positive and resilient way forwards, for trees and all they are connected to.

There is currently a huge volume of conversation around trees; and research programmes around the globe are exploring the best way to increase tree cover, including consideration of the world that today's seeds and saplings will face when they are 50, 100 or 200 years old. Modellers are busy; climate change scientists are continually projecting and re-evaluating; arborists, foresters and dendrologists are designing plans that they hope will suit a future world. All the while they are building on a historic relationship with trees which is layered with survival, industry, craft, spirituality and even, you could argue, with genetics. We came from the trees, some would say. But perhaps we haven't kept up our side of the bargain: trees offer so much to enrich our lives, but what do we do for theirs?

The installation was in place for the duration of the symposium, and we led a curated visit. Over the course of a few hours, we blended silent observation engaging all the senses with exercises that shifted perception. We considered the spaces between old and new, known and unknown, growth and decay, and explored the interconnectivity of things. How and who are we in relation to trees and the natural world? What is our connection to trees, and what is our responsibility going forwards? One of the workshop participants reflects:

> *'... it spoke to the questions that I had been asking and the challenges I was facing in my research project on human-forest relations. Research involves an infinite number of possibilities, in terms of what questions we ask, who we speak to, how we see the world, and what we write. At times we become lost.*
>
> *We could see the books from a distance hanging in the tree, and you asked us to walk towards one of them. I was drawn to the blue book. The*

Installing seven books in the Duddon Valley, Cumbria, 2018

words inscribed on the spine — 'A New Narrative' — were the same as the words on a little card that you'd given me. The message inside the card asked 'What rises above the white noise? Which voices are heard and how?'

Those two simple questions and the prospect of a new narrative were a clarifying moment in a long creative process.'

Art can continue to ask how new narratives concerning human relationships to the natural world may be formed. Since the symposium, Covid-19 has shifted mindsets. For many people, it has forced or triggered new lifestyle habits and shaken social, economic and political systems. The pandemic has many lessons to teach about the danger of disregarding the wonder and the fragility of the natural world, and our responsibility to nurture ecosystems and wildlife on our doorsteps and in places that are far from us yet are still affected by our choices.

Now is a time to step into the world beyond the walls we build around us, and to listen. Somewhere in the space between the greens of an oak are truths that may never be articulated or understood but can be felt and need to be valued alongside the revelations of data and models: truths about interconnectivity and about potential, and the beauty of a system that is respectfully loved and cared for. And the spaces between old trees that reach deep into the ground might well be crying out for new growth. According to the 2016 UK State of Nature report (since when things haven't got any better) over half of all woodland spaces show continuing declines; and over 100 woodland species are categorised as threatened. Trees are vital not just for their own sake and their connections to other vegetation and animal and insect species — they are also important as stepping stones to the kind of landscape we, as humans, will shape as our climate shifts. Their presence among us offers a direction of travel as we help restore the natural world to reach a state where it can, once again, begin to thrive.

As individuals, as families, communities, researchers, artists, policy makers, voters … what do we dare to imagine, what do we want to stand for?

Harriet with workshop participants at *Evolving the Forest*, with the Oak in the background, 2019

Data of the Heart
III

One of seven books suspended from the Troutbeck Alder, Cumbria, 2017

Muddy and wind-torn, hemmed and zipped, loose tree.
Bonnets
front of strolling top hats;
behind, Celts cloaks kneel Fagus god beech.
This garden – a library of trees –

The soul of the forest moves with stillness, speaks with silence. Here, with the trees, my words arise and rest.

My first poetry installation was at Westonbirt Arboretum, where eight poems appeared in the trees along their Autumn Trail, and featured on BBC Autumnwatch *(www.MarchantBarronWords.org/bbcvideo). For the Wye Valley Festival, I showcased my words at The Kymin — a National Trust Site — and Tintern Abbey, alongside Luke Jerram's* Museum of the Moon. *At Dartington, my poems also found a home during the international symposium. The stories behind these installations can be found on my website (www.MarchantBarronWords.org).*

My writing journey began at Bristol Grammar School, who honoured me by awarding an annual creative writing prize in my name. I graduated from Bath Spa University in 2020 with First Class Honours and an Alumni Award for Excellence.

photo: Oliver Raymond-Barker

The Poetry of Trees

Marchant Barron

drawing: Simon Barron

Beginnings

In the sky's eye, this land is changing.
A stretch of saplings, row on row,
Reaches to dawn a thousand mantras.
Murmurs of wych elm and willow
Whisper with hazel and oak.
In an uprising of sap,
We rewild and
Awake a woodland.

Beginnings was written for the charity 'Moor Trees'

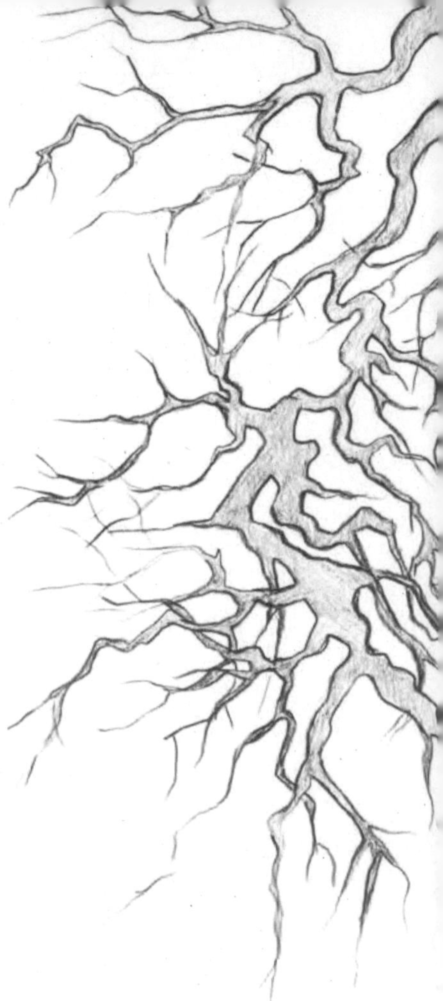

Roots

My great-grandfather bound books and his great-grandfather made paper. In the earth of my family, I find my roots in words. Our DNA trickles down the years, patterned in every handshake.

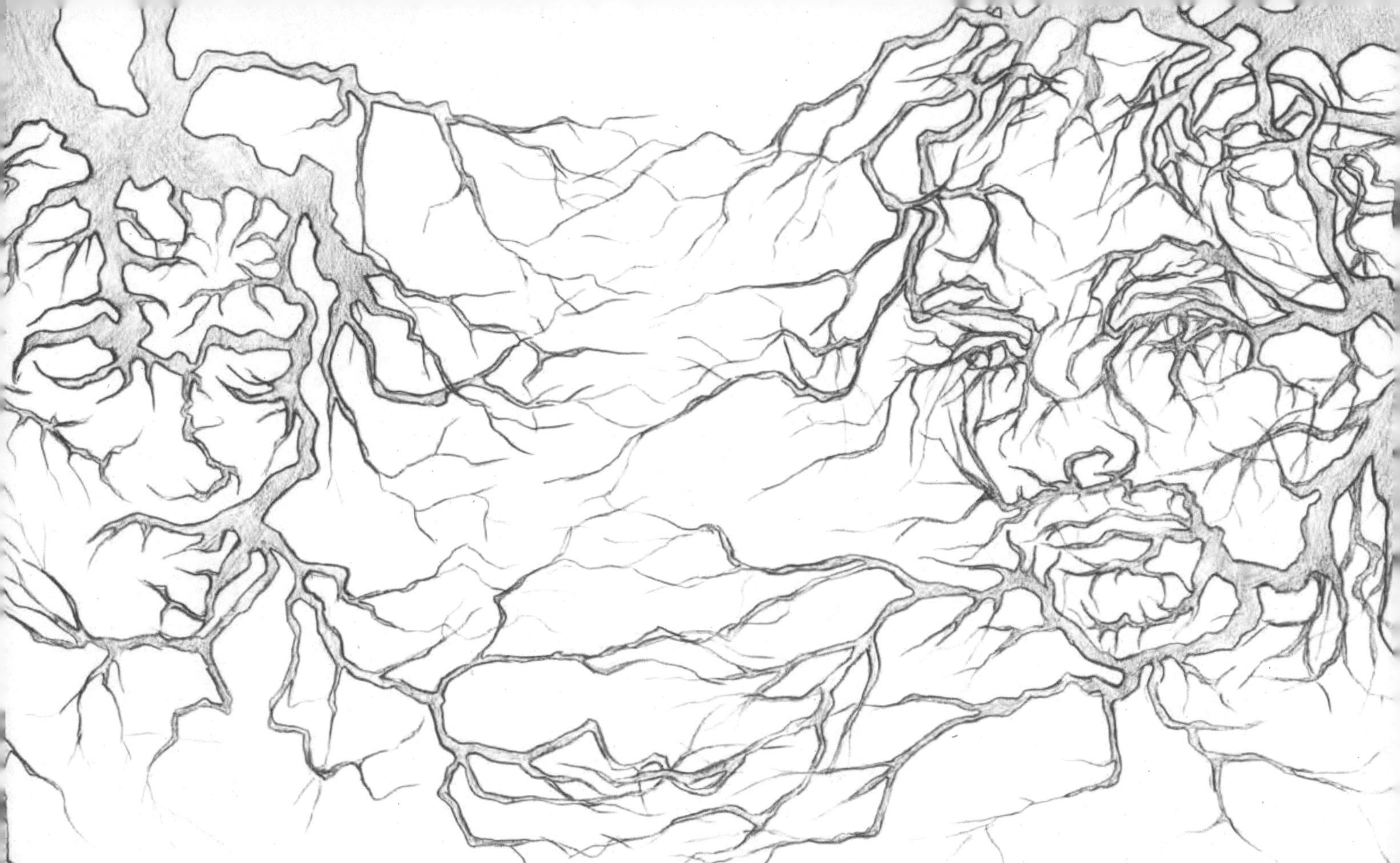

drawing: Amy Robins

In the woods, no tree stands alone — the true story is underground. A diaspora of roots journeys beyond the canopy; a mesh of trails that meet and meld, each tree tied to another. Each tree speaks to another, messages tapped by fingers of fungi that braid the roots — gossamer whispers feed the soil.

Roots are needed for a tree to wander.

Hear This

Listen, the woods are full of knotted words
that twine the trunks and twist within the leaves.
Wood seals the blood on blistered bark that seeps
beneath. The winded words unfold; leaves drop
and burrow deep and damp, intent to hide.
The voices rot and sing their requiem,
through chandeliers of broken rain, which fall
on trees that hear our words when we are lost.

From my book: *Autumn, Caught*

photo: Oliver Raymond-Barker

on blistered bark that seeps
beneath the winded words unfold;
and burrow deep and damp, intent to hide.
The voices rot and sing their requiem,
through chandeliers of broken rain, which fall
on trees that hear our words when we are lost.

Art Connects Deep in the Woods

Trees speak to me, they speak to us. They quieten our minds so we can hear their truths.

Earthbound — skyborne.

Trees bend with the wind. An arabesque of branches brushes the sky, birthing grace. In the woods, everywhere, wild beauty gilds as each tree turns to find its place. Storms weathered, their crowns inch towards the light.

In the budding and falling of leaves, I find my words shaped by trees. On red banners these words float, my poems part of the tree — a piece of art. In acts of serendipity people come across my installations and, in that moment, we see the tree together — we connect. I am sustained knowing my humanity is seen in our shared love of trees. Many people write to me via my website and email:

> *'I lose myself among the giants.' — Antony B.*
>
> *'Marchant, the trees do know you. We are all as one, we all resonate together.' — Judith H.*

In the breathing in and the letting go, we are at one with the trees. Our breath their breath, our lives held in the circles deep within forests far and near.

Coronavirus stripped us bare, revealing that we are all fragile — leaves in the wind. During lockdown, I went to live with my father in the countryside. The rural lanes filled with butterflies and people with time to watch them while, at home, the butterflies on screens were less serene. Trees witnessed the slowing down and showed us how, in the standing still, we see each other more clearly. Under the canopy we recognised dappled light, the softness inside us.

Coronavirus turned down the volume of our greeds grinding. The sky, once loud with contrails, then filled with swallow song and the tumbling tones of the willow warbler. In this quiet isolation, we came together to look beyond to what really matters. The trees already knew this, the planet was trying to tell us, now we have to listen.

photo: Emma Drabble

Thank you to the Snowdon Trust for helping fund these displays

Margaret LeJeune is an image-maker, curator, and educator from Rochester NY. Working predominantly with photographic-based mediums, LeJeune explores our precarious relationship to the natural world. Her work has been widely exhibited at institutions including The Griffin Museum of Photography (USA), The Center for Fine Art Photography (USA), Circe Gallery Cape Town (South Africa), Science Cabin (South Korea), and more. LeJeune has been invited to create work at several residency programs which foster collaboration between the arts and sciences including The Ephemeral River (art.earth), University of Notre Dame Research Center, and University of Wisconsin - Madison Trout Lake Research Station. Her work was recently published in Culture, Community, and Climate: Conversations and Emergent Praxis from art.earth Books. LeJeune currently serves as Associate Professor of Photography at Bradley University in Peoria, Illinois.

photo: Richard Povall

Shifting Halo

Margaret LeJeune

Shifting Halo explores the impact of climate change and logging in the Boreal Forest (also known as The Emerald Halo). Working at the University of Notre Dame's Environmental Research Center (UNDERC), I examine the ways humans are altering the landscape and habitat of the Boreal Chickadee, an indicator species in this region. Bird call sound waves punctuate the works to silently echo the depleting number of avian species in this shifting landscape.

a photo essay

Bird Song #1

The Cut

Viewing Glass

Marked

Buttercups

Bird Song #2

I have been a wildlife filmmaker for many years, so the natural world informs my practice. I work with earth, wood, wild plants, trees, and found objects, combining drawing, painting, photography, text, and print, to explore the "spirit of place." I am fascinated by the impact of time and human history on the fabric and texture of both the urban and the natural world..

Selected exhibitions include the Royal Academy Summer Exhibition, where I received a British Institution Award, the RWA, Black Swan Arts, Wells Art Contemporary, and The London Group. I have participated in artist residencies in Southern Italy and Lisbon and with art. earth in the UK.

photo: Richard Povall

Lockdown Time & Tree Time

Petra Regent

Lockdown Time & Tree Time Petra Regent

I work with earth, stones, wood and found objects, combining drawing, print and text to explore 'the spirit of place'. I am fascinated by the impact of time and human history on the fabric of the natural world.

During the Coronavirus lockdown I became mesmerised by the slow unfolding of Spring , as tight buds split and unfurl, unzipped by the gradual tilt of the earth towards the sun.

Nearly every day during lockdown, I documented the infinitesimal transition from bud to leaf, in a series of drawings of twigs gathered on my daily 'exercise' walks in the local park and Ashton Court near Bristol.

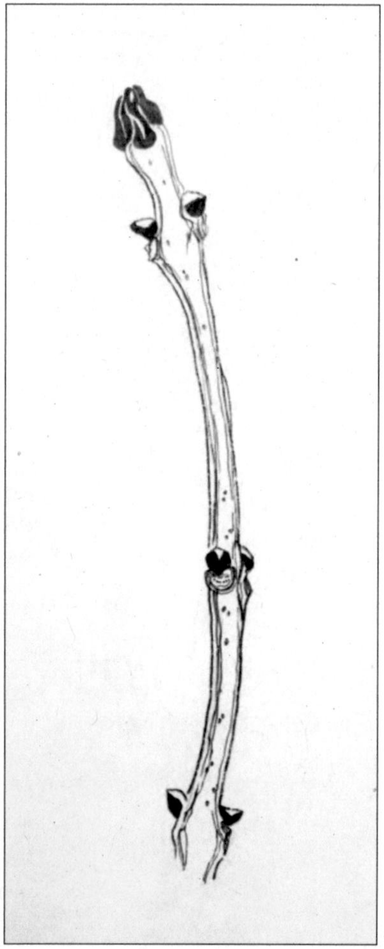

ash buds, March 5

First ash flower, March 24
Lockdown day 2

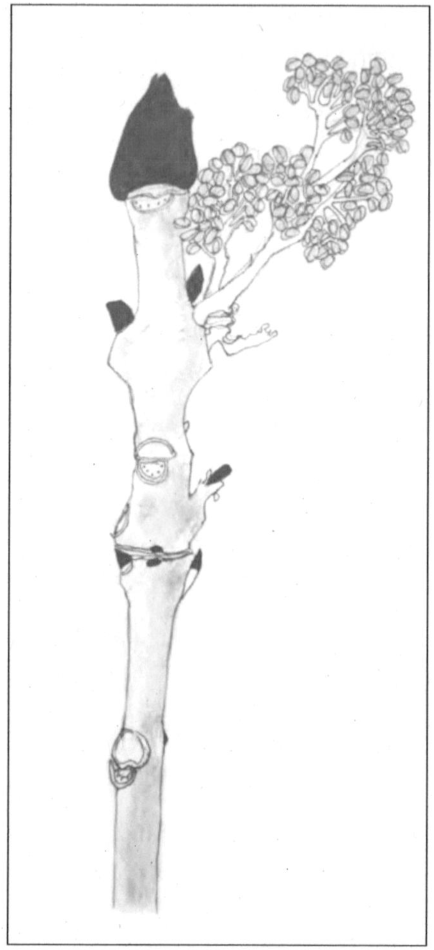

ash flowers, March 31
Lockdown day 8

As well as normal ink, I use home-made oak gall ink for many of my drawings, following a recipe little changed since *Magna Carta*.

The ink is remarkably light-fast, which is why so many Medieval documents are still legible centuries later. Depending on how long the acorns are steeped, the tannins in the ink vary from tawny ochre through to velvety black. The galls are formed by the oak in response to a parasitic oak gall wasp, creating a round cocoon around the developing wasp larva.

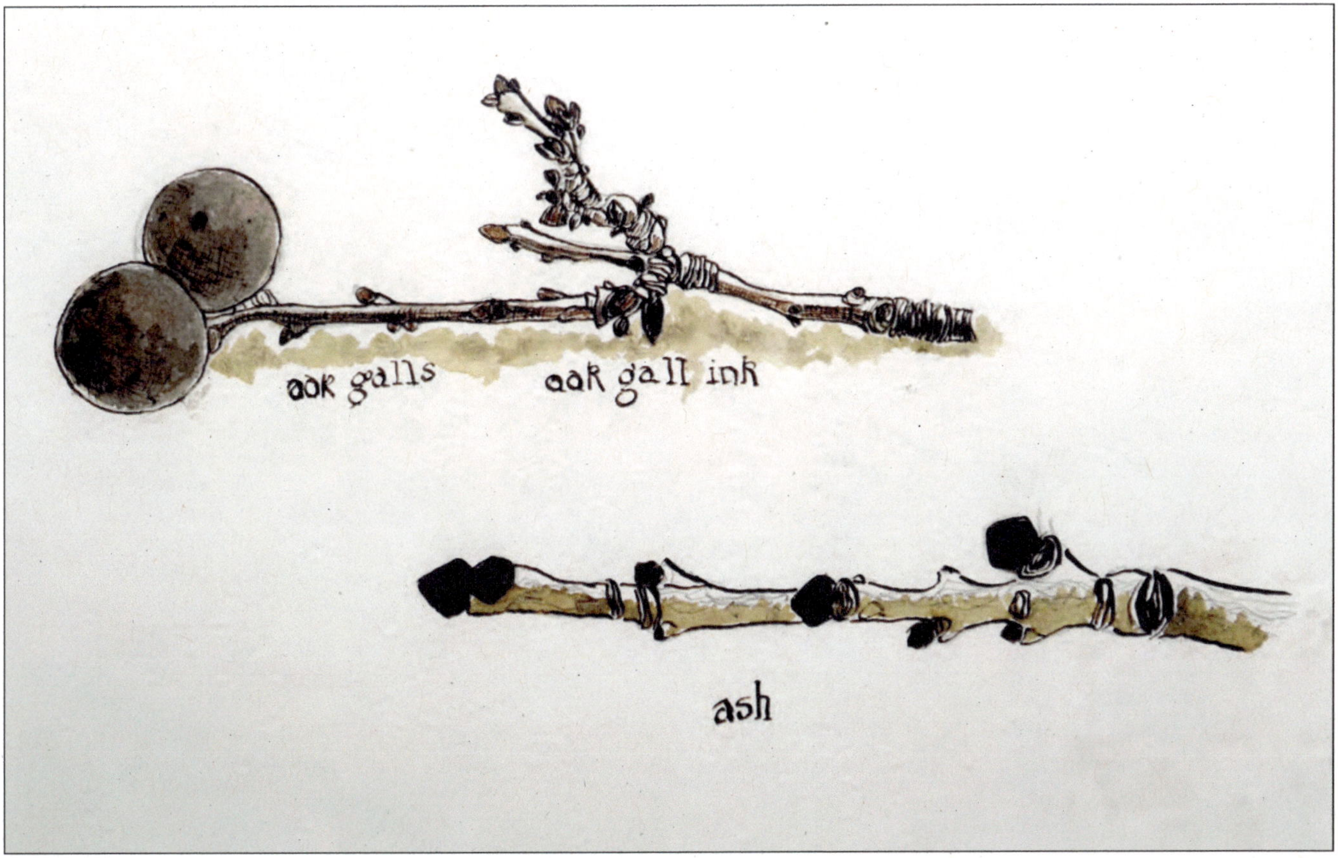

This brief concentrated 'snapshot of time' as measured by the unfurling of a leaf, was in stark contrast to my on-going project exploring the concept of 'tree-time': the huge scale of a tree's life, set against world events and the relatively brief lives of friends and family.

Oak leaves (oak gall ink), April 18 2020
Lockdown day 27

Oak leaves (oak gall ink), April 18 2020
Lockdown day 27

Oak leaves (oak gall ink), May 3 2020
Lockdown day 42

Sycamore leaves & flowers, April 21 2020
Lockdown day 30

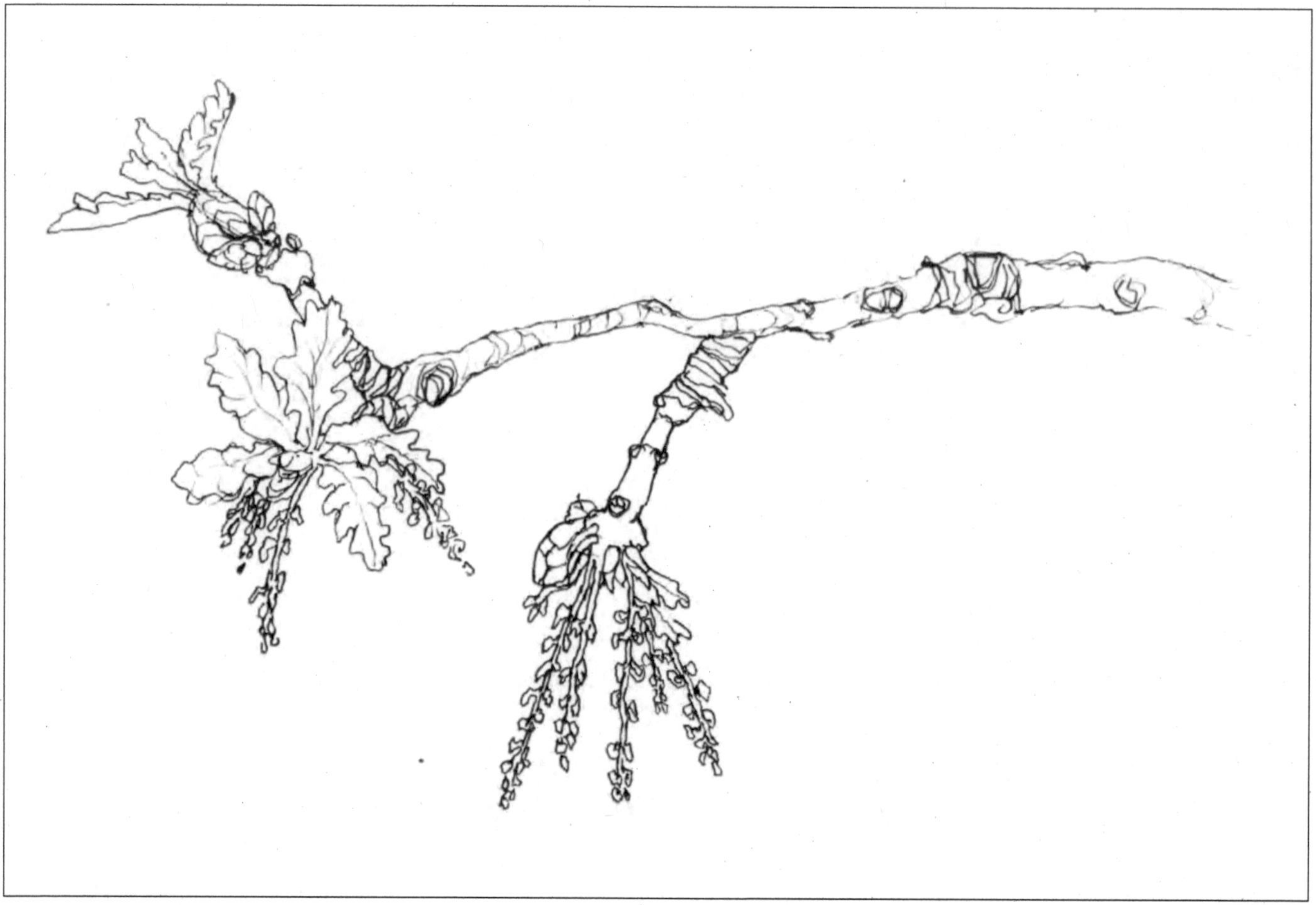

Male oak flowers & first leaves, April 11 2020
Lockdown day 20

Oak leaves & flowers, April 14 2020
Lockdown day 23

Tree Time

I have always been drawn to trees, and in particular, to their longevity: the oldest yew in Britain is believed to be almost 3000 years old, and many oaks and chestnuts are probably close to a thousand years.

In 2015 chance brought me to a huge red oak log, grown from an acorn in 1934 in Pill, near Bristol, and felled in 2013. This massive stump formed the basis of my depiction of one tree's life, using print, text, enamel, and clay for my MA in 2015.

When a tree is felled, each annual ring on the trunk represents a year in the tree's life, written in wood. It's no surprise that the science of dendrochronology refers to 'reading' tree rings - for they are a text, a tree's unique autobiography.

Only trees growing in temperate regions with four seasons have easily visible annual rings.

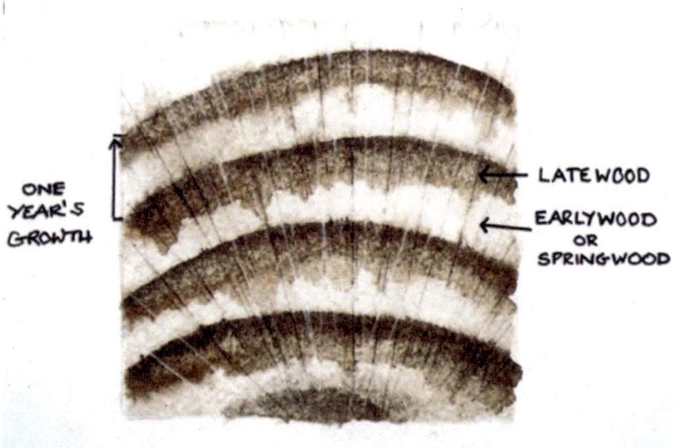

In the spring, as days grow longer, the tree increases its girth, adding a concentric circle of large, thin-walled cells called 'earlywood or springwood'. When conditions are perfect for growth, such as cool wet summers this layer of cells increases. In less favourable conditions, such as drought, the earlywood layer is narrower. This explains why annual rings are so irregular.

As autumn approaches, the days grow shorter and growth slows down. The tree starts laying down smaller cells with thick walls, creating a narrow, darker layer, called 'latewood'. It is the alternation of these two layers that gives rise to the classic 'tree ring' — each layer of earlywood representing one year's growth.

I find it fascinating that each annual ring is a representation of the amount of sunshine, transformed into wood — which, (as we know from burning wood) is stored energy.

My intention was to create an exact relief print of every ring for that oak's life. Though annual rings are visible to the eye, the surface is surprisingly smooth, so in order to create a printing template, the surface has to be charred. The latewood being harder, resists the heat and stands proud, while the softer earlywood burns away.

The surface is rolled with ink, and a large sheet of hand-made Japanese Kozo paper laid on top. Kozo paper is very thin, but remarkably strong, made from the fibres of the paper mulberry tree.

'Kozo' sticks are coppiced and thin strips of white bark fibre are soaked in river water, beaten with wooden clubs to create pulp, and left to dry in the sun. To make paper, the pulp is mixed with water & neri — from the tororo plant, producing mucous which helps to suspend the fibre evenly in the water before being scooped up onto a bamboo screen, rocked backwards and forwards several times to interlock the fibres, depositing a thin layer evenly

on the surface. This is then rolled out onto a cloth and left to dry — producing a sheet of paper that is translucent and light as gossamer.

First I run my hands over the paper, smoothing it down over the surface to reveal the precise location of each annual ring, including the bark perimeter . Then I hand-burnish, using a Japanese barren.

Even though I am applying immense pressure, generating heat through friction, the paper withstands the rough treatment and doesn't tear or bleed. Its translucency makes it easy to monitor the progress of burnishing through the back of the paper.

Of course I counted the number of rings — 79 years. If the tree could tell us its story, what would it say?

Following the contours of each annual ring, I replaced the tree's journal with handwritten text of human landmarks and personal events. My mother's escape from Nazi Germany as a child on the *Kindertransport* in 1938 is right in the centre of the tree. I have gone on to create tree journals for friends .

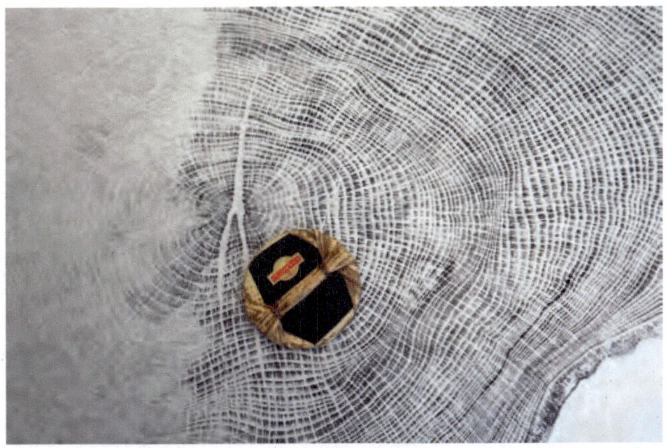

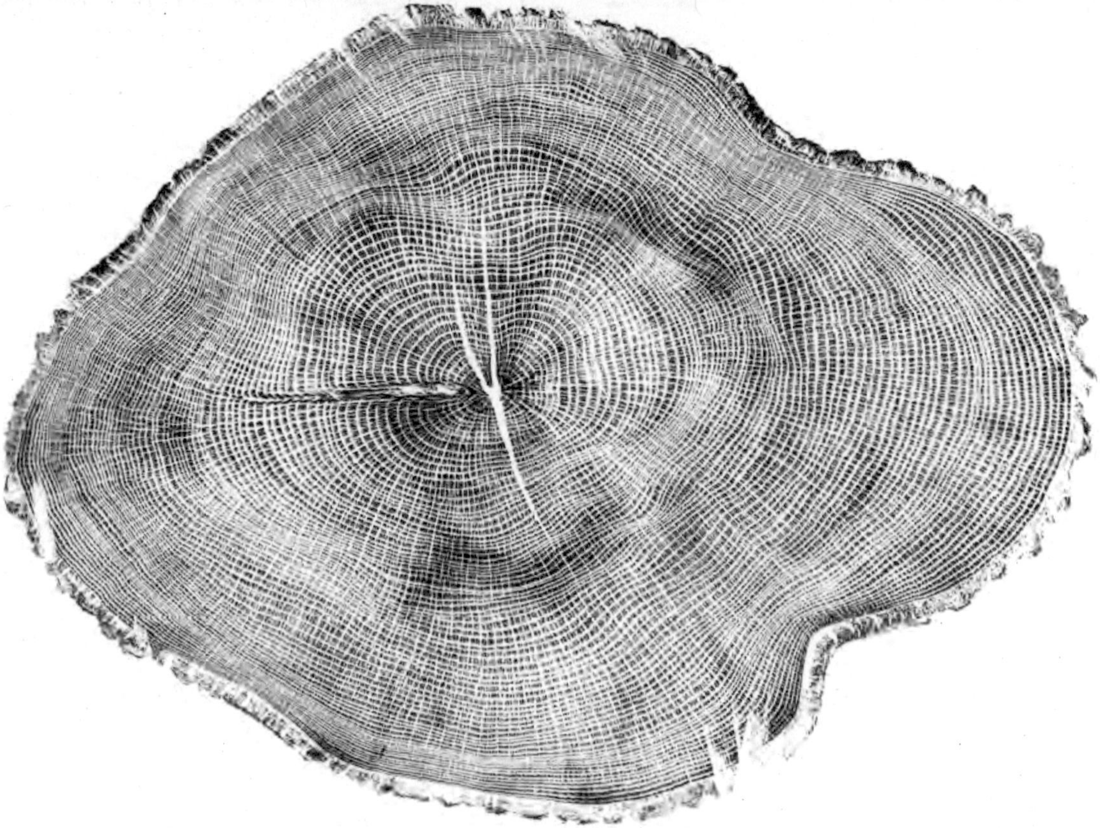

Red Oak 79 Years 2015 MA

Red Oak Journal II (2018)

My partner has a five-acre wood in Herefordshire that he planted in an old potato field, and I have watched it grow from spindly saplings to a forest where it's possible to get lost.

My sister-in-law's ashes are scattered here, and wild raspberry, foxglove, and orchids appear from nowhere, carried by the wind, birds, and other creatures. We collect hazelnuts in autumn, and the wood provides fuel for our winter fires.

Of course burning wood for warmth goes back to prehistory. It is this that I think of when transforming the timber cut from the living tree to flickering flames. It's as though the essence of the sun captured by the tree is remembered in the ash.

Ash is never far away from burning — burning books and bodies. In many religions, fire releases the spirit of a person allowing it to be reborn in another being: burning the body, and in so doing, creating ash, is perceived as an act of renewal.

Annual Rings 2015 MA

Most ceramic glazes contain wood ash, and I wanted to make my own, using wood ash from our woodland to fuse wood (in the form of ash) with earth (in the form of clay) by mixing the ash from our fires with feldspar and clay.

I used 'paper-clay' — porcelain clay that is mixed with paper (made from wood) providing structural strength to clay that would otherwise collapse, allowing me to create spiral forms, using 'paper-thin', clay. By drawing rings of ash glaze around concentric spirals of paper-clay, I hoped to create an homage to a tree's annual rings. Emerging from the heart of the spirals is a copper-plated acorn from the forest floor.

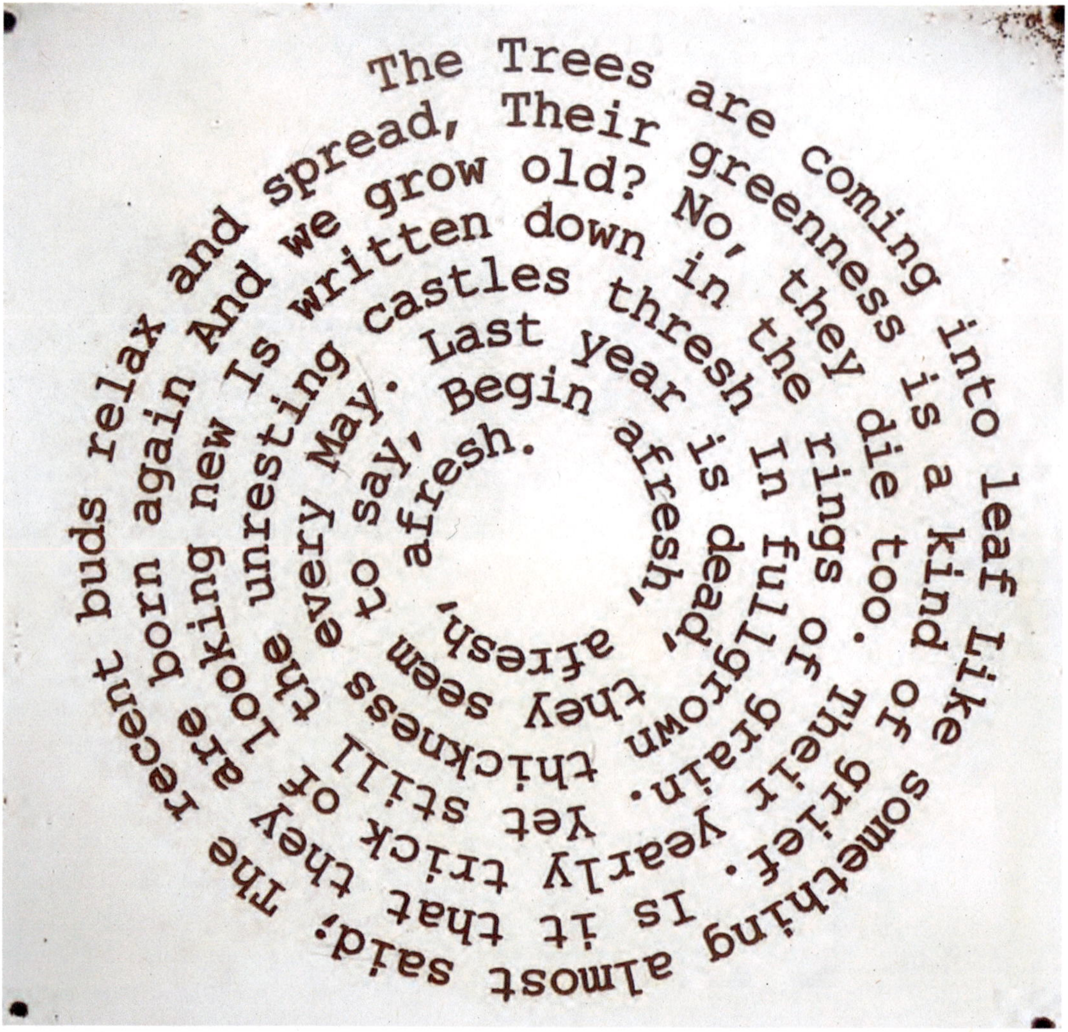

The Trees (from a poem by Philip Larkin) 2015 MA

Philip Larkin's poem, 'The Trees' perfectly describes this eternal cycle of renewal, ageing and death that I hoped to capture in my drawings of buds and new leaves during the months of March & April 2020

Enamel is one of mankind's most resilient materials. By embedding the text of Larkin's poem in circular form in enamel, I wanted to celebrate the fact that trees outlive us by thousands of years, and in doing so, bring hope every spring

Robin Walter began his work with trees by picking up sticks for a tree surgeon. He has since worked as an arboricultural climber in London, 'on the saws' in Dorset, as forest manager on private estates and as a site officer for the Woodland Trust. Since 2010 he has been working independently as a forester and writer. Throughout all this time he has held a vision of communal cultural change, most recently expressed through activism with Extinction Rebellion. His work seeks to restore the web of life, and our place in it, starting with trees.

Robin's book 'Living With Trees', written for Common Ground, was published in November 2020 and the poem beautifully presented here is an original work which reflects the essence of the book.

www.livingwithtrees.co.uk

#LivingwithTrees

Robin Walter

~ mantle

in eden first a circle dance
amidst the trees
a steady state
birth growth death
chthonic base

then cycles accelerating spin ever outwards
till the centre cannot hold and
pluck the apple
we are sent fleeing on our lonely tangent
our knowers arc

are we still rising
or are we sinking
or do we teeter on the hinge of history?

dry land achieves its aspiration
in the tangled forests of the holocene now moist and fecund
old growth language of the earth in raucous song
the harpstring warp of tree and vine
the slalom weft of bee and bird
the rooting clutch in earth
connect to woodwideweb of hyphae
collaborating kingdoms of makers and miners

vital fabric net strung in between in pattern tells of soil and sun and rain the silken
buzzing threads each species with a speaking role each plant a coloured strand
enmeshed in give and take this anarchy of equals this nexus of exchange
is
the web of life
each holding up the other

~ dismantle

now beached we are denizens of the forest
already in our glade
gone the low hanging fruit
oh sun give us light amongst the shade
come the thirsty crop
oh marvel see what we have made
by taming grass and tempting in the wolf
we furnish all we lack
choosing which shall serve us best
and riding on their back

(more)   push back the forest
(need)   widen the glade
(make)   this is ours
(fight)   not yours

the forest cloak now threadbare
we can do without the wasted hinterland
for we are novel citizens of light
ascending to lounge bloated in the net
repurposed as our hammock of repose
usurpers throne

enslaving nature for our use we hold the whip
an occupying force
the wild songs of ragged partisans
grow fainter in the hills
burn chop dig cut
the blunt axe hacks
bark phloem cambium xylem sapwood heartwood pith
creaking trees crash down
loose the forest grip
raze the moderating mantle
bare the raw earth for service

and our shattered forest fragments
scattered to the margin
taught a new song of exile
in a strange and othered land
the quirky native urge repressed in sullen ranks
a grudge to fester and to brood
in dwindling hollow woods
and splintered hollow minds

~ remnants

whats left?
the seamless mosaic floor depicting pan amongst the dryads
reduced to odd shards of tile
left glinting there and here
still hinting at the erstwhile whole
while slabs of our intent lie heavy on the land
a field of wheat
a field of cows
a carpark
nothing grand

pillars of the community
trees host generous and keep order
among the tribes of the diaspora
the court of quercus stately strong
the austere fagus palace grey
the hardy pinus outposts on the moor
and on the hillside fraxinus excels

yet trees push up thru cracks in our intent
weeds in our crazy civic pavement
whisper of the lands desire
to restore her ravished honour
so why not trees?
weve had a better offer

~ companions

already always there
the trees stand by us
persistent quiet content
their stubborn grace bestowed for free

each garden an oasis of opportunity
to test our kinship with the trees
a living laboratory
clipped and poodled
fanned against a wall
a shaven pollard
or freely running wild

go on a journey
go into the woods
in the lawless wilds you may find natural justice
in foreboding shadows you may find welcome refuge
in the frisson of terror an enchanted ecstasy
the lost may be found

drawn into the shady woods
drawn into their mediate shelter
between earth and sky
between inside and out
between solitude and crowd
they stand firm while we move within
shield us from the raw elements
they listen as we speak
they reflect as we project
they absorb as we bleed
they hold as we release
they have seen it all
and will see more again

~ timber

love forests but can we take a cut?
can we still hear that earthy song
behind the buzzing saw?

drop the whip and listen soft

can we frame our world in wood again
count the rings
learn to live within
respect their incremental discipline?

wood
strong supple live
draws food from earth
draws breath from air
draws power from fire
draws blood from water
to make the fifth element
the one to crown and bless them all

trees gather slowly make with light
true alchemists transforming elements
tree feed tree the spanning generation
fibre breath shelter home delight

~ belong

can the eye conquer the elbow
can the liver conquer the larynx
can the bee conquer the blossom?
so how could we conquer nature?

our long lonely arc has brought us here
to this moment
to this moment of reckoning
this moment of recognition
can we see our fractured faces in the shattered mirror
here on the morning after?

we have taken
we have taken long and hard
the earth our mine
creatures our slaves
landscapes our service providers

we can belong
if we so choose
we can be of service
be long deep service

stitch earth and sky with trees
knit land and sea with streams
weave multitudinous strands of energy
to make our urgent safety net
let dismantled hills reclothe
let weary land relax
back into natures lap
let every field
and every face
express its nature
find its rightful place

Fig 1. Tim Craven: *Twin Pillars* Casin on canvas 2018 61x 91.5cm

George Peterken is a forest ecologist who worked principally in nature conservation. During a career with the Nature Conservancy he negotiated the conservation aspects of the 1985 Broadleaves Policy, started the Ancient Woodland Inventory and maintained a research interest in ecological isolation and natural woodland. Latterly, he held a fellowship at Harvard University and advised the Forestry Commission on nature conservation. His books include Woodland Conservation and Management (1981), Natural Woodland (1996) and, with Edward Mountford, Woodland Development: a long-term study of Lady Park Wood (2017); and Wye Valley (2008). He is currently associate professor at Nottingham University.

Stella Carr is an artist and horticulturalist, and has exhibited widely and worked across multiple art forms in public art, design, installation, gardens, arts education, and arts policy including transnational cultural collaboration. Exploring the energetic relationships between species, Stella's fine art practice currently uses the mediums of printmaking, drawing, painting and topiary. Stella's work is held in Public and Private Collections in the UK and abroad. @stellacarr.artlandscape

Art Meets Ecology in Lady Park Wood

Stella Carr & George Peterken

Art Meets Ecology in Lady Park Wood

Stella Carr and George Peterken

Ecologists and artists both meticulously observe woods and trees, but they do so separately and present their understanding and appreciation of woods in contrasting ways to different audiences. Ecologists record objectively and act impersonally when they analyse the results. The product, usually a peer-reviewed paper, is presented in journals where one paper looks superficially just like another. All use neutral, precise, quantitative terms and specialist terminology. In theory, ecologists are interchangeable: if different research ecologists were to tackle exactly the same topic in the same place, they would come up with the same product.

Artists in contrast act subjectively and personally. Their paintings and drawings are designed to attract attention, stimulate imagination and open the observer to several lines of thought and feeling. Artists are individuals: no two artists will produce the same artwork, even when observing identical scenes. Their styles are personal and usually recognisable, even without labels. The end-results of an ecological research project in woodland are precise, often narrow conclusions, whereas artworks created in woodland are open-ended invitations for the viewer to form their own impressions.

But, are artists and ecologists really that different? Would not both groups appreciate and enjoy the woods more if they could see them from the other's standpoint? And would they be able to convey their interest in, and concern for, the woods better together than separately? In a world of increasing concern for the environment and rapidly developing interest in woods and trees as part of the solution, working together could be stronger than working apart. Here we summarise one such project and explain our individual perceptions.

The project

In 2017, The Arborealists, an informal group of professionally-trained artists, were invited to work in Lady Park Wood, an ancient semi-natural wood on the steep and rocky flanks of the Wye gorge that was set aside in 1944 to study the development of natural woodland, and which has been recorded in detail ever since. In fact, the wood has by design developed into a 'wildwood', now almost devoid of obvious signs of human activity so it presented a rare artistic opportunity to work in an environment lacking human reference points.

Having observed the wood for 40 years, the ecologists started to publish their findings in peer-review, specialist journals in 1987 and have continued in that vein ever since. This work continues: at the present time, the progress of disease is being studied in a population of several hundred ash that has been known and recorded for over 70 years. The research project has recently been published as a book (Peterken & Mountford 2017) which, even with a liberal allowance of photographs, will inevitably have a limited audience. This details the three main processes: the on-going growth with competition between individual trees; disturbances or events which disrupt the steady growth at unpredictable intervals; and regeneration of new trees when growth and disturbances present opportunities. The main events have been the

Fig 2: Lesley Slight: *Late Afternoon* Oil on canvas 30 x 40cm

Fig 3: Richard Bavin, *Regeneration* Oil on panel 2019 40 x 50cm

arrival of elm disease in 1971, the great drought of 1976 and the arrival of ash disease in 2017. The broad conclusion is that we cannot predict how the wood will develop in future: it may be blown flat in a storm next winter, or it may grow serenely on for decades without disturbance.

The artists therefore encountered a wood that has been left to itself for up to 150 years and now looks primeval, with: trees of all sizes and ages, many leaning at sharp angles; great trees standing dead or dying; gaps in the canopy where groups of large trees have fallen together; an all-pervading litter of decaying trees; and clusters of new growth which will eventually make good the losses. All this and the findings of the ecological research were presented to the artists during an initial tour of the wood.

Collectively, the resulting drawings and paintings displayed a remarkably wide variety of styles and aspects of woodland. Some were exhibited in the Nelson Museum, Monmouth, as part of the Wye Valley River Festival, which in 2018 took trees as its theme, but the main exhibition followed in 2019 and continued into 2020, partly because it was 'locked down' for several months. In 2020, the artworks were brought together in a book (The Arborealists 2020) together with short essays setting out the ecological trains of thought they generated.

The ecological commentaries (GP)

We can illustrate this combination of artworks and ecological commentary with a selection of examples. Tree fall gaps, the defining feature of natural woodland in Britain, are represented in their contrasting styles by Tim Craven's *Twin Pillars* (Fig 1) and Lesley Slight's *Lady Park Wood Late Afternoon* (Fig 2). Trees are blown over, lose their balance or rot at the base and, when they crash down, they leave a gap and the doleful spectacle of great trees fallen. Some piles of broken timber form impressive barriers to movement until the heaps of entangling small branches rot down. Visually, natural woodland that has not been levelled by a hurricane forms a grid of vertical trunks and horizontal fallen trees, with a few diagonal trees that fell against neighbours that stood their ground. In

Fig 4 Julian Perry: *Vestigal Birch* oil on panel 30 x 25cm

Lady Park, fallen trees tend to lie parallel, because trees fall downslope.

Awesome scenes of destruction though they are, tree-falls are also the focus of regeneration: the trees are dead, long live the trees. Richard Bavin's *Regeneration* (Fig 3) includes a few slow-growing beech saplings in an old gap. They just sit there, enduring the shade as the crowns in the remaining canopy trees expand, and moderately proof against deer, which prefer to eat other trees. There were actually clusters of saplings in his Fallen (not shown here), but for artistic reasons he chose to exclude them: the artist has license, but the ecologist must observe objectively.

As woods grow they change. Trees become larger, but fewer, and woodland composition shifts inexorably towards taller and long-lived species. Julian Perry's *Vestigal Birch* (Fig 4) shows a fragment of one of the post-war generation of birches that sprang up after parts of the wood were felled during the Second World War, but which have now reached their dotage. Birch dies on its feet, quickly rots, falls and the trunk fragments, but the bark lasts longer than the wood. These rolls of birch parchment tell a story — of the wood's contribution to our survival and the decline of the wood's baby-boomer generation.

Jacqueline Wedlake Hatton's *Presence* (Fig 5) immediately suggests a combination of seclusion and observation. In prosaic terms, the artist stands behind a group of trees looking into a small clearing containing the dark root plate of a fallen tree. In the artistic imagination, she has seen a mystical presence meditating in the quiet of the woodland interior.

To the ecologist and woodsman, this is just the place where deer would stand hidden looking for dangers ahead; and where the hunter would stand concealed in order to kill the deer feeding in the clearing. However, neither hunter nor hunted would frame the scene like the artist: both would remain acutely aware of what was happening in the wood to either side.

Susan Peterken's *Interspatial* (Fig 6) draws attention to a surprising fact. Woodland is defined by trees, but most of its volume is space between trees. We have a measure of this in a wood's basal area, which at 40m2/ha show that the trees occupy less than 1% of the soil surface. It also incorporates a property of light in a sloping woodland. Look up-slope and trees stand against a dark background of the higher ground. But look down-slope, and they stand out as silhouettes against the sky.

Abi Kremer's *Lady Park Wood 3* (Fig 7) might be unkindly labelled the 'flying root plate'. Like her other fantastical images, it is far from anything that might illustrate an ecological text, but this is the only image in the whole Arborealist output that makes one reflect on how the wood looks from below. The inspiration is the upturned root plate of a large tree that tipped over in a gale, but we have a hint that the worm's eye view of natural woodland is a scatter of starfish shapes linked by a fine mesh of roots and mycelia, now given an identity as the wood-wide-web.

Linkages are the underlying idea of Stella Carr's *We Are All Connected* (Fig 8). Above ground, entangled thickets form when brambles scramble over fallen brushwood and branches to form impenetrable barriers to human progress (but perfect hideaways for the newly arrived wild boar). They form also when the wild, anastomosing growths of ivy bring down the weaker ash trees, or when great looping lianas of Clematis finally lose their grip on the trees they were attempting to climb. Contrary to popular imagination, however, tangles and thickets are localised: most natural woodlands are easy to navigate.

Fig 5 Jacqueline Wedlake Hatton, *Presence* oil on canvas 50 x 40cm

Natural woodland is, according to a long-held ecological view, completely free of human influence, but it has lately become increasingly apparent that even pre-Neolithic

Fig 6 Susan Peterken: *Red Interspacial* pastel on paper 2018 45.5 x 38cm

Fig 9 Stella Carr: *Arborealists in Lady Park Wood*. Monoprint on washi 2019 61 x 76cm

Fig 7 Abi Kremer: *Lady Park Wood 3* Watercolour on paper 2018 46 x 39cm

Fig 8 Stella Carr: *We are all connected* Relief print on Fabriano paper 2019 60 x 50cm

Fig 10. Stella Carr: *Fagus Metanoia.* Raw pigment gouache and ink on paper 42.5 x 68cm

woodland was not pristine, unaffected by people. Mesolithic and earlier hunters had removed or reduced the megafauna, and thereby initiated changes in woodland structure and composition. This emergence of people into our view of natural woodland is exactly mirrored by Stella Carr's *Arborealists in Lady Park Wood* (Fig 9). At first glance we see only the trees, then gradually notice the people emerging from the background.

The artworks speak for themselves and the responses of viewers will be individual and open-ended, but many, perhaps all, artists have a clear philosophy or theme underlying their works. These are necessarily different and personal to each artist, but we can illustrate the depth of background with Stella Carr's explanation of ecology as immersion in response to Lady Park Wood.

An artistic viewpoint (SC)

My work involves the symbiotic relationship we have with our environment and specifically trees. This boundary-less connection with ecology takes its form from a sensed system that we all cohabit.

As David Abram describes Van Gogh's paintings, objects 'are not situated in space but actively deploy or secrete the space between them.' (Abram 2010). For me this space is inhabited by the ecology of a place, from woodland floor to top canopy, one may feel this connection. To make works in this context is to be challenged by scale, i.e. how to depict macro and micro networks, the reality of an ecosystem that has no beginning and end, microscopic organisms having as valued influence as enormous mature trees. There are blurred edges in the ecosystems of woodland; multitudes of species, each growing with individual characteristics, whilst existing as one linked system:

This perspective of seeing is due to being influenced by the Biological Sciences as much as the Arts whist growing up. Stimulus for my work stems from understanding the cycle of growth and decomposition in woodlands is interrelated, recognising the patterns of mycorrhizal fungi are mirrored in the growth of roots and branches. The work *Fagus Metanoia* (Fig 10) celebrates decomposition as part of woodland regeneration in Lady Park Wood. Incorporating images of this fungi from under a microscope I use these through pattern texture and colour in and through the entire painting, I draw attention to this vital life-giving invisible organism.

In woodland dynamic growth and decay is consistent and may be experienced as one interconnected circle. Circles may be seen to represent trees, humans, and in fact all living things. In the relief print We Are All Connected, (FIG 8) branches and root systems are abstracted, a network with no beginning and no end. With infinite reach as a growing tree, the circle is applied over an embossed surface, reflecting trees as organisms that seed into existing ecosystems that, over time, evolve into a new ecosystem supporting new life cycles. The study of interconnectedness is also explored in the work *Arborealists in Lady Park Wood* (Fig 9), a blended scene of woodland and humans merged.

In the painting *Pollen With A Feather Touch Has Swept Away Granite Mountains*, (Fig 11) I record the immersive experience of being within an ecology, amongst ancient *Pinus sylvestris* in the Caledonian Forest. There is no one characteristic species in the terrain but multitudes, each aspect talking with an individual voice, at the same volume, just different pitches in symbiosis.

This way of defining Art and Ecology is clearly explained in the essay *Art in co-relationship with Nature* by Anne Douglas and Mark Hope (2020). 'Eco' comes from the Greek 'oikos' meaning 'home' or dwelling. Ecology shares this root with 'economics'. By tracing back to an etymological root associated with dwelling, 'economics' could mean the management of resources in relation to survival in the place that we call home. Ecology by association may be defined as the dynamic interrelationship between living beings within natural systems that continuously evolve and transform the environments in which they are situated (their 'home'). An ecology artist might draw out, uncover and reveal such dynamics, experiencing them by developing awareness of our entanglement with every component of our environment, a process in which we, the 'audience', become 'participants'. Ecology art is a

Fig 11. Stella Carr, *Pollen with Feathertouch Has Swept Away Granite Mountains*. Oil on lead ground on paper 2020 45 x 64cm

dialogue of sorts between the artist, the natural world and ourselves'.

For the work *Infinity* (Fig 12) I travelled to Lady Park Wood in mid-December, arriving in the gloaming and sleeping within its canopy. The morning light was slow to come and I realised mist from the Wye had risen like a silver veil, leaving only vague outlines and textures visible within a few feet in front of me. I spent a few hours walking, keeping warm clambering over fallen trunks and sliding down muddy deer tracks with the Wye boiling in spate below. The wood completely wrapped itself around all my senses, the woods and I were infused with moisture rising from the river, immersed together. Then the mist cleared enough for me to make the work, leaching colours and washes a contribution from the brume holding us together in time and space.

Within the arboreal environ, we recognise the seasonal cycle and its part of endlessly contributing to the whole. This may be viewed as an allegory to our layered human experience that, over time, leads to additional learning, added layers of wisdom and known truths in our own evolving.

Reflections (GP)

From the standpoint of an ecologist and conservationist, it was heartening to find the artists expressing strong views on conservation issues, including woodland preservation and the need for contact with nature, even though only two to my knowledge have any direct involvement with nature conservation organisations. They form part of the concerned general public, yet they also have the skills to arrest attention and communicate aspects of woodland that professional ecologists and conservationists may neglect. We might debate whether they reach a wider public than scientifically based ecologists, but their public is certainly different.

As an ecologist from a scientific background, I have been required to look at woods objectively and quantitatively. As a conservationist I was expected to present my case in terms of scientific interest, environmental services and maintaining biodiversity. These are crucial aspects, but they placed social aspects in the background and excluded aesthetics and feeling. In practice, like many colleagues, I did my best to bring landscape and social implications into my work, and was not

Fig 12. Stella Carr: *Infinity* Ink on paper 2020 32 x 45cm

blind to the interplay of light, shape, texture and ambience, but the aspects of woodland to which many people respond were excluded.

The Arborealists all have a strong interest in trees and woodland, yet some seemed to know little about woodland ecology. Despite observing woods intently, their thoughts had evidently been on other aspects, blind to features and implications that are meat-and-drink to ecologists. Ecologists, of course, have been much the same in reverse. It is as if both artists and ecologist know one side of the coin, but not the other.

The artists also reinforced my interest in trees as individuals. A peculiarity of the Lady Park long-term ecological study is that we know the detailed history of 20,000 individual trees. Most are short-lived and long gone, but some are old friends who I know have had their ups and downs. This fascinated the artists, who generally seemed to have greater interest for trees as individuals than for trees collectively. They were drawn to individual and distinctive trees, whereas the ecologist publishes papers that seek generalisations, preferably backed by statistical tests.

Artists appeared to be just as selective as ecologists in their perceptions but perhaps less subject to fashion. The Arborealists produced work in a wide variety of styles. Ecologists on the evidence of, say, papers in *Journal of Ecology* have preoccupations that could be described as fashions. As for selection, the artists seemed most interested in beech and yew, and least in oak, lime and hazel. Many gravitated to features that were essentially legacies from previous management, but that was more because such trees had interesting shapes, not because they obviously presented a human reference point.

Did the artists change my view of a wood I had studied in detail for decades? I knew all about individuality of trees, but had not thought this would be so important to others, even though television producers had previously built their items round individual trees. I had dismissed the unique trees and concentrated on the collective. Equally, I had never previously thought of the view from below as a collection of starfish caught in the net, nor had I previously thought of woods as space defined by trees, though I was well aware that the collective basal area of the trees was a small proportion of total area. More generally, I had never gazed round the wood seeing tree shapes as spectral presences in human form and had not bothered to focus my attention on the changes in a woodland's appearance as the daylight changes. None of this changes how one would describe the ecology of Lady Park to an ecological audience, but it could make all the difference to our attempts to present this ecology and its implications to people in general.

Generally

Along the way, the artists and ecologists gained a new appreciation of the wood and each other's interest in woodland, and now hope to interest a wider audience than either would normally reach.

Evolving the Forest

Epilogue

Jeremy Ralph

A year has gone by since the *Evolving the Forest* conference, two years since its inception, one-hundred years since the Forestry Commission was formed. When we started formulating the conference there was always a plan to publish the Proceedings, the conventional way to go about leaving a post-conference legacy. But *Evolving the Forest* was anything but conventional.

The conference had a feeling of being in the moment, of being about the interaction of people there and then. The feedback we received was not only of the exceptional range of speakers but also of the chance to mix with those at other ends of the forestry and tree worlds. People felt it is was unique and we felt that there was something about it that couldn't be expressed in a publication of conference proceedings but did reflect the zeitgeist of forward-looking forestry. Instead we have waited a year, we have invited submissions from those who attended and those who didn't and we hope that we have recaptured, in written form, that breadth and of-the-moment thinking that started at the conference.

When we set out on this *Evolving the Forest* adventure the idea seemed ludicrous, challenging and exciting. Our aim was to bring together people from all walks of life involved in forestry to one place under one umbrella — parts of the forestry world that at some points have almost been at war, parts that are anathema to others — to consider the future of our treescapes. Our earliest meetings saw art.earth, The Royal Forestry Society and Timber Strategies sitting in a room, wondering how we were going to work together from such disparate arenas, connected only by a vision.

That over 230 people responded to our call for proposals we found invigorating and humbling. In the space of a few weeks we had moved from a vague idea to something that obviously had resonance. It seemed that within forestry and architecture, science and arts, policy and philosophy, this was a moment to reach out to others and talk about the critical issues of our evolving relationship with trees.

That the conference filled up, that we took over the Dartington estate, itself a crucible for forestry innovation in the past, with three days of activity was even more of a surprise. To watch senior policy-advisors taking part in, and enjoying, performance art in the forest (albeit with the help of some fine wine), was the realisation of our ambitious imaginings.

We are now a year on and find ourselves in very different circumstances. Global pandemic has altered how we view the world in the short-term as well as long-term. Yet our trees keep growing, rightly unconcerned by our troubles. This upheaval, along with escalating climate change, has thrown into relief the difference between our humanity-driven speed of life and the natural world we inhabit. It seemed more urgent than ever to revisit *Evolving the Forest*.

Like the conference, this book could have been twice the size. The scope and number of submissions is recognition of the increasing importance of trees across many sections of society. Many, if not all, of our authors have transgressed boundaries. They have shown how difficult it is to talk of trees from a purely scientific, or artistic or policy points of view. They have shown how complex our relationship with trees is now and how increasingly complex it may become. For many the start point is of our past mistakes or future climates, for most, but not all, the journey is one of optimism for the future. Throughout runs a caveat that this is a pivotal moment that must be grasped by all to reconnect and reconsider what our treescapes mean to us.

The complexity of forest ecologies is wrapped up in the complexity of how we view forests. As submissions came in we realised that creating a narrative through the book was going to be difficult. Our own fault for asking people to challenge us.

From a personal perspective *Evolving the Forest* has been the biggest and most stimulating project, a defining point in a career. To have access to such a wide variety of passionate people from all walks of life and to be small part of bringing them together has re-invigorated a belief in our ability to evolve how we think of forests. To be able to talk to a scientist about the mechanisms of forest fire; a historian about The Charter of the Forest and an artist about tensions in eco-art within a half day has been an ambition fulfilled.

I'd like to take this opportunity to thank Richard Povall and his team at art.earth for the immense amount of work realising the conference and this publication. Without their experience we would still be dithering in discussion about whether it was a good idea. And also Simon Lloyd and all at the Royal Forestry Society without whose contacts and forestry knowledge we would have had a skeleton of what we have achieved.

We challenged our audience at *Evolving the Forest* to go out of their comfort zone, to go to sessions they would otherwise dismiss, and go with an open mind. We challenge you as readers to do the same, skip the comfort-zones for later and immerse yourselves in parts of the forestry world so far unfamiliar to you.

Jeremy Ralph
Timber Strategies
Dartington, November 2020

Building workshop at Evolving the Forest (photo: Oliver Raymond-Barker)

Works referenced

Abbott, Sarah. *Filming with nonhumans*. In Vannini, Phillip. (Ed.), *The Routledge international handbook of ethnographic film and video* (pp. 224-233). Routledge 2020

Abram, David. *Becoming Animal: an Earthly Cosmology*. Pantheon Books, 2010.

Abram, David. *The Spell of the Sensuous: Perception and Language in a More-than-Human World*. Vintage Books, 1997.

Adnanes, J. H. (2012, December 18). *Bugs in the Christmas tree*. Science Daily. Retrieved from https://www.sciencedaily.com/releases/2012/12/121218081830.htm

AFP *Bolsonaro shrugs off German aid cuts, as deforestation surges*. Climate Homes News. (August 12, 2019). Retrieved from https://www.climatechangenews.com/2019/08/12/bolsonaro-shrugs-off-german-aid-cuts-deforestation-surges/.

Agamben, Giorgio, and Kevin Attell. *The Open: Man and Animal*. Stanford University Press, 2004.

Agyepong-Parsons, J. . Interview: What the Forestry Commission chair thinks about rewilding, invasives and growing supertrees. ENDS report 2019, October 24. Retrieved from https://www.endsreport.com/article/1663584/interview-forestry-commission-chair-thinks-rewilding-invasives-growing-supertrees.

Alexander, Christopher, et al. *A Pattern Language: Towns, Buildings, Construction*. Oxford University Press, 1977.

Alexander, K., Butler, J. & Green, T. *The value of different tree and shrub species to wildlife*. British Wildlife, 18(1). 2006

Allen, C. D. et al.. *A global overview of drought and heat-induced tree mortality reveals emerging climate change risks for forests*. Forest Ecology and Management, 259:660–684; 2010.

Alpi, Amedeo et al. *Plant neurobiology: no brain, no gain?* Trends in plant science. 12:135-6. 10.1016/j.tplants.2007.03.002.

Anderson, W. Green Man: *The Archetype of Our Oneness with the Earth*. COMPASS books, 1990.

Anstis, Ralph: *Warren James and the Forest of Dean Riots. Coalway, Forest of Dean* Albion House, 1986.

Anstis, Ralph. *Four Personalities from the Forest of Dean: Sir John Wyntour, Catharina Bovey, Timothy Mountjoy, Sir Charles Dilke*. Albion House, 1996.

Aubrey, Allison. *Forest Bathing: A Retreat to Nature Can Boost Immunity and Mood*. Segment on *Morning Edition*, National Public Radio (NPR). July 17, 2017. https://www.npr.org/sections/health-shots/2017/07/17/536676954/forest-bathing-a-retreat-to-nature-can-boost-immunity-and-mood. Accessed October 16, 2020.

Baker, N.. *The intelligence of plants and the problem of language: A Wittgensteinian approach* in Gagliano, Monica, et al. *The Language of Plants: Science, Philosophy, Literature*. University of Minnesota Press, 2017.

Barnosky, Anthony et al. *Has the Earth's sixth mass extinction already arrived?* Nature, 471, 51-57; 3 March 2011.

Beatty, Laura. *Pollard*. Vintage Books, 2009.

Bekoff, Marc. *Animal Passions and Beastly Virtues Reflections on Redecorating Nature*. Temple University Press, 2006.

Bertini, Enrico., Plaisant, Catherine & Santucci, Guiseppe. *BELIV'06: Beyond Time and Errors: Novel Evaluation Methods for Information Visualization*. 2006. Retrieved from http://www.dis.uniroma1.it/~angelini/VisDis/Papers/interacts07.pdf, 30 November 2020.

Beurteaux, Danielle. "*Winemakers Worry Wildfires Will Leave Whiff of Ashtray in Their Wine*", NPR The Salt, December 13, 2017, https://www.npr.org/sections/thesalt/2017/12/13/570188980/winemakers-worry-wildfires-will-leave-whiff-of-ashtray-in-their-wine.

Bladon, F. Evolving the forest, Dartington, 19-21 June 2019.

Quarterly journal of forestry, 113(4): 11-15; October 2019.

Blake, W. (1799). *Letter to Revd Dr Trusler*. in Wu, Duncan. *Romanticism: an Anthology*. Blackwell, 1994.

Braidotti, Rosi. *Posthuman critical theory* in Banerji, Debashish, and Makarand R Paranjape. *Critical Posthumanism and Planetary Futures*. Springer India, 2016: 13-32.

Brasier, C.M., *The biosecurity threat to the UK and global environment from international trade in plants*. Plant Pathology, 57(5 (19 Sept 2008): 792-808.

Brass, M.). *Indigenous climate action: Why land-based, Indigenous-led responses are crucial to effectively addressing the impacts of climate change* [Lecture]. Academics for climate community series. University of Regina, Regina, Saskatchewan. (March 2, 2020)

Bratman, Gregory, et al. *Nature and mental health: an ecosystem service perspective*. Science Advances, 5, (24 July 2019). DOI: 10.1126/sciadv.aax0903

Brend, Yvette. *Forget Smokey the Bear: How First Nation fire wisdom is key to megafire prevention*, CBC News British Columbia, July 15, 2017, https://www.cbc.ca/news/canada/british-columbia/fire-fighting-first-nations-firekeepers-annie-kruger-penticton-bc-wildfire-mega-fire-1.4205506.

Brock, Adam. *Change Here Now: Permaculture Solutions for Personal and Community Transformation*. North Atlantic Books, 2017.

Brown, Colum. *Fish Intelligence, Sentience and Ethics*. Animal Cognition, 18 (1), 1-17; January 2015.

Buhrich, Alice. et al. *Attributes, preservation and management of dendroglyphs from the Wet Tropics rainforest of northeast Australia*. Australian Archaeology, Volume 80:91–98; June 2015.

Buijs, Arjen, and Lawrence, Anna. *Emotional conflicts in rational forestry: Towards a research agenda for understanding emotions in environmental conflicts*. Forestry Policy and Economics, 33: 104-111; September 9, 2012.

Butler, Rhett. *Amazon destruction. Mongabay* Retrieved from https://rainforests.mongabay.com/amazon/amazon_destruction.html August 16, 2020

Cajete, Gregory, and Leroy Little Bear. *Native Science: Natural Laws of Interdependence*. Clear Light Publishers, 2000.

Calvo, P., Sahi, V. P., & Trewavas, A. *Are plants sentient?* Plant, cell & environment, 40(11), 2858-2869. DOI: 10.1111/pce.13065; September 6, 2017.

Camden, William. Camden's *Britannia, Abridg'd; with Improvements and Continuations to This Present Time*. Printed by J.B. for J. Wild, 1701. Available at: https://play.google.com/books/reader?id=fHBbAAAAQAAJ&pg=GBS.PP8 [Accessed 13th February 2020]

Canadian Press. *Harmful effects of wildfire smoke are immediate and could make Covid-19 symptoms worse, UBC study warns*, accessed September 7, 2020. https://www.cbc.ca/news/canada/british-columbia/wildfire-smoke-covid-19-symptoms-ubc-1.5625438.

Cantarello, Elena. et al. *Quantifying resilience of multiple ecosystem services and biodiversity in a temperate forest landscape*. Ecology and Evolution, 7(22), 9661-9675; 16 October 2017.

Carlson, Allen. *Is environmental art an aesthetic affront to nature?* Canadian Journal of Philosophy, 16(4), 635-650; December 1986.

Carrington, Damien. *Public concern over environment reaches record high in UK*. The Guardian, 5th June, 2019

Carson, Rachel. *Silent Spring*. Boston: Houghton Mifflin, 1962.

Clark, Leonard. *A Fool in the Forest*. Dennis Dobson, 1965.

Coghlan, Andy.. *Trees may have a 'heartbeat' that is so slow we never notice it*. New Scientist, April 20, 2018. https://www.newscientist.com/article/2167003-trees-may-have-a-heartbeat-that-is-so-slow-we-never-noticed-it/

Collett, Anne & Jones, Dorothy. *Gendered tree-scapes in the art of Emily Carr and Judith Wright*. Mosaic (Winnipeg), 42(3) 2009

Cooper Alan., McCann Thomas. *Technical report of the Northern Ireland Countryside survey*, University of Ulster & the Department of Environment & Heritage Service. 2002

Coops, Nicholas et al. *A thirty year, fine scale, characterization of area burned in Canadian forests shows evidence of regionally increasing trends in the last decade*, PLoS One, 13(5), e0197218; May 22, 2018.

Crowe, Sylvia. *The Landscape of Power*. Architectural Press, 1958.

Crowther, T. W. et al. *Mapping tree density at a global scale*. Nature, 525(7568), 201–205; 2 September 2015.

Cunningham, Sophie. City of Trees: *Essays on Life, Death & the Need for a Forest*. Text Publishing Company, 2019.

Dalton, Jane). *More than half of world's forest wildlife lost in 40 years*. The Independent, August 14. 2019. Retrieved from https://www.independent.co.uk/environment/wildlife-forest-climate-change-wwf-a9056516.html.

Daston, Lorraine and Mitman, Greg, eds., *Thinking With Animals: New Perspectives on Anthropomorphism* Columbia University Press, 2005

Davies, J. *On Ancient Statutes Relating to the Marches of Wales and the Border Counties, Considered In Connexion with the Political Geography of Wales*. In: Journal of British Archaeological Association (1871) London [online] Available at: https://books.google.co.uk/books?id=_RUrAAAAYAAJ&pg=PA408&dq=Henry+Vi+river+severn&hl=en&sa=X&ved=0ahUKEwiqoq-Z6qDZAhWjKsAKHXc_DAEQ6AEIKTAA#v=onepage&q=Henry%20Vi%20river%20severn&f=false [Accessed 12th February 2018]

Defra 25 Year Environment Plan available at *https://www.gov.uk/government/publications/25-year-environment-plan* (January 2018)

Defra. *Agriculture in the United Kingdom 2019*. Published online 25th June 2020 https://www.gov.uk/government/statistics/agriculture-in-the-united-kingdom-2019

Defra. *Code of Good Agricultural Practice (COGAP) for Reducing Ammonia Emissions* 2018 Available at https://www.gov.uk/government/publications/code-of-good-agricultural-practice-for-reducing-ammonia-emissions/code-of-good-agricultural-practice-cogap-for-reducing-ammonia-emissions

Demos, T. J. *The Politics of Sustainability: Contemporary Art and Ecology*. In *Radical Nature: Art and Architecture for a Changing Planet 1969–2009*, published in conjunction with the exhibition of the same name, shown at the Barbican Art Gallery, edited by Francesco Manacorda, 16–30. London: Barbican Art Gallery, 2009.

Douglas, Anne and Hope, Mark *Art in Co-relationship with Nature* in Newling, John: *Ecology Works* Beam Editions 2020

Drayton, M. (1612) Poly Olbion: the seventh Song [online] Available at: http://poly-olbion.exeter.ac.uk/the-text/full-text/song-7/ [Accessed 12th January 2018]

Drengson, A. et al. *The Deep Ecology movement: origins, development, and future prospects (toward a transpersonal ecosophy)*. International Journal of Transpersonal Studies, 30 (1–2), 101–117. 2011

Drew, C. (1841) *A Collection of Poems on the Forest of Dean and Its Neighbourhood*. Reprint, Coleford: John Saunders Past and Present Books, 2002.

Ducarel, P. J. *A Tale of Dean Forest, in Five Cantos*. Longman, Rees, Orme, Brown, Green & Longman, 1836.

EarthTalk *Deforestation and Its Extreme Effect on Global*

Warming. Scientific American, November 13, 2012. Retrieved from https://www.scientificamerican.com/article/deforestation-and-global-warming/

Edwards, David., Collins, Timothy., Goto, Reiko.. *An arts-led dialogue to elicit shared, plural and cultural values of ecosystems*. Ecosystem Services, 21B: 319-328. 2016

Evans, P.M. et al. *Thresholds of biodiversity and ecosystem function in a forest ecosystem undergoing dieback*. Scientific Reports, 7, 6775 doi: 10.1038/s41598-017-06082-6 2017

Evelyn, John. *Sylva*. Rarebooksclub.com, 2012.

Fish, Robert. Church, Andrew. Winter, Michael. *Conceptualising cultural ecosystem services: A novel framework for research and critical engagement*. Ecosystem Services, 21: 208-217; October 2016.

Fisher, Chris. *Custom, Work and Market Capitalism: the Forest of Dean Colliers, 1788-1888*. Breviary Stuff Publications, 2016.

Foley, W. *A Child in the Forest* British Broadcasting Corporation 1974

Foley, W. Interview recorded for Forest of Dean Radio, 19th October 2002. Interviewed by Ralph Anstis, produced by Jason Griffiths. (Author's collection).

Foley, Winifred et al. *A Quat 'an A Chat*. Dubbin Productions 1984

Forest Research *Carbon in live woodland trees in Britain, National Forest Inventory Report* Forest Research 2014

Forester TV. Mark Harper, MP flees after public meeting [video online] Available at: https://www.youtube.com/watch?v=5gioBLu-aps [Accessed 26th October 2020]

Forestry Commission. *Forestry Statistics 2018: A compendium of statistics about woodland, forestry and primary wood processing in the United Kingdom*, IFOS-Statistics 2018

Frank, Arthur W. *The Wounded Storyteller: Body, Illness & Ethics*, 2nd Ed. University of Chicago Press. 2013.

Frank, B. *On the nutritional dependence of certain trees on root symbiosis with belowground fungi (an English translation of AB Frank's classic paper of 1885)*. Mycorrhiza 15.4 (2005): 267-275.

Fudge, Erica. *Animal*. Reaktion Books, 2010.

Fuller, Rob, et al. *Effects of woodland structure on woodland bird populations: An assessment of the effects of changes in woodland structure on bird populations as a result of woodland management practices and deer browsing*. DEFRA Project WC0793. 2016

Gadon, Elinor. *The Once & Future Goddess: A Sweeping Visual Chronicle of the Sacred Female and Her Reemergence in the Cultural Mythology of Our Time*. Harper & Row, 1989.

Gagliano, Monica, et al. *The Language of Plants: Science, Philosophy, Literature*. University of Minnesota Press, 2017: vii-xxxiii

Gagliano, Monica. *Thus spoke the plant: a remarkable journey of groundbreaking scientific discoveries and personal encounters with plants*. North Atlantic Books, 2018

Gallego-Sala, A. V., Charman, D. J., Harrison, S. P., Li, G., and Prentice, I. C.: *Climate-driven expansion of blanket bogs in Britain during the Holocene*, Clim. Past, 12, 129–136, https://doi.org/10.5194/cp-12-129-2016, 2016.

Garbutt R.A., Sparks T.H. *Changes in the botanical diversity of a species rich ancient hedgerow between two surveys (1971-1998)*. Biological Conservation 106 (2): 273-278., 2002

Garrard, Greg. *Ecocriticism*. Routledge, 2012.

George M. Church, Yuan Gao, Sriram Kosuri. *Next-Generation Digital Information Storage in DNA*. Science 337.6102; 2012.

Gigerenzer, Gerd. *Adaptive Thinking: Rationality in the Real World*. Oxford University Press, 2002.

Gilmurray, J. *Ecological sound art: Steps towards a new field.* Organised Sound, 22(1), 32-41. 2017

Greenfield, Susan. *A Day in the Life of the Brain: the Neuroscience of Consciousness from Dawn till Dusk*. Penguin Books, 2017.

Grieve M, *A Modern Herbal*, Penguin Books, 1976

Grusin, Richard. *The Nonhuman Turn*. University of Minnesota Press, 2015.

Hall, Clare. O'Brien, L. Atkinson, M. *Tribute to Trees*. Forest Research 2019.

Hall, Matthew. *Plants as Persons: a Philosophical Botany.* State University of New York Press, 2011.

Hamilton, Clive. *Requiem for a Species: Why We Resist the Truth about Climate Change*. Routledge, 2015.

Hammond, Claudia, *The Art of Rest – How to Find Respite in the Modern Age*. Canongate, 2019.

Harrison, Robert P. *Forests: the Shadow of Civilization*. Univ. of Chicago Press, 2009.

Hart, Cyril Edwin. *Royal Forest: a History of Deans Woods as Producers of Timber*. Oxford University Press, 1966.

Harvey, F. W. *In Pillowell Woods and Other Poems*. F. W. Harvey Society 2017. First published by Frank H. Harris, Lydney in 1926.

Hauge, Åshild Lappegard. *A critical comparison of three identity theories*. Architectural science review, 50(1), 44-51; 9 June 2011.

Havins, P. J. N. The Forests of England. Readers Union of Book Clubs 1976

Health Link BC. *Wildfires and Your Health*, accessed September 7, 2020 https://www.healthlinkbc.ca/health-feature/wildfires.

Heddon, Dierdre. *Autobiography and Performance*. Palgrave MacMillan 2008.

Hercus, L. *Trees from the dreaming*. Artefact: The Journal of the Archaeological and Anthropological Society of Victoria, The, 35, 40-49 2012

Hillman, James, and Thomas Moore. *The Essential James Hillman: a Blue Fire*. Routledge, 1990.

Hobson-West, Pru, and Ashley Davies. "Societal Sentience: Constructions of the Public in Animal Research Policy and Practice." Science, Technology, & Human Values, vol. 43, no. 4, July 2018, pp. 671–693, doi:10.1177/0162243917736138.

HOOF Submission to the Independent Panel on Forestry 2011. Available at http://www.handsoffourforest.org/documents/submissionlight.pdf [Accessed 30th October 2020]

How to Hygge a Tree – Wellbeing at Westonbirt https://www.fowa.org.uk/uploads/documents/2018-03-16/1521198364-how-to-hygge-a-tree-book.pdf

Ingold, Tim, and Gísli Pálsson. *Biosocial Becomings: Integrating Social and Biological Anthropology*. Cambridge University Press, 2013.

Innis, H. A. *The bias of communication*. Canadian journal of economics and political science/revue canadienne de economiques et science politique, 15(4), 457-476. 1949

IPBES (Intergovernmental Science-Policy Platform on Biodiversity and Ecosystem Services). Media release: *Nature's dangerous decline 'unprecedented'; species extinction rates 'accelerating.* May 2019. Retrieved from https://www.ipbes.net/news/Media-Release-Global-Assessment.

Johnston, George. *My Brother Jack, George Johnston: One of a Series of Support Documents*. Dept. of Education North Coast Region, 1982.

Jones A.Y., Hayes M. J., Sackville Hamiliton N. R. The effect of provenance on the performance of Crataegus monogyna in hedges Journal of Applied Ecology, 38 (5): 952-962; 12 January 2002.

Jung, C. G. *The Archetypes and the Collective Unconscious.* Princeton University Press, 1980.

Karban, R. *Plant sensing and communication*. University of Chicago Press, 2015.

Karban, R. *The language of plant communication (and how it compares to animal communication)*, in Gagliano, Monica, et al. *The Language of Plants: Science, Philosophy, Literature.* University of Minnesota Press, 2017

Keith, Sallw. et al. *Plant metacommunity structure remains unchanged during biodiversity loss in English woodlands*. Oikos, 120(2), 302-331; 15 September 2011.

Keith, Sally, et al. *Taxonomic homogenisation of woodland plant communities over seventy years*. Proceedings of the Royal Society Series B, 276 (1672), 3539-3544. 2009; 22 July 2009.

Kennedy, Gayle. *Viewing the Carved Trees Exhibition*. Southerly, 71(2):196 2011 (Extract)

Kennedy, Jo. *Initiating ecological change through sound art - a review and short manifesto.* https://www.jokennedysound.com/blog/initiating-ecological-change-through-sound-art

Kenter, Jasper (Ed). *Shared, plural and cultural values of ecosystems.* Full report of WP6 UK NEA follow on project. pp211. 2014

Kenter, Jasper O., O'Brien, Liz et al.. *What are shared and social values of ecosystems?* Ecological Economics, 111: 86-99 2015

King James Bible. Thomas Nelson, 1991.

Kinver, Mark. *World 'losing battle against deforestation.'* BBC News (2019, September 12). Retrieved from https://www.bbc.com/news/science-environment-49679883

Kopnina, Helen *Wild Animals and Justice: The Case of the Dead Elephant in the Room*. Journal of international wildlife law & policy, 19(3), 219-235. 2016

Krause, Bernie. *The voice of the natural world*. TEDGlobal 2013. Retrieved from https://www.ted.com/talks/bernie_krause_the_voice_of_the_natural_world?language=en

Krien, Anna. *Into the Woods: the Battle for Tasmania's Forests*. Black Inc., 2012.

La Rue, Frank. *Report of the Special Rapporteur on the promotion and protection of the right to freedom of opinion and expression.* Human Rights Council. 2011.

Laing, S. *Images of the Rural in Popular Culture 1750-1990*. In Short, Brian. ed. *The English Rural Community*. Cambridge: Cambridge University Press.. 1992

Laland, Hilton F. Japyassú & Kevin N. *Extended spider cognition.* Animal Cognition 20: 375-395; 7 February 2017.

Lam, Paulina. *5 big causes of deforestation and how you can stop it. One green planet*. (March 2019). Retrieved from https://www.onegreenplanet.org/animalsandnature/5-big-causes-of-deforestation-and-how-you-can-stop-it/

Larkin, Philip, and Anthony Thwaite. *Collected Poems*. Farrar, Straus and Giroux, 2004.

Latour, Bruno. *Visualization and cognition*. Knowledge and society 6.6:1-40. 1986

Leadbeater, Simon. *Ancient roots to untruths: Unlearning the past and seeing the world anew*. Quarterly Journal of Forestry, 113(1): 51-56. 2019

Leopold, Aldo. *A Sand County Almanac* Oxford University Press 1949

Lewis, C. S., and Walter Hooper. *Poems*. Harcourt Brace & Co., 1992.

Long, Andrew *Scarred Trees An Identification and Recording Manual* (prepared for Aboriginal Affairs Victoria) 2003 https://www.aboriginalvictoria.vic.gov.au/sites/default/files/2019-09/Scarred-Trees_0.pdf retreived 25/08/2020

Lorde, Audre. *The Cancer Journals: Special Edition*. Aunt Lute Books 2006.

Louise Hill, Glyn Jones, Nick Atkinson, Andy Hector, Gabriel Hemery, Nick Brown. *The £15 billion cost of ash dieback in Britain*, Current Biology,Volume 29, Issue 9 2019

Lyons, O.. *Spirituality, equality and natural law.* In Little Bear, Leroy, Long, J. Anthony, & Boldt, Menno. (Eds.) *Pathways to self-determination: Canadian Indians and the Canadian state* 1984.

Macfarlane, Robert. *Understory*. Emergence magazine (August 25, 2019.. Retrieved from https://emergencemagazine.org/story/the-understory/

Mancuso, Stefano, *The revolutionary genius of plants. A new understanding of plant intelligence and behavior*. Simon & Schuster 2018

Mancuso, Stefano., & Viola, Alexandra. *Brilliant green: the surprising history and science of plant intelligence*. Island Press 2015

Mann, Michael E. and Lee R. Kump, *Dire Predictions: Understanding Climate Change. The Visual Guide to the Findings of the IPCC*. 2nd ed. DK Publishing, 2015

Marder, M. *Plant-thinking: A philosophy of vegetal life*. Columbia University Press, 2013.

Marino, L.. *Sentience*. In Breed, M. D., & Moore, J. (Eds.). *Encyclopedia of animal behavior*, Vol. 1 (pp. 132-138). Elsevier Science, 2010.

Martin, Phil. et al *Analysis of ecological thresholds in a temperate forest undergoing dieback*. PLoS ONE, 12(12), 2017. https://doi.org/10.1371/journal.pone.0189578

Martin, Phil. et al. *Stand collapse in a temperate forest and its impact on forest structure and biodiversity*. Forest Ecology and Management, 358, 130-138; December 2015.

Mather, A.S. *Forests of Consumption: post productivism, post materialism and post-industrial forest*. Journal of Environment and Planning C, 19: 249-268. 2001

McElroy, Justin. *Kamloops experiencing worst air quality in its recorded history*, CBC News British Columbia, August 3, 2017, https://www.cbc.ca/news/canada/british-columbia/kamloops-air-quality-1.4234720.

McKimm, Michael, & Simon Armitage. *The Tree Line: Poems for Trees, Woods and People*. Worple Press, 2017.

Mendelssohn, J. *When the wind changed: 'Albert Namatjira' at the Araluen Arts Centre, Alice Springs, 1984*. Art Monthly Australia; Acton Iss. 273, (Sep 2014): 54-63 2014.

Mitchell, Ruth .J. et al. *Collapsing foundations: the ecology of the British oak, implications of its decline and mitigation options*. Biological Conservation, 233, 316-327. 2019.

Mitchell, Ruth .J. et al. *The potential ecological impact of ash dieback in the UK*. Report No. 483. Joint Nature Conservation Committee, Peterborough, UK. 2014

Mitchell, Ruth .J. et al.. *Assessing and addressing the impacts of ash dieback on UK woodlands and trees of conservation importance (Phase 2)*. Natural England Commissioned Reports, Number 151, 2014.

Morgan, Keith. *Albert's Dree Wiker and Other Poems*. The Forest Bookshop, 1985.

Morris, Jake, O'Brien, Liz, Ambrose-Oji, Bianca, Lawrence, Anna. and Carter, Claudia. *Access for all? Barriers to accessing woodlands and forests in Britain*. Local Environment. 16: 375-396. 2011.

Morse, Richard, et al. *A Native Forester: the Life and Poems of Richard Morse* of Yorkley. Yorkley A & E, 2012.

Moxey, Tricia, et al. *Loughton and Its Trees: Community Tree Strategy for Loughton*. Loughton and District Historical Society, 2013.

Nagel, Thomas. *11. What Is It Like to Be a Bat*? The Language and Thought Series, doi:10.4159/harvard.9780674594623.c15.

Nelson Kathryn., Nelson Roy., Montgomery W. I. *Colonisation of farmland deciduous plantations by woodland ground flora*. Arboricultural Journal: The International Journal of Urban Forestry. 2021

Newton, Adrian. C. (ed.). *Biodiversity in the New Forest*. Pisces Publications, 2010.

Newton, Adrian. C. and Oldfield, Sara. *Red Listing the world's tree species: a review of recent progress*. Endangered Species Research 6, 137-147, 2008.

Newton, Adrian. C. et al. *Towards a Global Tree Assessment*. Oryx, 49(3), 410-415. 2015

Newton, Adrian. C. et al. *Trends in natural capital, ecosystem services and economic development in Dorset*. Bournemouth University, UK, 2019.

Newton, Adrian. C., *Ecosystem collapse and recovery*. Cambridge University Press, 2021.

Newton, Adrian. C., *Forest ecology and conservation*. Oxford University Press, 2007.

Nicholls, Rev. H.G. (1863) *The Personalities of the Forest of Dean; being a relation of its successive officials, gentry, and commonality, drawn from numerous sources, but chiefly from unpublished data and local information, forming an appendix to 'An Historical and Descriptive Account of the Forest of Dean'*. John Murray, 1858.

Nicholls, Rev. H.G. *The Forest of Dean; An Historical and Descriptive Account, derived from personal observation, and other sources, public, private, legendary and local*. John Murray, 1858.

Nolan, Ken. *Only the Brave*. DVD. Directed by Joseph Kosinski. Culver City: Columbia Pictures, 2017.

Nugteren, Albertina. *Belief, bounty and beauty: rituals around sacred trees in India*. Brill, 2005.

O'Brien, Liz and Morris, Jake. *Well-being for all? The social distribution of benefits gained from woodlands and forests in Britain*. Local Environment, 19, 4: 356-383, 2013.

O'Brien, Liz and Murray, Richard.. *Forest School and its impacts on young children: case studies in Britain*. Urban Forestry and Urban Greening 6: 249-265, 2007.

O'Brien, Liz, and Forster, J,. *Sustaining and changing sport and physical activity behaviours in the forest: An evaluated pilot intervention on five public forest sites in England*. Urban Forestry and Urban Greening, 55; November 2020.

O'Brien, Liz, et al.. *Situating risk in the context of a woodland visit: A Case Study on Lyme Borreliosis*. Scottish Forestry, 66: 14-24, 2012.

O'Brien, Liz. *Carrying out Physical Activity as Part of the Active Forests Programme in England: What Encourages, Supports and Sustains Activity?—A Qualitative Study* Environmental Research & Public Health 16(24:5118) 2019.

O'Brien, Liz. Engaging with and shaping nature: a nature-based intervention for those with mental health and behavioural problems at the Westonbirt Arboretum in England. International Journal for Environmental Research and Public Health, 2018. doi: 10.3390/ijerph15102214

O'Brien, Liz. *Learning outdoors: the Forest School approach*. Education 3-13, 37: 45-60, 2009.

O'Brien, Liz. *Publics and woodlands: well-being, local identity, social learning, conflict and management*. Forestry, 78: 321-336, 2005.

O'Brien, Liz.. *Human values and their importance to the development of forestry policy in Britain: a literature review*. Forestry 76: 3-17, 2003.

O'Connor, M.R. *A Day in the Life of a Tree*. The New Yorker, August 27, 2019. Retrieved from https://www.newyorker.com/science/elements/a-day-in-the-life-of-a-tree

Oakes, Timothy S. and Price, P. L. *Identity and Place in a Global Context: Introduction to Part Five*. in: Oakes, Timothy S., ed. *The Cultural Geography Reader*. Routledge, 2008.

Oliver, Mary. *Upstream*. Penguin Press, 2016.

Parish, Roberta, and Joe Antos. *Plants of Southern Interior British Columbia*. Lone Pine, 1996.

Parker, Matt. *Things to Make and Do in the Fourth Dimension: A Mathematician's Journey Through Narcissistic Numbers, Optimal Dating Algorithms, at Least Two Kinds of Infinity, and More.* Macmillan, 2014.

Parks Canada Science and Conservation. *2020 prescribed fires*, accessed September 7, 2020. https://www.pc.gc.ca/en/nature/science/conservation/feu-fire/feuveg-fireveg/dirige-prescribed/projet-projects#revelstoke.

Parrott, Lael and Mayne S Meyer. *Future landscapes: managing within complexity*, Frontiers in Ecology and the Environment 10, no. 7, (2012): 382-389, doi: 10.1890/110082.

Pascoe, Paul, & Julia Jones. *Pride and Prejudice, Jane Austen*. Pearson, 2015.

Peterken, George, and Mountford, Edward. *Woodland development. A long-term study of Lady Park Wood* by George. Commonwealth Agricultural Bureau International, Wallingford, 2017

Peterken, George, et al. *Art Meets Ecology. Arborealists in Lady Park Wood*. Sansom & Co., 2020.

Pierotti, Raymond John. *Indigenous Knowledge, Ecology, and Evolutionary Biology*. Routledge, 2012.

Pope, Alexander, and George Sherburn. *The Best of Pope*. Ronald Press, 1940.

Potter, Dennis. *The Glittering Coffin*. Victor Gollancz Ltd., 1960.

Potter, Dennis. *The Singing Detective*. Faber and Faber Ltd., 1986.

Powers, Richard. *The Overstory*. Vintage, 2019.

Purcell, Leigh. *Gamilaroi Country*. In H. Cummings (ed.), *Carved Trees Aboriginal Cultures of Western NSW*, 2011:.4. State Library of New South Wales. https://www.anbg.gov.au/aboriginal-resources/Carved-Trees-Guide-State-Library-NSW-3449.pdf

Rackham Oliver. *Trees and woodland in the British landscape*. Dent, 1976.

Rahmani, Aviva. The Blued Trees Symphony. *An artwork for the Anthropocene era at the nexus of justice and science*. 2019 https://storymaps.arcgis.com/stories/

Reber, Arthur S. *The First Minds: Caterpillars, Karyotes, and Consciousness*. Oxford University Press, 2019.

Reglitz, Merten. *The human right to free internet access*. Journal of Applied Philosophy 37.2 (2020): 314-331.

Richard Ennos, Joan Cottrell, Jeanette Hall, David O'Brien *Is the introduction of novel exotic forest tree species a rational response to rapid environmental change? – A British perspective*. Forest Ecology and Management Volume 432, 15 January 2019, pp 718-728

Rosenberg, Douglas. *Screendance: Inscribing the Ephemeral Image*. Oxford University Press, 2012.

Rowe Ed, et al. Trends Report 2020: Trends in critical load and critical level exceedances in the UK. Report to Defra under Contract AQ0843, CEH Project NEC05708. 2020 https://uk-air.defra.gov.uk/library/reports?report_id=1001

Ryder, R. D., *Speciesism*. In Chadwick, Ruth, ed. *Encyclopedia of applied ethics*, 2nd ed. (pp. 213-219). Academic Press, 2012.

Sallmannshofer, Markus, et al. *Health benefits of forests: opportunities for the forest sector* in Marusakova, Laura, and Sallmannshofer, Markus, eds. *Human Health and Sustainable Forest Management*. Forest Europe, Slovakia, 2019.

Sample, Ian. *Group of biologists tries to bury the idea that plants are conscious*. The Guardian, July 3, 2019. Retrieved from https://www.theguardian.com/science/2019/jul/03/group-of-biologists-tries-to-bury-the-idea-that-plants-are-conscious?CMP=Share_iOSApp_Other

Sandall, Simon. *Industry and Community in the Forest of Dean, c.1550-1832*. Family and Community History: journal of the Family and Community Historical research Society, Vol. 16/2, October, 2013, pp87-99.

Schechner, Richard. *Performance Studies: A Critical Introduction* (2nd Ed.). Routledge, 2006.

Schmitz M.F., Sánchez A., de Aranzabal I. *Influence of management regimes of adjacent land uses on the woody plant richness of hedgerows in Spanish cultural landscapes*. Biological Conservation, 135, 542–554, 2007.

Sepänmaa, Yrjö. Professor Emeritus, University of Eastern Finland, Joensuu. In conversation with the artist/author, 2011, during Sampson's 2011 Core Scholar Fulbright period in Finland.

Sharp, Buchanan. *In Contempt of All Authority: Rural Artisans and Riot in the West of England, 1586-1660*. Breviary Stuff Publications, 2010.

Sheldrake, Merlin. *Entangled Life: How Fungi Make Our Worlds, Change Our Minds & Shape Our Futures*. Random House, 2020.

Shiva, Vandana. *Rights of Nature Ethics Tribunal: Vandana Shiva's Closing Statement*. 2014 Retrieved from https://therightsofnature.org/vandana-shiva-president-tribunal/

Silvia, Paul J., *Emotional responses to art: from collation and arousal to cognition and emotion*. Review of General Psychology, 9 (4), 342–357, 2005.

Simard, Suzanne W., David A. Perry, Melanie D. Jones, David D. Myrold, Daniel M. Durall, and Randy Molina. *Net transfer of carbon between ectomycorrhizal tree species in the field.* Nature 388.6642 (1997): 579-582.

Simon, Herbert A. *Rational choice and the structure of environments* Psychological review, 63, 129- 138, 1956.

Skar, Margrete. Gunderson, Vegard and O'Brien, Liz. *How to engage children with nature: why not just let them play?* Children's Geographies, 14: 527-540, 2016.

Smith A.G., Goddard I.C. *A 12,500 year record of vegetational history at Sluggan Bog, Co. Antrim, N. Ireland (incorporating a pollen zone scheme for the non-specialist)* New Phytol, 118, 167-187, 1991.

Society for Integrative Oncology (SIO) website. https://integrativeonc.org/integrative-oncology-guidelines. Accessed October 11, 2020.

Steinman, Louise. *The Knowing Body: The Artist as Storyteller in Contemporary Performance*. North Atlantic Books, 1995.

Stevenson, Robert Louis. *Essays of Travel.* Chatto & Windus, 1925.

Stiegler, Bernard. *Technics and time: The fault of Epimetheus. Vol. 1.* Stanford University Press, 1998.

Stone, Christopher D. *Should trees have standing?—Toward legal rights for natural objects.* Southern California Law Review (45): 450-501, 1972.

Stork, Nigel E., Hammond, Peter M., Russell, B. L., & Hadwen, Wade L. *The spatial distribution of beetles within the canopies of oak trees in Richmond Park, UK.* Ecological entomology, 26(3), 302-311, 2001.

Summerfield, Angela. *Empathy*. Canwood Gallery, 2018.

Sweet, Victoria. *Rooted in the Earth, Rooted in the Sky: Hildegard of Bingen and Premodern Medicine*. Routledge, 2010.

T. Helgason, T. J. Daniell, R. Husband, A. H. Fitter & J. P. W. Young. *Ploughing up the wood-wide web.* Nature 394.6692 (1998): 431.

ten Brink Patrick, et al. *The Health and Social Benefits of Nature and Biodiversity Protection (Executive summary).* Institute for European Environmental Policy, 28 April 2016.

Thunberg, Greta. *The world is waking up*. Address to the UN Climate Summit, New York City, 2019.

Toubman, Will. *Inside the Megafire*. Online. Directed by Laurie Cahalane. Boston: WGBH Educational Foundation, 2019. https://gem.cbc.ca/media/media/the-passionate-eye/episode-7/38e815a-0119be921c4.

Trewavas, Anthony. *Plant behaviour and intelligence*. Oxford University Press, 2014.

Truth and Reconciliation Commission of Canada. *Honouring the truth, reconciling for the future: Summary of the final report of the truth and reconciliation commission of Canada*. 2015 Retrieved from http://publications.gc.ca/site/eng/9.800288/publication.html

Tuan, Yan. Place: An Experiential Perspective. Geographical Review, Vol.65, No.2, April, pp151-165, 1975. [online] Available at: https://www.jstor.org/stable/213970 [Accessed 15th February 2014]

Tversky, Amos, Kahneman, Daniel. *Extensional versus intuitive reasoning: the conjunctive fallacy in probability judgment* Psychological Review 90, 293–315, 1983.

Vaillant, John. *The golden spruce : A true story of myth, madness, and greed* W.W. Norton, 2006.

van den Berg, Magdalena M. H. E., *Autonomic Nervous System Responses to Viewing Green and Built Settings.* International Journal of Environmental Research & Public Health 12(12:15860-15874. December 2015. https://www.ncbi.nlm.nih.gov/pmc/articles/PMC4690962/

Vidal, John. England forests sell-off: Government outlines plans. The Guardian, 27 January, 2011 [online] Available at: https://www.theguardian.com/environment/2011/jan/27/government-england-forest-sell-off [Accessed 26th October 2020]

Viso, Olga. *Ana Mendieta: Earth Body, Sculpture and Performance, 1972-1985*. Exhibition catalog, Hirshhorn Museum, Washington DC. 2004.

Wagamese, Richard. *Wagamese: 'All my relations' about respect*. In The Kamloops Daily News (June 11, 2013). Retrieved from http://www.kamloopsnews.ca/article/20130611/KAMLOOPS0304/130619980/0/kamloops/wagamese-all-by-relations-about-respect&template=JQMArticle .

Whitinui, Paul. *Indigenous autoethnography: Exploring, engaging, and experiencing "self" as a native method of inquiry*. Journal of Contemporary Ethnography 43(4) 456–487 (December 11, 2013)

Whittet, Richard, Cavers, Stephen, Ennos, Richard and Cottrell Joan. *Genetic considerations for provenance choice of native trees under climate change in England*. Forestry Commission Research Report 2019. Available at https://www.forestresearch.gov.uk/research/genetic-considerations-provenance-choice-native-trees-under-climate-change-england/.

Wickenden, Rev. William. A Tale of the Forest of Dean. Household Words, Volume 3, pp461-464; 1851. Dickens Journals Online [online] Available at: http://www.djo.org.uk/household-words/volume-iii/page-463.html [Accessed 10th December 2018]

Wiking, Meik. *The Little Book of Hygge: Danish Secrets to Happy Living*. William Morrow, an Imprint of HarperCollins Publishers, 2017.

Williams, Kathryn, O'Brien, Liz, and Stewart Amy. *Urban health and urban forestry: how can forest management agencies help?* Arboriculture Journal, 35: 119-133; 2013.

Willis, Ken, Garrod, Guy, Scarpa, Riccardo, Macmillian, Douglas.. *Non-market benefits of forestry*. Report for the Forestry Commission, 2000. Available at https://www.researchgate.net/publication/238730003_NON-MARKET_BENEFITS_OF_FORESTRY_Phase_1.

Withrow-Robinson, B. et al. *Seeing the forest. Art about forests and forestry*. Journal of Forestry, 100(8), 8-14; 2002.

Wordsworth, William. *Collected Works of William Wordsworth: Poems in Two Volumes*. BiblioBazaar, 2010.

World Wildlife Fund. *Forest habitat overview*. 2019. Retrieved from https://www.worldwildlife.org/habitats/forest-habitat

Wright, Ian. *The Life and Times of Warren James: Free Miners From The Forest of Dean*. Bristol Radical Pamphleteer, 2008.

Wulf, Andrea. *The invention of nature: Alexander von Humboldt's new world*. Knopf, 2015.

Yamaguchi, H. S. K., et al. *We Japanese*. Yamagata Press, 1946.

Yong, Ed. *I Contain Multitudes: the Microbes within Us and a Grander View of Life*. Ecco, an Imprint of Harper Collins Publishers, 2018.

Zlinszky, András, Molnár, Bence, Barfod, Anders S., *Not All Trees Sleep the Same—High Temporal Resolution Terrestrial Laser Scanning Shows Differences in Nocturnal Plant Movement*. Frontiers in Plant Science, October 20, 2017.

photo: Simon Leadbeater

Index

A

B

C

D

E

F

G

M

N

O

S

V

Logging in North Wood, Dartington (photo: Bob Budd) ▶